Scientific genius

Scientific genius

A psychology of science

DEAN KEITH SIMONTON

University of California, Davis

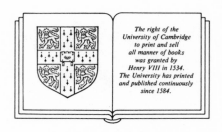

The right of the
University of Cambridge
to print and sell
all manner of books
was granted by
Henry VIII in 1534.
The University has printed
and published continuously
since 1584.

CAMBRIDGE UNIVERSITY PRESS

Cambridge
New York   New Rochelle   Melbourne   Sydney

Published by the Press Syndicate of the University of Cambridge
The Pitt Building, Trumpington Street, Cambridge CB2 1RP
32 East 57th Street, New York, NY 10022, USA
10 Stamford Road, Oakleigh, Melbourne 3166, Australia

First published 1988

Printed in the United States of America

Library of Congress Cataloging-in-Publication Data
Simonton, Dean Keith.
Scientific genius.
Bibliography: p.
Includes index.
1. Creative ability in science.   2. Science –
Philosophy.   3. Scientists – Psychology.   I. Title.
Q172.5.C74S57   1988   501'.9   87–27823

ISBN 0 521 35287 8

British Library Cataloguing-in-Publication Data
Simonton, Dean Keith
Scientific genius : a psychology
of science.
1. Science – Psychological aspects
I. Title
501'.9   Q180.55.P75

ISBN 0 521 35287 8

To Dad, Mom, Keith, and Grandma Rena

Contents

Tables and figures

Tables

Figures

Acknowledgments

This book owes its existence to several outside stimuli. The most immediate and important impetus was the invitation to participate in the conference "The Psychology of Science" in the spring of 1986, chaired by William Shadish and sponsored by the Center for Applied Psychology at Memphis State University. It became evident as I prepared my paper for presentation that I had a book-length manuscript inside my head, and therefore I had to resign myself to reading just a preliminary abstract at the conference. Barry Gholson, Arthur Graesser, Arthur Houts, and Robert Neimeyer, all members of the "metascience" group at the Center, offered detailed comments on that draft, which helped improve the current product as well. Moreover, at the conference itself I benefited from my conversations with Donald Campbell, Arthur Miller, and Ron Westrum, as well as the encouraging response of Howard Gruber.

Another motivating force was an earlier conference, "Scientific Excellence: Origins and Assessment," held at the University of Western Ontario, London, and organized by Douglas Jackson and J. Philippe Rushton. It was at that meeting that I first tried to synthesize my research on the multiples phenomenon. Much of chapter 6 emerges directly from that first attempt, although my thoughts on that subject have developed considerably since then. At that conference, too, I was stimulated by interactions with Janet Bavelas, Eugene Garfield, and Lee Sechrest.

These two conferences encouraged me to consolidate my thinking on a topic that has intrigued me for many years—the scientific genius. Along the way I have gained from the advice, criticism, and miscellaneous reactions of numerous researchers in this area. Many years ago Donald Campbell generously gave me photocopies of various articles relevant to his model of creativity, articles that were otherwise obscure, inaccessible, or outright unavailable. A long if sporadic correspondence with the late Derek de Solla Price encouraged me in the early stages of my empirical work on science, and he was a major factor in helping me publish my first book on genius-grade creativity. Robert K. Merton would send me, from time to time, a brief note that suggested that my ideas were attracting some appreciation. Kenneth Craik, by inviting me to the Institute for Personality

Assessment and Research (University of California, Berkeley) as Visiting Research Psychologist in 1985, allowed me to extend my sabbatical leave to over a year of uninterrupted research, thinking, and writing, during which the first draft of this book took form. I also have gained from correspondence or conversations with Robert Albert, Arthur Diamond, Zhao Hongzhao, William McGuire, and Harriet Zuckerman.

Finally, I must thank my wife, Melody, and my stepdaughter, Mandy, who tolerated my long absence in my upstairs study. Their patience is all the more outstanding, as I said that I would write only one book during my sabbatical year, and ended up composing two.

1 The chance-configuration theory

The psychology of science

With the launching of the Soviet sputnik into space, American psychologists were alerted to the urgency of enlarging our understanding of scientific creativity. J. P. Guilford, in his 1950 Presidential Address before the American Psychological Association, had already called for closer attention to the study of creativity, but current events injected this need with more significance (Golovin 1963). About this time the National Science Foundation sponsored a series of conferences, "The Identification of Creative Scientific Talent," at the University of Utah, the central papers of which were published in the 1963 volume *Scientific Creativity: Its Recognition and Development,* edited by Calvin W. Taylor and Frank Barron. We thus had every reason to believe that the discipline was on the threshold of a respectable "psychology of science," the first comprehensive science of science (see also Maslow 1966; Stevens 1939). But matters progressed little further, and the concerted effort largely petered out within a decade (Singer 1971). By the time that the psychology of science had, for all practical purposes, vanished as a distinct field of inquiry, the sociology of science had taken wing as a scholarly enterprise, joining the already high-flying disciplines of the philosophy of science and the history of science. There were accordingly three "metasciences" dedicated to the scholarly examination of science, two of these humanistic and only one scientific in analytical emphasis – with psychology patently excluded (see Houts 1988). This is not to say that psychologists ignored the subject altogether but only that any efforts were sporadic, inconsequential, or noncumulative (Fisch 1977). Many psychological studies were oriented more toward idiographic case studies than toward the abstraction of nomothetic principles that govern scientific discovery and invention (cf. Simonton 1983c). General laws were applied to specific instances rather than adducing those generalizations from multiple particulars. Howard Gruber's *Darwin on Man* (1974) may illustrate this approach at its best.

Nonetheless, in the past few years several psychologists have come to the realization, however delayed, that when opportunity had knocked at the

1

door, the discipline was found asleep. Psychological processes permeate all scientific activities, and this is particularly true in regard to creativity and problem solving. The recent coming of age of the cognitive sciences perhaps accelerated the dawning awareness that psychology may have something to contribute beyond what had already been offered by sociology, philosophy, and the history of science (see Faust 1984). In any event, psychologists have again received invitations to attend conferences devoted to the examination of science, especially the study of scientific creativity. Articles by psychologists have become more common in professional journals, including the interdisciplinary journals specializing in science studies, such as *Scientometrics* and *Social Studies of Science*. And books are once again concentrating on the psychological aspects of science (e.g., Faust 1984; Gholson, Houts, Neimeyer, & Shadish 1988; Jackson & Rushton 1987; Mansfield & Busse 1981; Tweney, Doherty, & Mynatt 1981). It is always dangerous to engage in prophecy, yet it seems that this growing movement may constitute a renaissance of that very psychology of science whose development was arrested two decades ago. At this moment in this miniature narrative, I as an investigator enter the story.

Over the past dozen years or so I have been engaged in research on exceptional personal influence. That is, I have been interested in determining why certain individuals have an inordinate and enduring impact on others in a given domain of achievement. For the most part, although not exclusively, this compelling interest has taken the form of historiometric studies of "geniuses" – of eminent creators and leaders – with much of this work focusing on scientific creativity. Some of the greatest geniuses in science – like Aristotle, Newton, and Einstein – exerted a tremendous and long-term influence not only on their scientific colleagues but on the general intellectual community besides. I have endeavored to understand the personal and social basis for such monumental impact, concentrating especially on the connection between age and achievement, the consequences of political conditions, and the role of the zeitgeist in the generation and acceptance of discoveries and inventions.

In addition to my own empirical and theoretical labors, I have tried to keep abreast of the vast literature on genius, in general, and scientific creativity, in particular. During this research and reading, I have spotted what I consider a consistent theme pervading the phenomenon of outstanding scientific discovery and invention. This theme expanded first into some empirical hypotheses and now can be developed into a full-fledged psychological theory. I style this explanatory and predictive framework the *chance-configuration theory*. This conception, I maintain, facilitates both the organization of past research findings and the formation of new research hypotheses regarding scientific creativity.

I shall begin by sketching the chief tenets of the chance-configuration theory. This chapter will conclude by outlining what I consider to be the theory's explanatory scope. The remainder of this book is largely devoted to an empirical development of the basic ideas presented in this chapter – their enlargement into a comprehensive interpretation of exceptional scientific creativity.

The theory

At the most superficial level, there is little if anything original about the chance-configuration theory. I have always been impressed with Darwin's theory of evolution by natural selection and have often been fascinated with attempts to apply Darwinian ideas to innovation and sociocultural change. In particular, my own theoretical outlook can be said to have roots in Donald Campbell's (1960) blind-variation and selective-retention model of creative thought. To some degree, the current theory is an elaboration, albeit with a shift in nomenclature, of Campbell's ideas – ideas that were recently identified as holding "promise as a possible integrative framework for the psychology of science" (Tweney et al. 1980, p. 405). I shall outline those aspects of Campbell's model that I find most useful before I present my own rendition.

Campbell's scheme purports to be rather general, applicable to virtually any variety of knowledge acquisition or environmental adaptation, including biological evolution by natural selection, trial-and-error learning, creative thought, and social evolution (Campbell 1960, 1965). Furthermore, the model has provided the basis for his "evolutionary epistemology" (Campbell 1974a), a descriptive theory of knowledge that has certain affinities with Karl Popper's philosophy of science (see Schlipp 1974). Although I am in essential sympathy with all of these developments, we need to discuss only that portion of Campbell's thinking that deals specifically with the creative process and the growth of scientific knowledge. For our purposes, then, Campbell's position may be summarized as the following three core propositions:

1. The acquisition of new knowledge, the solution of novel problems, requires some means of producing *variation*. Campbell argues that this variation, to be truly effective, must be fully blind. To count as "blind" the variations must be unrelated to the environmental conditions, including the specific problem, under which the variations are generated, and the varia-

tions should be unrelated to one another (i.e., feedback from the failure of one variation is not used to formulate the next variation in a series of trials) (Campbell 1960). To the extent that the variations are shaped by the environment, whether past or present, they cannot be considered blind. Of course, many alternative qualifiers might be placed on the variations, such as chance, random, aleatory, fortuitous, and haphazard (Campbell 1974b, p. 147), but Campbell preferred the designation blind, for it retains the notion that the variations do not use any information already given, while at the same time it does not commit the variations to a particular generation mechanism. However, within the specific confines of creativity, I prefer the adjective *chance,* as will become evident later in this chapter.

2. These heterogeneous variations are subjected to a consistent *selection* process that winnows out all but those that exhibit adaptive fit (Campbell 1960). In other words, there must exist somewhat stable criteria by which those variations that offer viable solutions to the problem at hand are separated from those that embody no advance and hence are useless. In Darwinian evolution just such a selection procedure is the cornerstone of the theory: Natural selection chooses those genetic variations (whether chance mutations or random assortments of genes) that favor the fit between organism and environment. In scientific discovery, too, variations are judged against a set of criteria; those variations that fail to meet these requirements are weeded out from the body of scientific knowledge.

3. The variations that have been selected must be preserved and reproduced by some mechanism; without such *retention* a successful variation cannot represent a permanent contribution to adaptive fitness. The chromosomes retain fit variations in biological evolution; memory preserves knowledge acquired through learning; and cultural transmission through socialization and education saves valuable customs and techniques in sociocultural evolution.

Campbell noted the fundamental contradiction between the first and third propositions: Blind variation implies a departure from retained knowledge. A genetic mutation is a shot in the dark that ignores the wisdom contained in parental chromosomes, and thus mutant genes are often lethal; an excessive mutation rate would spell the extinction of a species. At the same time, however, a gene pool totally lacking in variation would be unable to adapt to changing circumstances, with consequences just as fatal to the species' survival; in time the genetically encoded wisdom would convert to foolishness. A comparable process operates on the level of the creative process. Any society has a rich repertoire of skills and concepts that enable its members to survive and prosper, and accordingly the cross-generational preservation and transmission of these adaptive features are a high priority. But without any provision for variation, for creativity, the sociocultural system will eventually stagnate, lose adaptive advantages, and in the end be defeated in the competition with rival systems. In a sense, there is an intrinsic contradiction between preserving the fruits of past creative acts and sowing the seeds for future creative achievements. In regard to scientific creativity, Thomas Kuhn (1963, p. 343) referred to this conflict as an "essential tension," for "very often the successful scientist must simultaneously display the characteristics of the traditionalist and of the iconoclast."

Frequently the solution to this conflict is to place restrictions on the variations, limitations that use a priori or a posteriori information. Most biological variation is limited to recombinations of genes of proven environmental utility, and even then not all combinations are permitted. In trial-and-error learning, not all potential behavior patterns are attempted but, rather, merely a subset that has proved itself useful in the past experience of the species and the individual. Cultural variations, too, are normally not allowed to run rampant; certain types of behavioral combinations, in fact, are outright proscribed as criminal or insane. Consequently, many variations display some "insight" into narrowing the possible trials from the near infinity of conceivable alterations. In any event, in chapter 5 we shall see that the essential tension between variation and retention helps explain why success as a scientist is so often a curvilinear, concave-downward function of key developmental variables. Creative development requires a well-adjusted trade-off between the traditionalist and iconoclast dispositions (Simonton 1987a,c).

Campbell (1960) was willing to admit that his model had been anticipated by many thinkers before him, the latter half of the 19th century being particularly resplendent with philosophers who felt the influence of Darwin's revolutionary ideas. He cited, among many examples, the 1880 essay, "Great Men, Great Thoughts, and the Environment," by William James, which emphatically states that "the relation of the visible environment to the great man is in the main exactly what it is to the 'variation' in the Darwinian philosophy" (p. 445). In particular,

the new conceptions, emotions, and active tendencies which evolve are originally *produced* in the shape of random images, fancies, accidental outbirths of spontaneous variation in the functional activity of the excessively unstable human brain, which the outer environment simply confirms or refutes, adopts or rejects, preserves or destroys—*selects,* in short, just as it selects morphological and social variations due to molecular accidents of an analogous sort. (p. 456)

Even though these quotations require qualification to be palatable to modern ears, they do illustrate how Darwinian ideas might be extrapolated to creative behavior. Indeed, if anything, the analogy between biological and other forms of evolution or development has been treated too often and taken too seriously over the past century or so – from Herbert Spencer to the present day.

I consequently should emphasize that I do not wish to draw detailed correspondences among various knowledge–acquisition processes. There are many ways that the analogy between biological and sociocultural evolution breaks down, and human information processing, which constitutes a form of individual development, has its own characteristics as well (Campbell 1965, 1986). Even so, the three components of variation, selection, and retention unite all varieties of knowledge acquisition under a single generic form. The chance-configuration theory offered in the following sections clearly falls into this broad class, too. The key ideas of this theory are (1) the chance permutation of mental elements, (2) the formation of configurations, and (3) the communication, social acceptance, and sociocultural preservation of those configurations. It will become evident that I am here offering a truly social-psychological theory of scientific creativity, one that emphasizes both intrapsychic events taking place solely within the individual and interpsychic or interpersonal events depending on social communication and interaction.

Chance permutations

We shall begin with the assumption that the creative process entails operations on what I choose to call *mental elements*. These psychological entities are the fundamental units that can be manipulated in some manner, such as the sensations that we decide to attend to, the emotions that we experience, and the diverse cognitive schemata, ideas, concepts, or recollections that we can retrieve from long-term memory. In scientific creativity, the predominant mental elements are cognitions of some kind, such as facts, principles, relations, rules, laws, formulae, and images. Yet immediate sensations may also play a role in laboratory experimentation and field exploration, and feelings may figure in scientific thought and discourse as well (Mahoney 1976). Sometimes these mental elements can be evoked voluntarily (e.g., the deliberate retrieval of a stored fact from memory); at other times these elements enter mental processing involuntarily (e.g., via a conditioned emotional association). Moreover, these mental elements do not have to be fully conscious, but rather, many enter information processing at the periphery of consciousness. As Einstein observed, what we "call full consciousness is a limit case which can never be fully accomplished" because of the inherent "narrowness of consciousness" (quoted in Hadamard 1945, p. 143).

Whether voluntary or involuntary, conscious or unconscious, these mental elements must be free to enter into various combinations. In fact, according to the theory proposed here, the fundamental generating mechanism in scientific creativity involves the *chance permutation* of these elements. To clarify what I mean, let me start with the term *permutation*. I favor this term over the alternative more often employed, namely, *combination*. In probability theory, combinations are sets of elements that have no particular order, whereas for permutations the elements' order in the sets is critical to distinguishing among sets. In actual applications, the combinations are frequently more interesting than are the permutations. When calculating the odds of being dealt a royal flush in a card game, for example, the order in which one acquires the ace, king, queen, jack, and ten is immaterial to the chances of obtaining a winning hand. Nonetheless, in other applications the specific order of the elements is crucial, requiring that any given generic combination be separated into its specific permutations. As a case in point, "a mathematical demonstration is not a simple juxtaposition of syllogisms, it is syllogisms *placed in a certain order,* and the order in which these elements are placed is much more important than the elements themselves" (Poincaré 1921, p. 385). This distinction will become useful later in chapter 6 when we discuss the phenomenon of multiple discovery. Consequently, the term permutation is retained insofar as it connotes that we must discriminate among combinations that, although containing identical elements, differ in how those elements are arranged. This usage permits us to say that a combination can form two or more permutations with the same elements but with the elements assigned distinctive levels of importance or emphasis within each permutation.

The hard part is to define *chance*. In general, to claim that the permutations are generated by chance is equivalent to saying that each mental element is evoked by a myriad determinants, there being virtually no overlap in the determinants for any pair of elements defining a given permutation. Chance, after all, is a measure of ignorance, a gauge of the situation in which the number of causes is so immense as to defy identification. Though chance implies unpredictability, it does not necessitate total randomness. We do not need to argue that all permutations of a specific set of elements are equiprobable, in contrast with Mendelian genetics. We must merely insist that a large number of potential permutations exist, all with comparably low but nonzero probabilities. Later in chapter 3, when I relate the theory to the cognitive style of creative persons, I shall describe how chance permutations can come about, at that time drawing on a model originally proposed to explain intuitive thought processes (Simonton 1980a).

Configuration formation

At this point we have evidently postulated a process that yields variations. We next must introduce some principle of selection into the theory, for not all chance permutations can or should be retained. In the case of scientific creativity, selection mechanisms operate on both personal and social levels. At this stage in the argument let us focus on one personal, or intrapsychic, criterion: Here we propose that the primary selection procedure is predicated on the fact that chance permutations vary appreciably in *stability*. On one extreme are transitory juxtapositions of mental elements that lack sufficient coherence to form a stable permutation, so that the permutation process usually continues with little or no pause. These unstable permutations we may call mental *aggregates*. On the other extreme are permutations whose elements, though brought together by a chance confluence of multiple determinants, seem to hang together in a stable arrangement or patterned whole of interrelated parts. These stable permutations I label *configurations*. It must be stressed that aggregates and configurations are permutations of mental elements that fall along a continuum from the highly unstable to the highly stable, with many gradations between. Nonetheless, we assume that of the innumerable chance permutations, only the most stable are retained for further information processing, for the greater the stability is, the higher the probability of selection will be. Further, on a subjective plane, the more stable a permutation is, the more attention it will command in consciousness, as the unstable permutations are too fleeting to rise often above unconscious levels of processing. Thus, configurations of elements are selected out from the permutations to be saved for further conscious deliberation.

The crucial requirement, then, is to define *configuration*. I chose this word advisedly, over the many possible alternatives (schemata, associative fields, constructs, concepts, ideas, matrices, etc.), based on its etymology and common applications. The root of *configuration* is a Latin word meaning "to shape after some pattern." A configuration is thus a conformation or structural arrangement of entities and implies that the relative disposition of these entities is central to the configuration's identity. In chemistry and physics the relative spatial location of atoms in a molecule is often called a configuration. Likewise in astronomy the characteristic grouping of heavenly bodies is sometimes referred to as a configuration. Finally, in psychology and, most particularly, in Gestalt theory, a configuration is a collection of sensations, emotions, motor patterns, and concepts organized in such fashion that the collection operates as a unit in thought and behavior. Indeed, if a configuration becomes sufficiently refined, it can become a new mental element that can enter into further permutations. That is, if the diverse elements that make up the configuration become strongly connected, they all will become "chunked" so that they function as a single element, taking up less space in limited attention. This process of consolidation is analogous to that when the atoms forming a molecule become subordinate to that molecule, which then operates as a unit in physical transformations (e.g., Avogadro's number applies to molecules of gas, not to the separate atoms).

It may seem contradictory to assert that mental elements thrown together by happenstance can unite in a way that prevents disintegration, but we must recognize that what jumbles the elements together is different from what glues them together. The elements themselves contain properties that will determine how well they fit together. The intrinsic attributes of one element may dovetail nicely with other elements, creating a stable unit. Hence, even if two elements are tossed together by haphazard juxtaposition, those elements may stick together because of mutually compatible properties. This event is analogous to a chance encounter that brings two people together who then form a lasting relationship on the basis of similar and complementary interests and values. Or to offer an analogy from chemistry, the hundred or so chemical elements each have characteristics, principally valence, that decide how they will behave in chemical reactions. For example, an atom of sodium tends to give up an electron in order to acquire a complete outer electron shell, whereas chlorine, because it lacks only one electron to finish out its outer shell, tends to take up an electron. Thus, sodium and chlorine atoms are intrinsically compatible elements, the former yielding an electron to the latter so that both can form a stable "molecule" of sodium chloride (Na^+Cl^-). Therefore, the random impact of gaseous chlorine on solid sodium will corrode the metal into sodium chloride. On the other hand, helium, which already possesses a full outer shell and thus is placed in the column of inert elements on the periodic table, will not combine with either sodium or chlorine, no matter how many random impacts are permitted between the molecules.

Because certain elements have intrinsic affinities for each other, not only can a chance linkage of two elements produce a stable pairing, but large clusters of elements also can spontaneously form highly ordered arrangements out of chaos. Campbell (1974b) offered a striking example of crystal formation, in which under the proper conditions, a dissolved chemical will not precipitate into merely amorphous aggregates but, rather, fine crystals.

A specific crystalline structure is implicit in the ions or molecules leaving solution, and so a more organized spatial pattern is actually more stable than is one less organized, yielding a specific configuration from the mere random collisions of the ions or molecules.

To be sure, this last example is much simpler than what occurs in intellectual matters. It is not always apparent when two distinct mental elements contain a natural affinity, nor is it obvious how these affinities might lead to larger structures, or configurations. At least, such ideational compatibilities are less apparent on a priori grounds and are, rather, discerned retrospectively, on a post hoc basis. For instance, a number of studies have illustrated how specific combinations of philosophical beliefs have been more prone to appear than have others in Western civilization (Simonton 1976c,f). Nominalism, as a case in point, is more likely to be associated with empiricism, mechanistic determinism, and the doctrine of incessant change than with mysticism, monistic idealism, and eternalism, just as hedonistic and utilitarian ethics display a stronger a posteriori linkage with mechanistic materialism, nominalism, and extreme individualism than with monistic idealism, realism, and universalism or statism. Even if some were to argue that these affinities could be justified a priori (see, e.g., Sorokin 1937–1941), such arguments would be precarious at best. As is well known, Kant erred in holding that Euclidean geometry was true a priori, a belief dispelled with the advent of perfectly consistent non-Euclidean geometries that later became the foundation for Einstein's treatment of space in his general relativity theory.

Configuration acquisition. To appreciate how chance permutations may generate stable collections of elements, we first must note that very few configurations arise in this way. On the contrary, most configurations consist of mental elements that have been connected on either empirical or logical grounds. In particular, these mental givens that provide the material for chance configurations are of two types, a posteriori and a priori configurations (cf. Stevens 1939).

A posteriori configurations establish a correspondence between perceived events and their cognitive representations. If, for example, we have a set of world events $A_1, A_2, \ldots, A_n$ represented by a set of mental elements $A_1', A_2', \ldots, A_n'$ and if, in reality, the conditional probability of any one event given any one of the others is much greater than zero, so that $p(A_i/A_j) \gg 0$ for all $i \neq j$, we can expect the mental elements to be ordered so that the subjective association strengths approximate the objective conditional probabilities (e.g., the rank order of conditional probabilities positively correlates with the rank order of association strengths). That is, in some manner a posteriori configurations are internal images of the world, mental expectations matching the observed cooccurrences of events. There is no need to specify how this fitting of configurations to environmental probabilities is accomplished. Pavlovian (classical) and Skinnerian (operant) conditioning certainly contribute, but cognitive and social learning theories may apply in equal or greater force. For instance, in Piaget's developmental theory, beginning in the sensorimotor phase, the child constructs schemata that relate sensations and actions into a coherent view of the world, eventually acquiring concepts of objects, causal expectations, and other useful configurations that symbolize how the world works and how the child can work on the world. However, we shall show in chapter 5, which discusses developmental antecedents of creativity, that certain ways of acquiring associations are more conducive to the emergence of an efficacious chance-permutation mechanism.

Unlike a posteriori configurations, which derive from experience, *a priori configurations* emerge from given conventions. These conventions define a set of mental elements and the rules by which these elements can be combined into a proper order. In arithmetic, algebra, and other forms of mathematics, for instance, the members of a given tradition are provided with rules for the correct manipulation of numbers and abstract symbols, enabling a practitioner to perform long division, solve an equation to express an unknown quantity in terms of known quantities, and to accomplish like tasks. Logic, too, regulates how specific verbal propositions can be combined so that we can detect when a set of statements is consistent or inconsistent. It is, in fact, characteristic of a priori configurations that decisions of rightness or wrongness, truth or falsity, are absolute within a given body of rules; a number either is or is not the square root of another number, and a function either is or is not the integral of a given function. The adequacy of a posteriori configurations, in contrast, is decided on probabilistic grounds, based on the degree of congruence between observation and cognitive representation. This absolute, right-or-wrong nature of a priori configurations is seen not just in mathematics and logic but in linguistic conventions as well. Each language contains rules, such as grammars, that define how phonemes combine into morphemes, how morphemes form words, and how words are arranged into sentences.

When I call such configurations a priori, I do not consider them anything more than mere conventions. Although some rules may represent innate ways of organizing thoughts founded on the evolutionary history of the species, most are likely derived instead from cultural evolution (cf. Campbell 1974b). Hence, even if children initially evolve their own grammars based on an instinctive coordination of linguistic material, eventually all children end up with the grammars that characterize their particular language community. Likewise, logic and mathematics may overlay primitive, species-specific givens regarding the appropriate approach to structuring cognitions according to culturally provided principles of information-processing etiquette (see also Campbell 1986, 1987).

A priori configurations have one valuable asset relative to a posteriori configurations, namely, that mental elements are combined without any recourse to empirical experience. Even a child can generate sentences never before heard; a logician can produce propositions from a set of premises that are not immediately apparent; and a mathematician can derive equations that are merely implicit in a set of axioms (that may or may not constitute abstractions from experience). Thus in a sense, a priori configurations can be truly "inventive," just as we can claim that chance configurations are fully "imaginative." Even so, the inventiveness of a priori configurations is less extensive than is the imaginativeness of chance configurations. The former is bounded by the conventions that define the acceptable repertoire of elements and rules of permutation, whereas the latter is virtually unlimited, for chance can place in juxtaposition virtually any element, without regard to logic.

We observed earlier that configurations may be "consolidated"; that is, the elements can be so compacted that the configuration as a whole can function as a single unit in mental manipulations. This can occur for a posteriori and a priori configurations as well as for chance configurations. In the case of a posteriori configurations, certain events cooccur so frequently that they become definitive elements of a particular concept (e.g., birds as feathered egg layers). For a priori configurations, particular operations may be refined so that what once was a complicated procedure becomes conveniently simple. For instance, by using algebraic rules and the concept of limits, one can demonstrate how various functions are differentiated, yielding a new set of rules that allow a mathematician to circumvent the original derivations (e.g., except in introductory calculus courses, no one uses limits, with the δ/ε nicety, to take the first derivative of trigonometric, logarithmic/exponential, polynomial, and other standard functions). Once a priori and a posteriori configurations become consolidated sufficiently so that they can be manipulated as mental elements, they can enter the process by which chance permutations emerge. (However, if the configurations are too refined, they will be less able to participate in chance variations, for reasons that will become evident in chapter 3.) Hence, the fortuitous union of two or more established configurations can form a new configuration, a configuration that may later become an element in another configuration still.

Self-organization. We can now state why some chance permutations are more stable than others are. Sometimes two configurations, of whatever origin, will have similar structures, and so the elements can line up more or less one on one. In other words, an approximate one-to-one correspondence can be fixed between the two configurations so that the elements of one set are mapped onto the elements of the other set. One important and commonplace example of this matching of elements across configurations is one chance permutation's producing an analogy between two hitherto unrelated phenomena (see Poze 1983; cf. Sternberg 1977). When Huygens, Young, Fresnel, or Maxwell saw that light behaved as a wave phenomenon, they established equivalences between two a posteriori configurations, one encoding the diverse behaviors of light in experimental studies, and the other the known behaviors of waves. Thus, different colors correspond to distinct wavelengths, color intensity to wave amplitude, and complex hues to mixtures of various wavelengths and amplitudes. Reflection, refraction, diffraction, and interference are effects with counterparts in both light and wave phenomena. Because so many characteristics of light map successfully onto wave attributes, the junction of these two configurations itself forms a stable configuration (in classical physics).

A second example is the pairing of an a posteriori configuration with a configuration derived a priori. Sometimes a particular mathematical formula will describe relationships between two or more abstract variables that fit the observed relationships between a similar number of concrete variables. The Balmer series illustrates this sort of isomorphism: By means of induction, Balmer found a relatively simple equation that could predict the location of the spectral lines of hydrogen, in which the wavelengths are expressed as a function of integers. We do not know exactly how Balmer arrived at his equation, but some sort of trial-and-error process was involved. Not until Bohr introduced his quantum theory of the atom did the Balmer series receive a theoretical justification (i.e., was subsumed under a larger a priori configuration).

What is gained by merging two or more configurations? One answer is that one configuration is frequently better consolidated than the other is, which is less well defined. A good model of light, for instance, allows us to connect a range of phenomena that before would be deemed isolated facts. We not only link together the various light phenomena but also place the visual spectrum within a single, unidimensional scale (wavelength) that stretches from X-rays and ultraviolet to infrared and radio waves, all with the same set of definitive behaviors (reflection, refraction, diffraction, etc.). Moreover, once we consider light as a wave rather than a particle phenomenon, we are led to specific expectations that, if verified, will expand our knowledge of light (e.g., whether the velocity of light increases or decreases when passing from air to water). Thus, a tight analogy or model permits us to know more about the world with less work (see also Gentner & Gentner 1983; Kochen & Lansing 1985). The same gain in informational efficiency is even seen in the application of an arbitrary formula to empirical data. It takes less mental space to remember Balmer's equation than it does to memorize all the wavelengths appearing in the hydrogen spectrum. More generally, the integration of configurations makes us think more economically, for the number of unrelated elements with which we must cope is dramatically reduced. Even if the correspondences are not perfect, there may be a net economical gain if the elements neatly packaged outnumber the elements left unaccounted for. For example, in English we have the orthographic rule "*i* before *e* except after *c* or when sounded as *a* as in *neighbor* and *weigh*." It is easier to recall this verse and the rare exceptions, such as *weird,* than to memorize the spelling of all words with a paired *e* and *i*.

The gain in information-processing efficiency becomes especially apparent when configurations are united hierarchically, that is, when mental elements are ordered for the optimal retrieval of facts and the anticipation of events. This asset is perhaps most conspicuous in biological taxonomy, in which each living form is assigned to a kingdom, phylum, class, order, family, genus, and species. Knowing how a particular species falls in each category immediately produces relevant data about morphology, physiology, and behavior. Likewise in the case of classical physics, many phenomena can be grouped into particle and wave events, wave phenomena into transverse and longitudinal waves, and so forth. We thus postulate that the human intellect is programmed to self-organize its contents into hierarchical structures in which knowledge is most efficaciously distributed. On the plane of subjective experience, we might even posit that the mind receives subjective rewards, or pleasure, from noticeable enhancements in cognitive order, in which pleasure is merely the marking of an adaptive event, as in the sweetness of carbohydrates. In other words, cognitive events that reduce mental "entropy," by combining configurations into more comprehensive hierarchical formations, receive intrinsic reinforcement. These subjective rewards or gratifications may be identified with the "peak experiences" characteristic of Maslow's (1962) "self-actualizers." Conversely, stimuli, whether facts or ideas, that appear to disrupt or challenge the present order are perceived as obnoxious, provoking defensive displeasure and rejection. Yet however adaptive and pleasurable intellectual organization may be, configurations cannot be ordered into higher-order configurations unless they are sufficiently consolidated. Otherwise each component of a hierarchical structure would connect with so many other components that its organization would be lost. This is why Descartes was wise to ground his philosophy solely on ideas "clear and distinct."

This self-organization, which is here presumed to drive the creative process in great science, is not equivalent to the dispassionate quest for truth that is so often thought to energize the scientific enterprise. Epistemologists are fond of abstract schemes by which knowledge propositions can be discerned and demonstrated. Although some scientists have indeed claimed to have been guided by such prescriptions – Charles Darwin gave lip service in his notebooks to Baconian induction (Gruber 1974), and the Nobel laureate John Eccles (1975) maintained that he successfully applied Popperian falsification – the bulk of the evidence suggests that few scientists are so well behaved. On the contrary, a provocative research literature has accumulated on the "confirmation bias" in human reasoning (e.g., Mynatt, Doherty, & Tweney 1977; Wason 1968). When faced with having to infer the principle underlying a sequence of events, people are not inclined to seek out information that contradicts a favored hypothesis but, rather, to gather the most confirmatory evidence that the circumstances will allow. Even when disconfirmatory data unexpectedly appear, they often are ignored as a minor exception to the accepted rule. Not only is there reason to believe that practicing scientists betray this confirmatory bias (Mahoney 1976), but those scientists most admired by their colleagues may also be those most dedicated to proving a cherished hypothesis or theory (Mitroff 1974). The notion of the disinterested investigator calmly committed to pure induction and falsification is a myth (see also Faust 1984).

Self-organization motivates the mind, whenever possible, to assimilate unpleasant facts into the present cognitive order, for to give up one's intellectual framework willy-nilly simply to accommodate the confusion of random events is to risk expanding psychological disorder, with a corresponding loss in behavioral adaptiveness (Campbell 1986). Indeed, notwithstanding his advocacy of doubt as the foundation of philosophy, Descartes admitted that skepticism should not be extended to practical affairs. And judging by the confirmatory bias he exhibited in grounding his theories on a priori rather than a posteriori principles, Descartes apparently limited the application of doubt in the sphere of scientific practice. Thus, scientists, or at least the greatest among them, appear to be more oriented toward the discovery of regularity, structure, order, harmony, or, in a word, *beauty* (see, e.g., Dirac 1963; Einstein 1933; Hardy 1940; Poincaré 1921; Wechsler 1978). Although not repudiating the value of truth, creative scientists apparently operate according to the "psychologic" voiced by Keats in *The Ode on a Grecian Urn* that " 'Beauty is truth, truth beauty,'–that is all/ Ye know on earth, and all ye need to know." This intuitive equivalence will be documented in later chapters.

To summarize, we assume that human information processing is designed to select those chance permutations that significantly augment the efficiency of thought. The stable permutations, or configurations, can then be further consolidated, eventually forming a hierarchy. This process reflects "a fundamental tendency for the stable to replace the unstable" (Ashby 1952, p. vi) in an apparent (but only superficial) violation of the second law of thermodynamics (see also Prigogine & Stengers 1984).

Communication and acceptance

Although we now have the rudiments of a chance-permutation and selective-retention theory, scientific creativity cannot be fully explained without adding three more variation–selection processes. The first is also intrapsychic, but the remaining two are social. Because these represent a temporal sequence of selection processes that occur after the primary creative act, let us outline them in order.

Communication configurations. Once a configuration has been isolated and proved useful in structuring cognition, that discovery will remain an article of personal knowledge only until it is successfully expressed to others. Occasionally the stable permutation is already in suitable form, for the elements being varied may have been linguistic or mathematical. But far more often, further intellectual effort is demanded to articulate the discovery or invention. For example, if the new configuration is a visual image or model of a process, such as a chemical reaction or molecular structure, then that configuration must be linked with a verbal description in which a correspondence is set up between image referent and verbal symbol. In some disciplines, a coherent logical pattern must be imposed as well, especially the translation of the initial idea into mathematical forms. Finally, the sciences have formats for the accepted presentation of findings. These journal styles are arbitrary and artificial inasmuch as they no longer correspond to the simple narration of how a finding came about, as was common for scientific papers published centuries ago (e.g., in *Philosophical Transactions*).

Hence, this conversion of a configuration from the ineffable to the articulate yields an often more complex *communication* configuration. On most occasions this conversion process is relatively straightforward, conscious, and deliberate, but at times the isolation of an appropriate vehicle of expression itself mandates a creative synthesis, sometimes even to the point of having to scan through another series of chance permutations. Moreover, when the conversion cannot be perfunctory, the particular communication configuration arrived at may be so arbitrary that something is lost in the translation. A one-to-one correspondence is lacking between the original and articulated configurations, so that one cannot be completely mapped onto the other. Such misfits are especially likely when the structure of the language, logic, or mathematics used fails to parallel that of the new stable permutation. In the case of linguistic articulation, the Whorf–Sapir hypothesis that language determines thought may operate here, albeit deflecting more the communication of knowledge than the knowledge acquisition per se (cf. Whorf 1956). And for mathematical expression, a scientist is sometimes compelled to devise a novel mathematics in order to convey an original thought, as did Newton, Fourier, and Hamilton.

Interpersonal influence. If a workable communication configuration has been devised, it can be made available to other scientists via the standard vehicles of scientific exchange, most commonly an article in a technical journal or a patent application. At this point the selection mechanisms cease to be merely intrapsychic, becoming fully social instead. Specifically, the articulated discovery or invention must succeed in the domain of interpersonal influence; that is, it must be accepted by colleagues in the same discipline. Referees must agree that the offered idea represents an advance worthy of publication, and readers of the published article or monograph must be able to use the communicated configuration to restructure their own thinking habits in approximately the same manner as did the originator. Social acceptance signifies that a community of scientists have found the suggested configuration to be valuable to their own personal endeavors toward self-organization, toward augmented cognitive effectiveness – whether the idea be a key finding that helps fill in a puzzling gap in knowledge, an original technique or instrument that allows variables and relationships to be assessed that hitherto escaped scrutiny, or a novel revolutionary theory that mandates the remaking of thought. In the case of inventions, the offered creation must enable potential users to structure more effectively subsequent planned actions, thereby enhancing the organization of practical behaviors. Several requirements must be met before the creation can achieve acceptance, four perhaps standing out.

1. Each member of the community must have available a similar repertoire of mental elements, such as a shared body of facts, methods, and questions. This shared foundation may include "universally recognized scientific achievements that for a time provide model problems and solutions to a community of practitioners" (Kuhn 1970, p. viii).

2. Those mental elements must be in comparative disarray in the minds of potential acceptors, so that there is a need for a more efficient approach to structuring information. Darwin noted in the last chapter of his *Origin of Species* (1860, p. 240): "Although I am fully convinced of the truth of the views given in this volume . . . I by no means expect to convince experienced naturalists whose minds are stocked with a multitude of facts all viewed, during a long course of years, from a point of view directly opposite to mine." Hence, Kuhn (1970, p. 53) observed how the accumulation of *anomalies* – findings that cannot be assimilated into a given scientific framework, tradition, or paradigm – prepares the way for scientific revolution. "Discovery begins with the awareness of anomaly, i.e., with the recognition that nature has somehow violated the paradigm-induced expectations that govern normal science."

3. There must be a consensus on the meaning of the linguistic, logical, and mathematical elements making up the communication configuration. This consensus enables each member of the community to reconstruct the original configuration from its social representation. From this requirement arises the difficulties encountered by those compelled to devise a totally new language or nomenclature, even logic, to articulate an original idea.

4. The originator must have successfully translated and communicated the initial conception so as to facilitate the requisite reverse translation by fellow scientists. Anthony Hope may have held, in his *Dolly Dialogues,* that "unless one is a genius, it is best to aim at being intelligible," yet even a genius, and certainly a scientific one, must aspire to the same goal. The capacity to exert personal influence over others is undermined by unintelligibility, for people are seldom persuaded by those who insist on talking over their heads (Simonton 1985a). Galois and Heaviside are just two of numerous scientists whose ideas were not immediately comprehensible to potential colleagues, thus substantially delaying the time that they could effectively contribute to scientific advance. Thus, even if the idea is couched in understandable terms, the communication configuration must assume a proper form. For instance, in his *On the Nature of Things,* Lucretius could convey scientific concepts in verse; but long before Erasmus Darwin made a similar endeavor when announcing his evolutionary theory, prose, not poetry, became the only acceptable manner of presenting scientific ideas. Also, scientists who dare to publish their thoughts in languages outside the lingua franca of scientific exchange suffer comparable consequences. A final aspect of this fourth requirement entails choosing the best vehicle for publishing theoretical or empirical results. It is no accident that competent scientists today select their journals quite deliberately: Unless

their work reaches the best audience for their ideas, the odds of leaving an imprint on science will be small indeed (see Gordon 1984).

These four requirements assume that the innovator's intellectual constitution is somewhat closer to that of the traditionalist than the iconoclast. That is, the scientific genius must to some extent be representative of others in the same discipline. Both creators and potential acceptors must share a set of mental elements, which are in comparable states of disassembly, and agree on the referents and rules belonging to particular expressive symbols (e.g., nomenclatures and standards of proof or evidence). To the extent that scientists do not represent their colleagues on these matters, their personal impact will diminish. The history of science is replete with instances of great minds who failed to leave an imprint on their times, owing to their failure to put together a passable communication configuration, however correct and significant their ideas were. Indeed, as we shall point out in chapter 6, this lapse in communication is one of the chief causes of multiple discovery and invention. Nonetheless, as long as some communication configuration has been offered, even if only in the guise of an unpublished manuscript or working model, the proffered ideas may be acceptable to a future community that has caught up with the forerunner.

Sociocultural preservation. In simple terms, the magnitude of social acceptance is registered by a poll of scientific colleagues. The more fellow scientists who use the communicated configuration to reorganize their thinking, the more adherents the innovation can claim. If almost all scientists in a discipline (or, at least, all productive or influential ones) adopt the new way of looking at experience, then this selection process can be said to be maximally complete. Though this victory is desirable, in revolutionary results or concepts often only a subset of the potential population of acceptors is convinced, in which case the innovation may merely add a new school rather than supplanting the old ones. When this occurs, we have a selection process operating on a higher plane, for the schools will then be competing for adherents. The school that succeeds will be the one that most promotes cognitive efficiency in its membership. In Kuhnian terms, we have rival scientific paradigms competing for the devotion of the forthcoming generations of scientists (Kuhn 1970).

In some sciences, naturally, no one school or paradigm is superior to any other, and accordingly two or more traditions may exist side by side for some time. This "speciation" of a discipline is particularly likely when the amount of data is large and unevenly distributed throughout the community, thereby allowing each school to concentrate on a subset of elements for synthesis (which is analogous in biological evolution to specializing in a particular ecological niche). This is often the case in the behavioral and earth sciences. As an example, for a long time geology was bifurcated into Neptunists and Plutonists (or Vulcanists), the geographic distribution of adherents in each school roughly corresponding to the prominence of sedimentary versus metamorphic minerals and formations in the lands where the geologists did their field work. Only when geological information became more homogeneously disseminated could these rival systems fuse into a conception like that found in Lyell's *Principles of Geology*. More recently, the willingness to accept the theory of continental drift has been shown to have depended partly on which section of the world the geoscientists did their research training, with those working in South America being the most receptive (Stewart 1986). Likewise, the profusion of theories that currently permeate psychology may in part reflect the uneven distribution of raw facts, with psychologists diverging on the sources of phenomena to which they are exposed – animal versus human, abnormal versus normal, laboratory versus natural, behavioral versus introspective, developmental versus differential, and so forth.

Nonetheless, it is crucial to recognize that even when an original configuration recruits enough adherents to form a school or paradigm, it does not mean that all converts will subscribe to the exact same ideas. On the contrary, because the mental elements to be integrated will almost never be identical within each mind, the subsequent cognitive integration will rarely be equivalent from person to person. Those who accept a scientific innovation assimilate the configuration to match their own personal needs for self-organization. For instance, not all converts to Darwin's theory maintained the same set of theoretical propositions, even if all could be said to define a school in united opposition to the traditional creationist interpretation of the origins of life (Hull, Tessner, & Diamond 1978).

A chance permutation must therefore pass a series of tests before it can become part of what is considered to be general scientific knowledge. Two tests are intrapsychic or personal, and another pair is social. First, the chance permutation must be sufficiently stable to coalesce into an original configuration. Then this configuration must be capable of elaboration into a communication configuration that makes it accessible to other practitioners of the scientific enterprise. Given this articulation, enough colleagues must accept the new configuration by using it, however idiosyncratically, to reorganize their own conceptions of reality. Finally, when there are enough converts to form a new school, this school must win the competition with the other schools, including any handed down from previous generations. In a sense, this selection sequence represents a chaining of separate variation–selection processes. Of all chance permutations, only a small proportion is stable enough to constitute configurations. Of this set of configurations, sometimes only a subset is successfully articulated. And from the resulting variation in available communication configurations, just an élite number will be honored with social acceptance (e.g., only a small percentage of published articles is even cited in subsequent works by others). Should two or more schools form, their variation will enable further selection at the sociocultural level.

Scope of application

So far we have introduced such key theoretical concepts as the chance permutation of mental elements; the formation of chance, a priori, and a posteriori configurations; and the creation, social acceptance, and sociocultural survival of communication configurations – all driven by an intrinsic quest for self-organization. Still, the chance-configuration theory is currently just a bare sketch in need of elaboration. To develop the theory further, I shall draw on information published in several disciplines (especially psychology, education, sociology, anthropology, and history) concerning key aspects of scientific creativity: (1) impressionistic evidence concerning the creative process, including both introspections and anecdotes; (2) individual differences in personality, whether cognitive or motivational; (3) productivity, including both cross-sectional variation and longitudinal fluctuations in quantity and quality of contribution; (4) developmental antecedents, such as family background, role models, education, marginality, and the sociocultural milieu; and (5) the phenomenon of multiples, that is, independent and often simultaneous discoveries and inventions. These are the topics of chapters 2 through 6. Chapter 7 then consolidates and applies the chief conclusions.

Before we advance to the empirical development of the theory, however, I must set forth what I consider to be the theory's explanatory scope. Any scientific model or system is necessarily restricted to a subset of all known phenomena (Toulmin 1960). Here we have two fuzzy delimiters.

First, the emphasis is on explaining creativity in the pure or basic sciences, such as mathematics, astronomy, physics, chemistry, and biology. This is not to say that the chance-configuration theory is irrelevant to understanding innovations in the applied sciences, like technology and medicine, but only that little effort will be made to account for any peculiarities inherent in the practical applications of scientific knowledge. Actually, I have argued elsewhere that the chance-configuration theory handles quite well the chief empirical aspects of creativity in the arts and humanities, not just in science and technology (Simonton 1987b). Indeed, certain facets of leadership, whether political, military, or economic, might be constructively interpreted, *mutatis mutandis,* in the same theoretical language. At suitable places throughout this volume, I shall compare and contrast scientific creativity with other guises of creativity, even with leadership. Even so, these discussions will serve largely to clarify the nature of pure science. At the same time, I shall pay little attention to differences among the several disciplines of basic science. Creativity in physics is not identical with that in biology, for instance (Roe 1952a). Nevertheless, all forms of creativity, and especially all forms dedicated to advancing scientific knowledge, share a common basis for discovery and invention. It is this common ground that supports my main theoretical arguments in the following chapters.

Second, I shall stress enlarging our appreciation of scientific creativity in its most remarkable form – that of the genius. This concept is romantic and elusive enough to make difficult a comprehensive and precise definition. A tradition over a century old associates genius with an exceptional intellect, as psychometrically registered by an intelligence quotient, or IQ, at least two standard deviations above the mean (Cattell 1903; Cox 1926; Galton 1869). But even if this position does have advantages, it remains incomplete, for cognitive power means nothing at all in isolation from the drive to use it (Nicholls 1972). "Genius does what it must, and Talent does what it can," apologized Owen Meredith in his *Last Words of a Sensitive Second-Rate Poet.* Yet even the inclusion of this motivational side of scientific genius does not suffice, for many profound and energetic minds have labored away without leaving even the tiniest imprint on scientific progress. Ultimately, any meaningful definition of genius – in order to have real-world validity – must include a social component (cf. Brannigan 1981). I conceive creativity as a form of personal influence over others and therein as a special variety of leadership – sociocultural rather than political, military, or economic. Social psychologists frequently define a leader as that group member who exerts more influence in problem solving or decision making than does the typical member of the group (Simonton 1985a). According to this conception, clearly an Aristotle, Newton, or Einstein is a leader par excellence in the community of scientists. The scientific genius exerts a massive effect not just on contemporaries but also on posterity (Albert 1975). In the last analysis, genius is defined by enduring eminence or reputation. "By reputation," said Francis Galton (1869, p. 33), "I mean the opinion of contemporaries, revised by posterity . . . the reputation of a leader of opinion, of an originator, of a man to whom the world deliberately acknowledges itself largely indebted."

Eminence, to be sure, is not a perfect indicator of creative greatness. Even Thomas Carlyle, a stalwart proponent of the cult of genius, admitted that fame "is no sure test of merit, but only a probability of such." Indeed, in later chapters we shall discuss some of the capricious ways that intrinsic capacity is translated into outward success. And we shall dispel certain heroic notions about the attributes of scientific luminaries (see also Weisberg 1986). Still, I chose to concentrate on creative genius in science because I believe that the chance-configuration theory best applies to those who have achieved a truly illustrious and permanent position in the annals of science.

2 Impressionistic evidence

Chance permutation and configuration

Numerous philosophers and scientists have conjectured about the role of random processes in science (Campbell 1960, 1974b). Ernst Mach, a physicist and philosopher of science, published in 1896 a paper entitled "On the Part Played by Accident in Invention and Discovery." What we abstractly call the chance permutation of mental elements until a stable configuration arrives he described far more graphically: "From the teaming, swelling host of fancies which a free and high-flown imagination calls forth, suddenly that particular form arises which harmonizes perfectly with the ruling idea, mood, or design" (p. 174). Earlier still, in an essay mentioned in the first chapter, psychologist William James (1880, p. 456) described the thinking patterns of "the highest order of minds" in this way:

Instead of thoughts of concrete things patiently following one another in a beaten track of habitual suggestion, we have the most abrupt cross-cuts and transitions from one idea to another, the most rarefied abstractions and discriminations, the most unheard of combination of elements, the subtlest associations of analogy; in a word, we seem suddenly introduced into a seething caldron of ideas, where everything is fizzling and bobbling about in a state of bewildering activity, where partnerships can be joined or loosened in an instant, treadmill routine is unknown, and the unexpected seems only law.

In his discussion James refers to the work of his predecessor, William S. Jevons, an economist whose 1877 book *The Principles of Science* claims that

it would be an error to suppose that the great discoverer seizes at once upon the truth, or has any unerring method of divining it. In all probability the errors of the great mind exceed in number those of the less vigorous one. Fertility of imagination and abundance of guesses at truth are among the first requisites of discovery; but the erroneous guesses must be many times as numerous as those that prove well founded. The weakest analogies, the most whimsical notions, the most apparently absurd theories, may pass through the teeming brain, and no record remain of more than the hundredth part. There is nothing really absurd except that which proves contrary to logic and experience. The truest theories involve suppositions which are inconceivable, and no limit can really be placed to the freedom of hypotheses. (Jevons 1900, p. 577)

24

Although about a century old, these three quotations do an excellent job of sketching the phenomenological attributes of the chance-permutation process and, in the case of Mach, the identification of a configuration. To document these descriptions further and to make them more detailed and concrete, we shall in this chapter draw on impressionistic evidence, whether introspective reports or anecdotes. Despite the subjective and unsystematic nature of these data, they do suggest that the chance-configuration theory describes the actual thought processes of great scientists rather than the highly idealized (and frequently invalid) portraits so often conjured up by philosophers of science, from Francis Bacon and J. S. Mill up to the present day (see also Mahoney 1976; Medawar 1984; cf. Hanson 1958).

Introspective reports

Occasionally, creative persons, whether spontaneously or when prodded by queries, will leave an account of the mental processes behind their creative acts (see Ghiselin 1952). Although scientists have been perhaps somewhat more reluctant to engage or indulge in introspections than artists, composers, and writers have, enough have left reports to document the mental processes involved in chance permutation and configuration identification. In particular, we have instructive reports on three facets of the creative person in science: the nature of the mental elements, the operation of the permutation mechanism, and the unexpected illumination after an apparent incubation period.

The nature of the mental elements

Einstein consented to offer some introspections for a survey conducted by the French mathematician Jacques Hadamard; Einstein's report appears in appendix II of Hadamard's 1945 book *The Psychology of Invention in the Mathematical Field*. With minor rearrangement (required because Hadamard's questionnaire somewhat artificially structured the response), Einstein clearly described a two-stage process. The first stage is the free permutation of mental elements: "The psychical entities which seem to serve as elements in thought are certain signs and more or less clear images which can be 'voluntarily' reproduced and combined. . . . [T]his combinatory play seems to be the essential feature in productive thought" (p. 142). These "elements are . . . of visual and some of muscular type" (p. 143). In fact, even though "the desire to arrive finally at logically connected concepts is the emotional basis of this rather vague play with the above mentioned elements," the combinatory play takes place "before there is any connection with logical construction in words or other kinds of signs which can be communicated to others" (p. 142). Because "the words or the language, as they are written or spoken, do not seem to play any role in my mechanism of thought" (p. 142), "conventional words or other signs have to be sought for laboriously only in a secondary stage, when the mentioned associative play is sufficiently established and can be reproduced at will" (p. 143). In our terms, after a novel configuration has been identified through chance permutations and then sufficiently consolidated, an appropriate communication configuration must be constructed. This stage is only weakly aided by the presence of "a certain connection between those elements and relevant logical concepts" (p. 142).

As Hadamard (1945) noted, other scientists in the mathematical disciplines have likewise reported the prominence of visual images, and sometimes kinesthetic feelings, during the early phases of discovery and invention. Because mathematical, even verbal, thoughts participate so little, the process by which mental elements are combined is neither logical nor articulate. Curiously, when words do play a role in the jumbling together of largely nonverbal elements, that role is atypical from the standpoint of standard linguistic expression. Galton, for example, observed that nonsense words may appear "as the notes of a song might accompany thought" (quoted in Hadamard 1945, p. 69), and other scientists have recorded unusual verbal associations such as puns. In these instances, the physical characteristics of the verbal stimuli – how words actually sound – are what apparently mediate the free-associative process that underlies the location of truly exceptional chance permutations. In a sense, the mental elements in the creative act seem more compatible with what might prevail in poetry rather than in science.

To be sure, truly verbal, even mathematical, thought processes may be more common in certain scientific endeavors. In Roe's (1952a) study of eminent scientists, those in the social sciences were more dependent on linguistic cognitions than were those in the natural sciences; and in physics, the theoreticians relied more on verbalizations than did the experimentalists. Those scientists who exclusively use verbal mental elements sometimes proclaim that words are the sole vehicle of creativity – that one cannot have a thought unless it is embedded in words. Max Müller, the distinguished 19th-century language scholar, held that thinking must, without exception, be couched in linguistic symbols organized into proper sentences, a position with which Hadamard took issue (cf. Watson 1930, chap. 9). Perhaps when the phenomena under investigation are primarily verbal, as is frequently the case in many social sciences, the most suitable mental elements will tend to be verbal too. Nonetheless, because most scientists deal with natural phenomena that are not linguistic, it is likely that a star creator must go beyond words to obtain genuinely novel permutations. When words do mix with the nonverbal imagery, they will do so in ways that use nonlogical and nonlinguistic qualities of those words, such as their sonic attributes and emotional connotations. How this can come about will become more apparent in chapter 3, when we treat the several levels of information processing.

Granting this theoretical position, any stable permutation that emerges will not consist of mental elements that permit immediate communication to others. Rather, the chance configuration must be translated into a communication configuration, precisely as Einstein suggested. Hadamard (1945, p. 82) said of himself that "as to words, they remain absolutely absent from my mind until I come to the moment of communicating the results in written or oral form." Considering the remoteness of language and logic from the original configuration, this translation procedure is far from straightforward. Hadamard quoted at length Galton's description of the intellectual awkwardness frequently endured at this phase:

It is a serious drawback to me in writing, and still more in explaining myself, that I do not so easily think in words as otherwise. It often happens that after being hard at work, and having arrived at results that are perfectly clear and satisfactory to myself, when I try to express them in language I feel that I must begin by putting myself upon quite another intellectual plane. I have to translate my thoughts into a language that does not run very evenly with them. I therefore waste a vast deal of time in seeking for appropriate words and phrases, and am conscious, when required to speak on a sudden, of being often very obscure through mere verbal maladroitness, and not through want of clearness of perception. That is one of the small annoyances of my life. (p. 69)

Although Galton did not say so, it seems likely that the more original the chance configuration is, the more difficult the isolation of a suitable communication configuration will be. What did not directly derive from verbal or mathematical symbols may not lend itself easily to linguistic and logical conversion.

The permutation mechanism

One limitation in Einstein's response to Hadamard's (1945) questionnaire is his failure to discuss more fully the chaotic nature of the "vague . . . combinatory play," such as was suggested by our quotations from Mach, James, and Jevons. This deficiency was remedied by Henri Poincaré (1921), a famous mathematician and philosopher of science who, without a doubt, volunteered the most frequently quoted introspective report on the creative process in science. Campbell (1960) quoted Poincaré to demonstrate how the blind-variation and selective-retention model is consistent with the subjective experience of creators. Rather than reprint the same passage, I shall merely slice out and rearrange those segments that best illustrate the key features of the chance-permutation procedure.

Poincaré began by defining mathematical creation, showing that it entails both the combination of elements and the selection of that subset of all possible combinations that are adaptive in some sense.

> It does not consist in making new combinations with mathematical entities already known . . . [for] the combinations so made would be infinite in number and most of them absolutely without interest. To create consists precisely in not making useless combinations and in making those which are useful and which are only a small minority. Invention is discernment, choice. . . . [The most useful combinations] are those which reveal to us unsuspected kinship between other facts, long known, but wrongly believed to be strangers to one another. . . . [Accordingly,] among chosen combinations the most fertile will often be those formed of elements drawn from domains which are far apart. Not that I mean as sufficing for invention the bringing together of objects as disparate as possible; most combinations so formed would be entirely sterile. But certain among them, very rare, are the most fruitful of all. (p. 386)

We postulated that chance permutations differ greatly in their inherent stability and that that stability correlates with how long a given permutation lingers in consciousness, the most unstable passing by virtually without notice and the most stable staying on for possible consolidation. Poincaré, with only a slight change in terminology, maintained that "the sterile combinations do not even present themselves to the mind of the inventor. Never in the field of his consciousness do combinations appear that are not really useful, except some that he rejects but which have to some extent the characteristics of useful combinations" (p. 386). Later he qualified the criterion of usefulness by saying that in order for combinations to enter full consciousness, they must appeal to the mathematician's "emotional sensibility," the sense of "beauty and elegance" (p. 391). Thus, "among the great numbers of combinations blindly formed by the subliminal self, almost all are without interest and without utility; but just for that reason they are also without effect upon the esthetic sensibility. Consciousness will never know them; only certain ones are harmonious, and, consequently, at once useful and beautiful" (p. 392). Every so often "a sudden illumination seizes upon the mind of the mathematician . . . that . . . does not stand the test of verification; well, we almost always notice that this false idea, had it been true, would have gratified our natural feeling for mathematical elegance" (p. 392).

All this remains rather abstract, but one of Poincaré's introspections features more vivid imagery regarding the creation of configurations from chance permutations. This often-cited story also suggests why certain mental elements possess inherent affinities so that stable configurations can emerge simply by means of random collisions. One evening Poincaré found himself unable to sleep after drinking, contrary to his custom, black coffee: "Ideas rose in crowds; I felt them collide until pairs interlocked, so to speak, making a stable combination. By the next morning I had established the existence of a class of Fuchsian functions" (p. 387). Later he compared these colliding ideas to "the hooked atoms of Epicurus" that move about "like the molecules of gas in the kinematic theory of gases" so that "their mutual impacts may produce new combinations" (p. 393).

In a footnote, Hadamard (1945, p. 29) briefly mentioned two etymological curiosities that suggest some primitive wisdom about how novel ideas originate in the mind. First, he cited Max Müller's observation that the Latin verb *cognito* for "to think" once signified "to shake together," a clear intuition about the utility of permitting ideas to bounce randomly off one another. Second, Hadamard noted St. Augustine's comment that *intelligo,* from which came *intelligence,* means to "select among," indicating that only stable configurations, not mental aggregates, are selected and preserved for further information processing. Hence, the awareness of the significance of blind variation and selective retention appears to have a long if inexplicit history.

Unexpected illumination

Poincaré (1921, p. 388) mentioned one last characteristic of the creative process, namely, that a fully original solution to a given problem is seldom found at once but, rather, only after a long delay during which the problem is seemingly put aside for work on unrelated tasks:

Then I turned my attention to the study of some arithmetical questions apparently without much success and without a suspicion of any connection with my preceding researches. Disgusted with my failure, I went to spend a few days at the seaside, and thought of something else. One morning, walking on the bluff, the idea came to me, with just the same characteristics of brevity, suddenness and immediate certainty, that the arithmetic transformations of indeterminate ternary quadratic forms were identical with those of non-Euclidean geometry.

Other scientists have offered similar reports. For example, after years of failing to solve a problem, Gauss stated that "finally, two days ago, I succeeded, not on account of my painful efforts, but by the grace of God. Like a sudden flash of lightning, the riddle happened to be solved. I myself cannot say what was the conducting thread which connected what I previously knew with what made my success possible" (quoted in Hadamard 1945, p. 15). This suggests how the creative act came to be associated with "divine inspiration," or the whispering of the Muses, for the illumination appears automatic or involuntary. So dramatic are such spontaneous revelations that the precise moment in which the successful permutation emerges is commonly remembered in unusual detail. We see this not only in Poincaré's words just given but also in Darwin's *Autobiography* when he reminisced about when he arrived at his solution to the problem of the origin of species: "I can remember the very spot in the road, whilst in my carriage, when to my joy the solution occurred to me" (F. Darwin 1892, p. 43). As the examples so far given imply, the unexpected insight most often occurs when the scientist is engaged in a mundane behavior, such as walking or riding, although the instant of illumination sometimes appears just after waking: "One phenomenon is certain and I can vouch for its absolute certainty: the sudden and immediate appearance of a solution at the very moment of sudden awakening" (Hadamard 1945, p. 8).

That these episodes are commonplace was shown in a survey of 232 distinguished scientists conducted over a half-century ago (Platt & Baker 1931). Only 17% reported never having "received assistance from the scientific revelation or hunch in the solution of an important problem" (p. 1976). Typical responses to the questionnaire included "Freeing my mind of all thought of the problem I walked briskly down Tremont Street, when suddenly at a definite spot which I would locate today – as if from the clear sky above me – an idea popped into my head as suddenly and emphatically as if a voice had shouted it," and I "decided to abandon the work and all thoughts relative thereto, and then on the following day when occupied in work of an entirely different type, an idea came to my mind as suddenly as a flash of lightning and it was the solution" (p. 1977). Although many of the respondents who reported instances such as these asked to remain anonymous, a few permitted their names to be made known, including G. A. Abbott, E. T. Bell, E. S. Conklin, W. M. Grosvenor, M. H. Ittner, F. E. Ives, A. D. Little, and L. L. Thurstone, all of whom were honored with biographical entries in the *World Who's Who in Science* (Debus 1968) over a third of a century later.

In *The Art of Thought,* Graham Wallas (1926) surmised, on the basis of introspections offered by Helmholtz (1898), that an "incubation" period intervenes between the "preparation" stage, when a problem is originally formulated, and the stage of "illumination," when the solution is suddenly at hand. Poincaré maintained that the emergence of an unexpected inspiration was "a manifest sign of long, unconscious prior work" (1921, p. 389).

During the incubation phase, what he styled the "subliminal self" is seeking the right combination that completes the quest begun in the preparatory phase. According to the theory advanced here, the incubation period represents that portion of the creative process most specifically engaged in the chance permutation of mental elements. Hadamard (1945) apparently concurred, for he said that to find the fruitful combinations it is

necessary to construct the very numerous possible combinations. . . . It cannot be avoided that this first operation take place, to a certain extent, at random, so that the role of chance is hardly doubtful in this first step of the mental process. But we see that the intervention of chance occurs inside the unconscious: for most of these combinations – more exactly, all those which are useless – remain unknown to us." (p. 28)

Hence, when the right permutation is found, the configuration will seemingly emerge out of nowhere, with the discovery of invention appearing without prior announcement or volitional control.

In the next chapter, I shall sketch a model of intuitive information processing that indicates how this unconscious ideation may come about. At this point in our discussion, however, I would like to put forward three theoretical clarifications regarding the illumination process:

1. The isolation of a suitable chance configuration, though unexpected, is not necessarily unanticipated. Even if the interim separating the preparation and the illumination phase of creativity is highly variable and thus unpredictable, a preparation period does normally set the stage for the subsequent illumination. Seldom does a scientist conceive a solution to a problem that had not been previously pondered in some form. When a solution does appear that is not an obvious response to some given problem, that solution commonly consists of elements that were in fact evoked by some closely related puzzle. To return to the metaphor of the "hooked atoms," Poincaré (1921, pp. 393–394) maintained that

the role of the preliminary conscious work . . . is evidently to mobilize certain of these atoms, to unhook them from the wall and put them in swing. We think we have done no good, because we have moved these elements a thousand different ways in seeking to assemble them, and have found no satisfactory aggregate. But, after this shaking up imposed upon them by our will, these atoms do not return to their primitive rest. They freely continue to dance. . . . The mobilized atoms are . . . not any atoms whatsoever; they are those from which we might reasonably expect the desired solution. Then the mobilized atoms undergo impacts which make them enter into combinations among themselves or with other atoms at rest which they struck against in their course. . . . However it may be, the only combinations that have a chance of forming are those where at least one of the elements is one of those atoms freely chosen by our will. Now, it is evidently among these that is found what I called the *good combination*.

That stable permutation will often address the enigma that initially un-leashed the mental elements, yet the outcome may also be more relevant to some related issue that would have detached much the same collection of elements to set in motion the free-associative procedure. As we shall see shortly, a comparable phenomenon occurs in the case of serendipity.

2. It is not invariably true that the scientist is unaware of the thought sequences that link the preparation and illumination periods via the incuba-tion period. Much of this chaotic search will take place in what Galton termed the "ante-chamber" of consciousness, as other thoughts occupy the core awareness. Nonetheless, there are sometimes opportunities for a cre-ator to recognize these normally subterranean meanderings of the intellect. Poincaré's sleepless night is one case in point, and daydreams are another. In addition, because the amount of information-processing space assigned to a combination is correlated with its stability, every once in a while smaller chunks of the final configuration will momentarily enter conscious-ness only to recede into the periphery when these pieces are dismissed as only partial solutions. Without this intermittent awareness of the cognitions making up the chance permutations, we would not have access to the introspective reports quoted earlier. Even so, most frequently something more urgent is commanding the attention of the central consciousness just as the haphazard collection of elements happens to arrive at a cohesive arrangement. Thus, immediately before the illumination, the creator will not be privy to the train of thought leading to the solution. Again, this lack of awareness at the crucial moment makes the revelation unexpected but not unanticipated.

3. There is no particular reason that an incubation period *must* intervene between preparation and illumination, even when chance permutations must be scanned before a configuration obtains. Sometimes the investiga-tor will enjoy a nice stroke of luck and reach the desired destination in virtually no time, whereas at other times a long sequence of associations must be sifted through before the stable permutation appears. Because the permutation process is "blind," in the sense of being devoid of any a priori knowledge of the most profitable direction to search for combinations, the length of the quest is a random variable. An analogy is that if the goal is to toss four heads in a row, they can be obtained in the first four throws or only after a thousand flips of the coin. Hence, although it is possible for a creator to report virtually no delay between preparation and illumination for a particular discovery or invention, that same person may have much less luck in another instance, perhaps never arriving at a solution, even though all the required components are present in the mind. The highly unpredictable nature of this trial-and-error survey of combinations, need-

less to say, makes the concluding illumination equally unexpected. Nevertheless, one pattern is imposed on the random process: The more original the illumination is, the longer the incubation, on the average, will be. That is, if the elements that make up the chance configuration are not related to one another, so that they can be connected only by rather long and strange sequences of associations, then the odds are greater that the permutation mechanism must run longer before the stable combination will emerge.

This wait will be especially necessary if, to use Poincaré's apt picture, not all of the atoms needed for a good combination are unhooked off the wall at the start but, rather, some must be knocked off later on by the kinetic agitation of the original atoms. Accordingly, if the length of the incubation period is plotted as a function of the solution's novelty, a positive relationship will be seen, but with considerable scatter around the line of best fit, because of whimsical chance. Furthermore, because of floor effects that restrict the dispersion for highly probable configurations, the degree of scatter about the line will also increase with the expected incubation duration (an instance of heteroskedasticity, in statistical terms). To use again the coin-tossing example, if the aim is to toss two heads in a row, there will be less variability in the number of trials that suffice than if the purpose is to toss eight heads in a row, a rarer event.

This increased variability as a function of originality has a provocative implication: On the average, the more exceptional is the permutation of elements that make up the workable configuration, the wider will be the possible ranges in the duration of incubation, and consequently, the more unpredictable will be the outcome. Ironically, the more impressive is the achievement of a scientific genius, as gauged by how original the idea is, the *less* control that scientist can claim over finding a solution. This is why, in part, we stated in the first chapter that the chance-configuration theory is most applicable to those scientists who make landmark, even revolutionary, contributions. No scientist can make a complete break with tradition and isolate a viable alternative without first submitting to the caprice of chance, as the quest for a new synthesis compels a random search. In a loose sense, genius and chance become synonymous.

Anecdotes

The main conclusion to be drawn now is that the introspective reports provided by Einstein, Poincaré, Hadamard, and other distinguished scientists add some credibility to the chance-configuration theory. To be sure, introspective reports cannot always be trusted, for people are not privileged with error-free access to their internal mental processes, nor can the resulting introspections be granted objective validation by outside observers (see Nisbet & Wilson 1977). Even so, this congruence is coupled with the theory's ability to explain the more genuine empirical data reviewed in the next four chapters, thus inserting a small but sturdy piece in the total theoretical argument. Furthermore, anecdotal evidence, which is a slightly more objective source of information, falls in line behind the chief propositions of this theory. We shall begin by examining general descriptions of the creative act and then turn to the important phenomenon of serendipity.

The creative act

Certain similarities exist between the theory articulated in chapter 1 and that proposed by Arthur Koestler in his 1964 book *The Act of Creation* (cf. Mays 1973). Koestler maintained that all notable acts of creative synthesis entail the "bisociation" of two or more "matrices," the latter taken "to denote any ability, habit, or skill, any pattern of ordered behavior governed by a '*code*' of fixed rules" (p. 38). Clearly, his matrices are more or less equivalent to our a priori and a posteriori configurations. He made it evident, too, that the associative processes required for the bisociation of two matrices are quite different from those used in more routine modes of thought, which depend far more on habits.

Koestler's theory leaves something to be desired. His discussion frequently lacks conceptual clarity; he failed to derive any empirically testable propositions (which we shall do in chapters 5 and 6, for example); and he focused perhaps excessively on the intrapsychic aspects of the creative act (cf. Brannigan 1981). Even so, Koestler at least made a reasonable effort to use impressionistic information pertaining to the creative process, including anecdotes. Sometimes a discoverer or inventor leaves a record about how a particular creative product was found, emphasizing the external conditions or specific behaviors that led to the new idea (e.g., F. Darwin 1892; Helmholtz 1898; Watson 1968). In chapter 6 of his book, Koestler offered three illustrations: Gutenberg's invention of the printing press, Kepler's theory of the solar system, and Darwin's theory of evolution by natural selection. There is enough conceptual overlap between Koestler's ideas and those advocated here that much of his discussion can be taken to document the present theory, with only a minimal translation of terms. Gutenberg, for instance, described in some letters the route by which he came to the printing press (Koestler 1964, pp. 121–124). In line with the earlier quotation from Jevons, the route was by no means direct or deliberate, but rather roundabout. Gutenberg had to construct and consolidate a series of a posteriori configurations that, when properly positioned, could be collated into a method of printing inexpensive Bibles for pilgrims. These were the printing of playing cards from woodblocks via rubbing (for the mass production of identical copies), the coin punch and seal (for separate and hence movable type), and the wine press (for exerting the requisite pressure to imprint the ink on the page). The relevance of this last configuration, the last step in the origination of the printing press, occurred unexpectedly to Gutenberg as he was participating in a wine harvest.

W. I. B. Beveridge's *The Art of Scientific Investigation* (1957) also provides several anecdotes concerning the creative act in science (see also Beveridge 1980). Even though Beveridge, unlike Koestler, attempted no broad theoretical framework – instead proceeding more inductively – he amply documented the contention implicit in the book's title, that scientific research is more an art than a science. In those chapters on chance, imagination, and intuition, Beveridge showed why discovery and invention depend less on reason or logic and more on imaginative conjunctions of apparently dissimilar ideas. As we observed earlier, these original integrations often arrive without warning. Gutenberg's account of his invention of the printing press is actually fairly typical: The a posteriori or a priori configuration that provides the missing piece in the puzzle is often met when least expected. Perhaps the first "Eureka" episode on record took place in the bathtub when the accidental overflow of water gave Archimedes the notion necessary to solve the problem handed to him by Hiero of Syracuse. The unexpected nature of this creative act is especially conspicuous when chance seems to intercede on behalf of an idea's origination, which brings us to a phenomenon of immense theoretical significance for the chance-configuration theory.

Serendipity

There are many anecdotes regarding the influence of chance on discovery and invention. Mach's 1896 paper offers several incidents, including Grimaldi's discovery of interference, Arago's observation of the dampening of the oscillations of a magnetic needle in a copper envelope, Foucault's discovery of the stability of the plane of vibration, Mayer's observation that venous blood is more red in the tropics, Kirchhoff's discovery that a sodium lamp augmented the D-line in the solar spectrum, and Schönbein's discovery of the ozone produced by electric sparks. Other writers have added even more names to the list of scientists who have benefited from "luck." Koestler (1964, pp. 192–197) cited Haüy (geometric laws of crystallography), Pasteur (vaccination), Alexander Fleming (penicillin), Röntgen (X-rays), Henri Becquerel (radioactivity), and Edison (the phonograph); Beveridge (1957) devoted a whole chapter to the subject and then added an appendix that offers 19 more examples (see also Austin 1978; Beveridge 1980, chap. 2). But maybe the classic discussion of this topic is Walter B. Cannon's 1940 paper, "The Role of Chance in Discovery." Besides presenting illustrations from his own career and the careers of Columbus (the New World), Galvani ("animal electricity"), Oersted (electromagnetism), Bernard (nervous control of blood flow), Richet (induced sensitization), Dam (vitamin K), Nobel (dynamite), and Perkin (coal-tar dyes), Cannon revived a word coined by Horace Walpole to refer to this phenomenon – *serendipity*. He argued, as did Mach before him (in a paper that Cannon inexplicably failed to cite), that accident, or serendipity, has made, and continues to make, an impressive contribution to scientific and technological progress.

Given the ample literature on this subject, I shall not narrate each incident. Rather, I shall indicate how serendipitous creativity fits in with the chance-configuration theory. Here two points are worth making, one concerning the role of chance events in the permutation scheme and the other concerning the importance of configurations in making chance events pertinent to self-organization.

First, we must recognize that serendipity is nothing more than a special case of the more universal chance-permutation procedure that underlies scientific genius. The sole distinction is that at least one of the elements composing the new stable permutation is provided by outside experience. Rather than confine the permutations to cognitive elements, such as concepts and images retrieved chaotically from memory, one or more elements entail a sensation or perception of a current event, an external stimulus that often provides the scientist with the keystone for constructing a novel configuration. Indeed, many of the presumed sudden illuminations discussed earlier, which seemingly resulted from completely internal mental processes, may actually have been serendipitous events of a special kind. Once a scientist has entered an incubation period with respect to a certain problem, extraneous stimuli in the environment may introduce new elements into the permutations, either directly or indirectly through a divergent train of associations that is thus begun. Because most of this haphazard influx is subliminal, the scientist may not realize that the insight that appeared apparently without warning may actually have been elicited by some recent external stimulus that deflected the random search in the right direction toward synthesis. This possibility may help explain why the illuminations so often come when the scientist is engaged in some totally irrelevant activity, such as a walk in the woods or vacation travel, for just such circumstances would offer new input into the permutations in the guise of diverse recollections (see also Watson 1930, pp. 247–248).

Because a chance encounter with an environmental event acquires significance only when incorporated into a stable permutation, we are led to the second point: Pasteur was right when he maintained that "in fields of observation, chance favors only the prepared mind." Inside or outside the laboratory, daily life is crammed with unexpected events that might insert the lacking element into a potential configuration, yet these stimuli provoke nothing, passing through consciousness without joining other elements in a stable permutation. As Mach (1896, p. 169) characterized the difference, the fortuitous facts that inspired many critical discoveries "were *seen* numbers of times before they were *noticed*." Fleming was not the first bacteriologist to see a petri dish spoiled by a mold contamination, yet he was apparently the first to notice the far-reaching implications of the clear ring around the little fuzzy spot on the gel. Similarly, Archimedes was not the first to have seen a bathtub overflow, Newton the falling of an apple, or Watt the steam escaping a teapot, but these three did notice the broader implications of these trivial, almost everyday occurrences (Cannon 1940). Frequently investigators stumble on a discovery when looking for something quite different, though in the same realm of natural phenomena, so that the laboratory equipment is set up for generating the unanticipated event. This happened to Dufay, Fresnel, Fraunhofer, and Faraday, for example (Mach 1896; see also Barber & Fox 1958). Because these investigators likely already possessed an abundance of mental elements awaiting organization into more efficient configurations, the range of accidents that might stimulate a stable permutation would be rather large, making a serendipitous discovery highly probable. Creative scientists, even while confining themselves to a specific line of experimentation, are always on the lookout, however subliminally, for the needed linkages.

As Charles Darwin's research assistant for many years, Francis Darwin had plenty of opportunity to observe his father's working habits. One reminiscence not only exemplifies the intellectual priming necessary for a scientist to take full advantage of chance but also illustrates how the descriptions of the creative process given by Mach, James, and Jevons can be applied, *mutatis mutandis,* to the way a great scientist behaves in the laboratory. Francis spoke of his father's

instinct for arresting exceptions: it was as though he were charged with theorizing power ready to flow into any channel on the slightest disturbance, so that no fact, however small, could avoid releasing a stream of theory, and thus the fact became magnified into importance. In this way it naturally happened that many untenable theories occurred to him; but fortunately his richness of imagination was equalled by his power of judging and condemning the thoughts that occurred to him. He was just to his theories, and did not condemn them unheard; and so it happened that he was willing to test what would seem to most people not at all worth testing. These rather wild trials he called "fool's experiments," and enjoyed extremely. (F. Darwin 1892, p. 101)

Hence, Darwin projected the chance-permutation procedure onto his experimental activities, actively seeking serendipitous results rather than passively waiting for them to happen.

Discussion

Although the impressionistic evidence we have examined so far centers on scientific creativity, there is a firm foundation for claiming that the chance-configuration theory describes a generic process that applies to all forms of genius-grade creativity. The Nobel Prize–winning physicist Max Planck asserted in his 1949 autobiography that the pioneer scientist "must have a vivid intuitive imagination, for new ideas are not generated by deduction, but by an artistically creative imagination" (p. 109); this remark seemingly merges the two primary brands of creativity. Thus, most theories of the creative process presume that the mental manipulations demanded for a truly innovative synthesis are the same no matter which endeavor we may examine. Koestler (1964), for instance, held that all forms of creativity involve bisociation, whether in the arts or the sciences. Indeed, his book opens by applying this idea to humor, which is said to be based on "the sudden bisociation of a mental event with two habitually incompatible matrices [that] results in an abrupt transfer of the train of thought from one associative context to another" (p. 59).

The introspective reports of star creators in the arts provide ample documentation for generalizing the present theory to cover aesthetic creativity as well (see Allen 1949; Chipp 1968; Ghiselin 1952). Hence, the English playwright and poet John Dryden, in his "Dedication of the Rival-Ladies," spoke of his play beginning "when it was only a confused mass of thoughts, tumbling over one another in the dark; when the fancy was yet in its first work, moving the sleeping images of things towards the light, there to be distinguished, and then either chosen or rejected by the judgment" (quoted in Ghiselin 1952, p. 80). The French poet and essayist Paul Valéry provided a fine paraphrase: "It takes two to invent anything. The one makes up combinations; the other chooses, recognizes what he wishes and what is important to him in the mass of the things which the former has imparted to him" (quoted in Hadamard 1945, p. 30). These quotations offer thumbnail descriptions of the generation and selective retention of chance permutations.

Several artistic notables even speak of events that can be construed as analogues of scientific serendipity. The fiction author Henry James, in his preface to "The Spoils of Poynton," related how the germ of his story came from a casual dinner conversation that yielded "a mere floating particle in the stream of talk" that others merely heard but that James alone noticed had potential for literary expansion (quoted in Allen 1949, p. 156). Likewise, the surrealist artist Max Ernst described the method of frottage by which aleatory patterns are allowed to stimulate visual creativity:

I was struck by the obsession that showed to my excited gaze the floor-boards upon which a thousand scrubbings had deepened the grooves. . . . I made from the boards a series of drawings by placing on them, at random, sheets of paper which I undertook to rub with black lead. In gazing attentively at the drawings thus obtained . . . I was surprised by the sudden intensification of my visionary capacities and by the hallucinatory succession of contradictory images superimposed, one upon the other. (quoted in Chipp 1968, p. 429)

And Henry Moore, the modern sculptor, recounted that

sometimes for several years running I have been to the same part of the seashore – but each year a new shape of pebble has caught my eye, which the year before, though it was there in hundreds, I never saw. Out of the millions of pebbles passed in walking along the shore, I choose out to see with excitement only those which fit in with my existing form-interest at the time. (quoted in Chipp 1968, p. 595)

The last part of this quotation again highlights how these chance encounters acquire significance only when the mind is previously primed to detect specific configurations.

I do not wish to exaggerate the congruence between scientific and artistic creativity. Even if all guises of creativity can be subsumed under a single generic *modus operandi,* Koestler (1964, p. 658) noted some contrasts among separate creative endeavors: "The true creativity of the innovator in the arts is more dramatically evident and more easily distinguished from the routine of the mere practitioner than in the sciences, because art (and humor) operate primarily through the transitory *juxtaposition* of matrices, whereas science achieves their permanent integration into a cumulative and hierarchic order." As a necessary corollary, the utility of "altered states of consciousness" probably differs for these two types of creativity. A few scientists have reported important creative acts during dream states. Kekulé's visualization of the benzene ring of carbon atoms offers the best illustration: "I fell into a reverie, and lo! the atoms were gambolling before my eyes" (quoted in Findlay 1948, p. 37). Still, such instances are likely far less common in the sciences than in the arts (see also Hadamard 1945, pp.

7–8). Even more rare in science are creative ideas originating in drug-induced states of awareness, such as the opium experience described by the poet Samuel Taylor Coleridge in his prefatory note to "Kublai Khan" (see Ghiselin 1952, pp. 84–85). The safest conclusion at this point is that normal consciousness is probably better suited to the generation of those chance permutations that have the highest odds of yielding a useful configuration. When a scientist subjects mental elements to chance permutations, some constraints are in fact usually placed on the repertoire of elements. Dreams and other altered states of consciousness, in contrast, tend to have fewer restrictions, and thus a far higher number of permutations will be unstable, at least from a scientific perspective. Juxtapositions that are produced by such, to use Freudian terminology, deep regressions into primary-process thinking are more akin to random mutations in biology.

Of course, totally wild juxtapositions may be quite valuable in creating certain artistic styles, surrealistic art particularly so. But one difficulty from our point of view is that the sense of judgment (or secondary-process thinking) tends to deteriorate outside everyday consciousness. With the selection process turned off, chance permutations that are but randomly original are often taken as profound. William James (1902) reported his own experience with nitrous oxide, discovering that he found himself pondering apparently significant notions that merely turned silly as he returned to a normal conscious state. Poincaré (1921, p. 390) recorded something similar "in regard to ideas coming to me in the morning or evening in bed while in a semi-hypnagogic state," for the notions so derived are often deceptively creative in that they usually fail to survive more intellectually coherent scrutiny. The earlier quotations from the works of Mach, James, and Jevons suggest an imaginative flow of ideas, yet in scientific luminaries these chance permutations are probably still within the pattern available in regular awareness, such as reverie or daydreaming. It is instructive then to observe that Kekulé, when he visualized the benzene ring, claimed only to have fallen into a reverie or "half sleep" (*Halbschlaf*). In this respect Koestler's differentiation is sound: Artistic creativity may, on the average, exploit far more improbable chance configurations than does scientific creativity (see also Rothenberg 1986).

To determine the amount of overlap between scientific and artistic creativity, we must address the basis for individual differences in cognitive style and motivational disposition – the subject of the forthcoming chapter. We shall see then that the two classes of achievement are not qualitatively distinct but, rather, can be placed along a continuum. In addition, to anticipate the argument, this same dimension will reappear in chapter 5, when we discuss the developmental antecedents of genius-caliber creativity.

3   Personality and individual differences

How can the personality of the creative scientist be described? Can illustrious contributors to science be distinguished on some character traits that set them well apart from their more obscure colleagues? Someone familiar with research in personality psychology might infer that this last question may have a negative answer. In recent decades a controversy has raged over whether stable personality traits exist at all, for some critics have claimed that situational factors determine human behavior far more than do individual variables, thereby undermining the "cross-situational consistency" of personal attributes (see, e.g., Epstein & O'Brien 1985; Mischel 1968). Although this person–context debate continues, my own view is that at least some character traits are both stable over time and firmly entrenched in concrete behaviors. These traits are dependable both empirically and theoretically. That is, in certain instances we have definite theoretical reasons for believing that particular individual variables enjoy both cross-situational stability and predictive validity. Such is the case here. The chance-configuration theory implies that a special set of traits should differentiate the scientific genius from mere talent or mediocrity. After all, it seems reasonable to assume that individuals differ substantially in their ability to generate chance permutations and that individual differences in this capacity would also correlate with other personal attributes, owing to some causal connection, whether as antecedents or as consequents (cf. Weisberg 1986).

To make this argument, we must review the central findings of the massive research literature on the cognitive style and character of the creative person (see, e.g., Barron & Harrington 1981). Although much of this research fails to distinguish scientific and artistic dispositions – which are known to be distinct on some traits (Cattell 1963; Hudson 1966) – with sufficient care we can sketch a portrait of the exceptionally creative scientist (cf. Fisch 1977; Mansfield & Busse 1981). I shall also attempt to show how this portait can be integrated with the theory proposed in the first chapter. This picture of the scientific luminary has two main features, one cognitive and the other motivational.

41

Cognitive style

The experimental psychologist F. C. Bartlett (1958, p. 136) differentiated between original and routine information processing, contending that "the most important feature of original experimental thinking is the discovery of overlap and agreement where formerly only isolation and difference were recognized" – which echoes Poincaré's statement quoted in the preceding chapter. Carl Rogers (1954, p. 255), a humanistic psychologist, went one step further by observing that the creation of a "novel relational product" requires the "ability to toy with elements and concepts." These compatible assertions are substantiated in the empirical literature. In particular, the cognitive style conducive to creativity in science may be characterized by two components.

First, creative individuals are noticeably more intelligent than average (Cattell 1963), and a high IQ is especially helpful in scientific creativity (e.g., Hudson 1966; Knapp 1962; Roe 1952a). The average IQ of a physics PhD, for instance, is roughly around 140 (Price 1963; Roe 1952a; cf. Helson & Crutchfield 1970). To place this score in perspective, the median IQ of college students is 118, a BA graduate 123, honor graduates 133, and initiates to Phi Beta Kappa 137 (Roe 1952a). In Cox's (1926) analysis of 301 historical figures, the 39 scientists in her sample had IQs of somewhere between 135 and 180, depending on the particular operational definition. Newton, for example, had an IQ as high as 190, Copernicus 160, Galileo 185, Kepler 175, Huygens 175, Lavoisier 170, Linnaeus 165, and Darwin 165. However, a high intelligence no more guarantees creativity than it ensures leadership (Simonton 1985a, 1987e). Rather, a strong intellect provides a necessary but not sufficient condition for the exercise of creativity (Barron & Harrington 1981). Because intelligence operates largely as a threshold test, once that threshold is surpassed, IQ may bear a negligible correlation with measures of scientific accomplishment (Bayer & Folger 1966; Bloom 1963; Cole & Cole 1973, pp. 69–70; Gough 1976; cf. Jones 1964). Eminent mathematicians, for instance, do not have more impressive IQs than do their colleagues who hold a PhD in mathematics (Helson & Crutchfield 1970).

Second, for intelligence to be converted fully into creative potential, the intellect must be structured in a special way. For example, high scores on the Barron–Welsh Art Scale (Barron & Welsh 1952) – a measure of the preference for complexity and a good predictor of creativity (Stein 1969), including that in science (e.g., Helson & Crutchfield 1970) – are related to high verbal fluency, impulsiveness, originality, breadth of interests, independence of judgment, and flexibility (Barron 1963). Fluency of thought, whether verbal, associational, expressional, or ideational, has also been linked with creativity (Guilford 1963; Jones 1964), as has the capacity to generate remote associations to various ideas (Gough 1976; Johnson & Clark 1973; Mednick 1962). Highly creative individuals tend to be wide categorizers and to be more willing to take intellectual risks (Cropley 1967; Eisenman 1987; Jones 1964). Versatility may be an important attribute of eminent achievers as well (Raskin 1936; Schaefer & Anastasi 1968; White 1931; cf. Simonton 1976a). In the specific case of science, a strong interest in disciplines outside one's own chosen specialty area has been shown to correlate with distinction as a researcher (Manis 1951; Simon 1974; see also Andrews 1979).

It is evident that a person is more likely to see congruence between hitherto isolated elements if that person has broad interests, is versatile, enjoys intellectual fluency and flexibility, and can connect disparate elements via unusual associations and wide categories that force a substantial overlap of ideas. The capacity to play with ideas is facilitated by impulsiveness, flexibility, independence, and a risk-taking disposition. Finally, a high intelligence enables the acquisition of many interconnected mental elements for such combinatory manipulations. In brief, these various traits, which help define the cognitive style of the creative individual, form a constellation of interrelated attributes. Furthermore, we have reason to believe that this collection of cognitive traits holds for the specific case of creative scientists (e.g., Eiduson 1962). Price (1963, p. 107) summarized the relevant research as follows:

From modern studies of creative ability in the scientific fields it appears that general and specific types of intelligence have surprisingly little to do with the incidence of high achievement. At best, a certain rather high minimum is needed, but once over that hump the chance of becoming a scientist of high achievement seems almost random. One noted quality is a certain gift of what we may call *mavericity,* the property of making unusual associations in ideas, of doing the unexpected. The scientist tends to be the man who, in doing the word-association test, responds to "black" not with "white" but with "caviar."

To appreciate the causal basis for this mavericity, let me elaborate on a model that I published some years ago (Simonton 1980a). While outlining the etiology of individual differences in cognitive style, we should also obtain a conception of the mechanism by which chance permutations can be generated. Although I used this model specifically to explain intuitive and analytical thought processes and although the model employs a nomenclature that is somewhat awkward in the current context, an abstract of it is still helpful (cf. Bastik 1982).

A model of associative processes

We shall start by differentiating persons along two dimensions. First, people can be distinguished by the sheer volume of mental elements that they possess, a factor that directly determines the potential number of associations. Some individuals have relatively few mental elements, others a great many, and corresponding to this contrast is a difference in the quantity of associations that may link these elements. Second, independent of the number of elements, persons differ in the distribution of association strengths. At the one extreme are those persons so cognitively constituted that most of their associations between elements are quite strong, and at the other extreme are those for whom the majority of associations are far weaker, albeit still prominent enough to have behavioral and emotional effects (were it otherwise, an individual would be autistic). On the basis of these two dimensions we can put forward a fourfold typology of ideal types, each with a characteristic distribution of associations. This typology is depicted in Figure 3.1.

The vertical axis on each of the four graphs represents the number of mental elements, whereas the horizontal axis, labeled Association Probabilities (because the model is based on the distribution of conditional probabilities), shows the strength of the associations linking these elements. The area under each curve represents the total number of associations among the given elements. These areas are subdivided into regions by four thresholds that demarcate the psychological repercussions of an association of a given strength. The four thresholds are as follows:

1. *Attention* (θ_a), which determines when an association can direct the perception of environmental stimuli, orienting attention to promising contingencies. This threshold thus governs the exercise of curiosity or "diversive exploration" (cf. Berlyne 1960).

2. *Behavior* (θ_b), which decides when an association is strong enough to support a motor or visceral behavior, as in classical and operant conditioning. Associations that pass this threshold, but not the next, are not fully conscious but are only "infraconscious." Moreover, even though verbal associations are feasible at this level, words are linked not by logical or linguistic characteristics, such as denotative meanings, but rather by emotional connotations and their physical qualities as auditory and visual stimuli (cf. Brown & McNeill 1966).

3. *Cognition* (θ_c), which detects when an association becomes strong

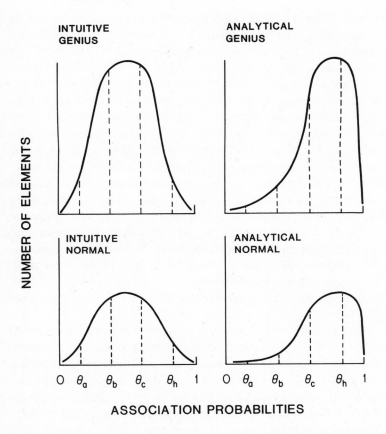

Figure 3.1. Four hypothetical personality types based on the probability distributions of conditional probabilistic associations: θ_a = Attention, θ_b = Behavior, θ_c = Cognition, θ_h = Habituation (from Simonton 1980a).

enough to be consciously represented and manipulated via symbolic representations, whether linguistic, logical, or mathematical. This threshold parallels the notion of a "quantitative threshold of consciousness" advanced by Leibniz, in which "our clear concepts are like islands that arise above the ocean of obscure ones" (Whyte 1960, p. 99). Here, too, words are linked according to denotative meanings, as restricted by grammatical and logical structure.

4. *Habituation* (θ_h), which specifies when an association becomes habituated and hence "ultraconscious" in execution. The habits that permit us to ride a bicycle, drive a car, or pursue some other everyday behavior with minimal awareness are located on this plane of automatic responses.

The "normals" have a considerably smaller supply of mental elements than do the "geniuses," and consequently fewer elements are available for chance permutations in the normals in comparison with the geniuses. This contrast is correlated with native intellectual ability as nurtured by the environment during early childhood and adolescence (cf. Simonton 1987c), a point that I shall elaborate in chapter 5. Nonetheless, being a genius is not enough to guarantee that one's mental elements can undergo chance permutation, for this capacity depends on the distribution of association strengths (or probabilities). Whereas the "intuitive genius" has many elements linked by numerous infraconscious but behaviorally and emotionally active associations, the "analytical genius" has a comparable number of elements linked by a smaller set of conscious and ultraconscious cognitions and habits – therein yielding the distinction between intuitive and analytical styles of thought. This contrast roughly parallels that between primary- and secondary-process thinking (Suler 1980) and between divergent and convergent thought (Guilford 1963). The implications of these opposed probability distributions are clarified by examining Figure 3.2, which shows a typical cross section of the mental organization for the two cognitive styles (again as ideal types).

On the one hand, the analytical genius has mental elements clustered into compact configurations arranged in a hierarchical order. The configurations are highly consolidated in that the elements within a configuration are linked by strong (cognitive or habitual) associations and in that the elements within a configuration have minimal links with the elements in other configurations. As we noted in chapter 1, configurations must be both "clear" (i.e., consist of strong associations among defining elements) and "distinct" (i.e., have minimal associations with elements outside the configuration) in order to form a hierarchical arrangement that might maximize the efficient distribution of knowledge.

On the other hand, the intuitive genius, though having roughly the same number of mental elements, has a dramatically different way of retrieving the information. Fewer connections are habitual or even properly symbolized, with an infusion of behaviorally active but infraconscious associations. Configurations are less "clear and distinct," and thus knowledge is distributed more equally. Because mental elements are more richly interconnected, there are more ways of passing from one element to another. This is immediately apparent in Figure 3.2 when we trace all possible paths between any two randomly selected elements. For instance, an analytical genius is very limited in the means by which element A'_{21} can be evoked by element A'_1, and that route is well ingrained by strong associations, whereas the possible avenues from A'_1 to A'_{21} in the intuitive genius are far more

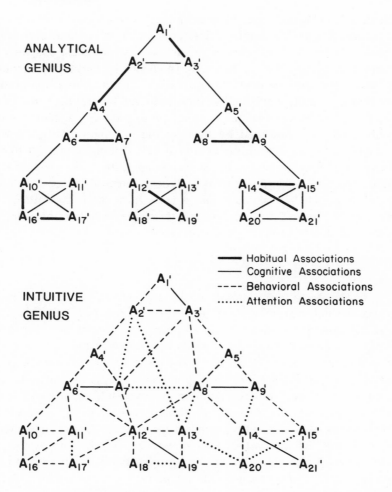

Figure 3.2. Typical associative connections among mental elements for analytical and intuitive geniuses.

numerous, and these are both weak and largely equiprobable. *This richness of associative interconnections provides the psychological vehicle for chance permutations.* Mach (1896, p. 167) recognized this key fact when after admitting the virtues of "a powerfully developed *mechanical* memory, which recalls vividly and faithfully old situations," he claimed that "more is required for the development of *inventions*. More extensive chains of images are necessary here, the excitation by mutual contact of widely different trains of ideas, a more powerful, more manifold, and richer connection of the contents of memory."

I stated in chapter 1 that chance is merely a confession of ignorance, the acknowledgment that potential determinants are abundant, each with approximately equivalent odds of impact, and so we must despair of any attempt to identify the causal nexus. In chance permutations, mental elements evoke other elements by such rare routes that any configuration so generated must be considered an essentially random (in the sense of virtually equiprobable) confluence of psychical events. The appearance of unpredictability is reinforced by the fact that so many of the associative linkages operate at the infraconscious level, making it difficult to reconstruct cognitively the origin of chance configurations. The product accordingly appears more intuitive than analytical, more an outcome of fancy or imagination than logical deduction. An analytical genius has little access to this "artistic power" to combine mental elements but, rather, must rely more on deductive, fully cognitive reasoning.

Implications of the model

Besides offering an account of the chance permutation process, this model helps explain the cognitive style of creative scientists (for details, see Simonton 1980a). In broad terms, the distribution of associative strengths seen in the upper left-hand quadrant of Figure 3.1 is necessarily related to the ability to generate remote associations. Because the configurations are less distinct, the corresponding concepts or schemata will be more inclusive, and thus the intuitive genius should feature wide categories. This property becomes apparent when we again look at Figure 3.2 and observe how in the analytical intellect the concept consisting of elements A_1', A_2', and A_3' is linked with fewer elements in adjacent concepts than is the case for the same elements in the intuitive mind. With such profusely interrelated thoughts, we also expect more fluency, flexibility, independence, and perhaps even risk-taking willingness, this last due to a greater awareness of alternative ways of perceiving and conceiving reality. In addition, a closer inspection of Figure 3.1 reveals two more ways that the subjective experience of the intuitive mind differs from that of the analytical intellect.

First, the intuitive genius has a much larger pool of associations that have just barely passed the threshold of attention, as is apparent from the area of the region between θ_a and θ_b in the figure. Such a profusion implies that the intuitive genius boasts a more impressive alertness to novel or unusual stimuli on the fringe of focused attention (see, e.g., Houston & Mednick 1963). This proclivity toward curiosity or inquisitiveness may explain the breadth of interests and preference for complexity displayed by creative individuals (as well as the incidental learning discovered by Laughlin 1967, and Laughlin, Doherty, & Dunn 1968). Naturally, this impulsive openness to experience could give a scientist *"sharpened attention,* which detects the uncommon features of an occurrence" (Mach 1896, p. 168) and thereby makes the gifted scientist more susceptible to serendipity.

Second, the intuitive intellect, in contrast with the analytical one, harbors many more infraconscious associations, that is, expectancies passing the threshold of behavior (θ_b) but still below the threshold of cognition (θ_c). Indeed, it is the very abundance of associations at this level of intuitions that gives this cognitive style its name. Because many of the chance permutations rely heavily on these behaviorally active but preconscious associations, the route that a chance permutation takes is often unknown to its creator, as Poincaré's introspections in the previous chapter illustrate. Reliance on these inarticulate but effective connections among elements was frequently reported in Roe's (1952b, p. 23) sample of eminent scientists: "All groups report a considerable amount of imageless thinking, particularly at crucial points." For example, one of her subjects noted in the interview that at certain times before a synthesis, "I just seem to vegetate; something is going on. I don't know what it is" (Roe 1952a, p. 144). The theory developed here considers these moments to represent occasions in which the "free-association" process that yields chance permutations dips into the infraconscious associations. In psychoanalytic terms, the scientist is "regressing into primary-process thinking," although this reverie may not entail repressed motives, sexual or otherwise. This regression is also revealed in the tendency, as mentioned in chapter 2, for words – when they do participate in the permutation process – to do so via emotional and physical attributes rather than rational connections.

The model just outlined presumes a high correlation between clarity and distinctness. That is, the stronger are the associations that tie the elements of a configuration, the fewer will be the active bonds among the configurations. Configurations range from small, tidy collections of elements that act as a unit (because all elements are strongly connected and minimally linked with outside configurations) to more diffuse configurations, or near aggregates, with weak associative bonds among elements and with minimal separation from kindred configurations, so that one concept easily flows into another. The act of consolidation serves as a sharpening process, accentuating the "ingroup" elements at the expense of the "outgroup" elements, producing configurations that are progressively clearer and more distinct. Recall that consolidation should count as an intellectual asset, for configurations, when sufficiently refined, can enter hierarchical structures for the most efficacious organization of information. Consolidation equally facilitates the permutation process insofar as configurations must behave more or less as a unit in order to be freely recombined. The goal of self-organization must be to advance from intuition to analysis. Yet the end result of consolidation is a population of configurations that do not lend themselves to chance permutations, owing to the dearth of interconnections among ideas. Herein arises one of the ironies of the creative act: Stable permutations are selected because they contribute to self-organization, but as these chance configurations become consolidated and the intellect becomes structured hierarchically the resources for chance permutations diminish. This self-defeating aspect of creativity has implications for the relation between career age and productivity as well as for innovation acceptance, as we shall discuss in chapter 4.

Motivational disposition

Assuming that a scientist has the requisite intellectual capacity to generate chance permutations, something more is required to translate potential into actual creativity. The scientfic creator must also possess the appropriate motivations that facilitate rather than inhibit the chance-permutation process. That is, according to this theory, we expect those motives that nurture creativity to be strengthened and those that discourage creativity to be weakened. Consequently, the motivational profile of the highly successful scientist consists of two sides, enhanced and suppressed motives.

Enhanced motives

According to Mach (1896, p. 170):

Supposing, then, that such a rich organic connexion of the elements of memory exists, and is the prime distinguishing mark of the inquirer, next in importance certainly is that *intense interest* in a definite object, in a definite idea, which fashions advantageous combinations of thought from elements before disconnected, and obtrudes that idea into every observation made, and into every thought formed, making it enter into relationship with all things.

An impressive inventory of empirical studies indeed suggests the crucial role that such motivations have in achievement (Nicholls 1972). In Cox's (1926, p. 187) classic historiometric inquiry into 301 geniuses (both creators and leaders), an exceptional IQ did not by itself ensure distinction, for intellect had to be accompanied by a tenacity of purpose, a perseverance in the face of obstacles; "high but not the highest intelligence, combined with the greatest degree of persistence, will achieve greater eminence than the highest degree of intelligence with somewhat less persistence." A follow-up study conducted years later again found that virtually anyone who attains fame in a given endeavor has an intense desire to excel, an exceptional need for achievement, and a willingness to persist in hard work (Walberg, Rasher, & Parkerson 1980).

Successful scientists are exceptionally energetic and hardworking (Bloom 1963; Knapp 1962; McClelland 1963), and their commitment to work is positively correlated with the number of publications and citations they receive (Busse & Mansfield 1984). In academic settings, the best predictor of the number of articles published in professional journals, as well as the productivity rate per unit of time, is the individual's fascination with research, and this is true even after controls are introduced for the effects of age and discipline: "Highest producers . . . express more of an interest in research, communicate more frequently with scholars at other institutions, and subscribe to more academic journals than do less productive faculty" (Blackburn, Behymer, & Hall 1978, p. 134; see also Fulton & Trow 1974). The influential researcher is unusually ambitious and enduring (Rushton, Murray, & Paunonen 1983; Wispé 1963), and in general, "great drive, as reflected in extraordinary commitment to work, is one of the personal characteristics that has often been found to differentiate creative scientists from their less creative peers" (Busse & Mansfield 1981, p. 66; see also Bloom 1963; Mansfield & Busse 1981; Taylor & Ellison 1967; Wispé 1963).

As a necessary corollary of this immense energy, we assume that the scientific achiever allots a disproportionate amount of time to research, for it takes time as well as force to search for stable chance permutations. Productivity in science is a positive function of the time given to scientific work (e.g., Boyce, Shaughnessy, & Pecker 1985; Chambers 1964; Gaston 1973, p. 51; Hargens 1978; Manis 1951; Simon 1974). Thus, one investigation found that distinguished researchers in the physical and social sciences worked around 8 to 10 hours per day, 300 to 335 days per year (Simon 1974). Indeed, a "Type A" or a "workaholic" personality (i.e., one who seldom feels that there is sufficient time to accomplish what must be accomplished) is positively associated with the number of times a scientist is cited in the literature (Matthews, Helmreich, Beane, & Lucker 1980). Anne Roe (1952b, p. 25) concluded from extensive interviews with 64 eminent scientists that they all were characterized by a "driving absorption in their work." The noted researcher "works hard and devotedly at his laboratory, often seven days a week. He says his work is his life, and has few recreations, those being restricted to fishing, sailing, walking or some other individualistic activity" (p. 22). As a group, "they have worked long hours for many years, frequently with no vacations to speak of, because they would rather be doing their work than anything else" (p. 25). This tremendous investment is succinctly expressed in Michael Faraday's motto "Work, Finish, Publish."

Suppressed motives

Roe's remarks hint that the drive to create, to do science, obliges competing drives to assume subsidiary roles, thereby inducing a distinctive motivational profile. The individualistic hobbies, for example, imply that great scientists prefer time for reflection to social interaction, and that is indeed the case; the notable scientist avoids interpersonal contact, social affairs, and political activities (Bloom 1963; Eiduson 1962; Helmreich, Spence, Beane, Lucker, & Matthews 1980; McClelland 1963; Roe 1952a; Taylor & Ellison 1967; Terman 1955). Although it is often maintained that science and religion are antithetical cultural enterprises (e.g., Sorokin 1937–1941; cf. Simonton 1976c)–a point that apparently is endorsed by eminent scientists' general lack of strong religious involvement (Chambers 1964; Eiduson 1962; Lehman & Witty 1931; Roe 1952a)–this latter tendency may actually reveal more about the creator's inherently unsociable nature than about any intrinsic hostility toward religion (but see chapter 5). Even academic duties of a more social nature hamper rather than help: Scientists who assign more time to administration duties are less prone to be prolific or to gain a wide reputation (Manis 1951; cf. Fulton & Trow 1974); and although the personality characteristics of successful teachers are orthogonal to (hence not negatively correlated with) those of successful researchers (Rushton et al. 1983; Wispé 1963; cf. Jex 1963), the more influential investigators tend to be less committed to teaching (Chambers 1964; Fulton & Trow 1974; Manis 1951; cf. Voeks 1962).

In his 1963 investigation of famous scientists, Cattell found a pattern similar to that found in studies of contemporary scientists, namely, that they were disposed to be "schizothymic" (i.e., withdrawn and internally preoccupied) and "desurgent" (i.e., introspective, restrained, brooding, and solemn) (cf. Chambers 1964). Cattell provided the specific instance of the chemist and physicist Henry Cavendish who "when dragged to a state function and about to meet some distinguished . . . foreign scientists, broke away and ran down the corridor, squeaking like a bat" (p. 121). Normally Cavendish never spoke more than a handful of words to a man and never spoke at all to a woman; he expressed his wishes to his female servants solely by written memos, fired on the spot any servant who crossed his path at home, and had a separate entrance to his house built to enable his coming and going without human contact! Cavendish was an extreme case, admittedly, but the following three theoretical considerations lead us to suspect that creative scientists tend to have personalities more introverted than the average.

As we quoted Jevons in chapter 2, the scientist does not grasp a new truth directly in some momentous flash of insight, but rather he or she must usually sift through a long and laborious parade of chance permutations before finding the solution to a problem. Faraday, another illustrious physicist and chemist, admitted that

the world little knows how many thoughts and theories which have passed through the mind of a scientific investigator have been crushed in silence and secrecy by his own severe criticism and adverse examinations; that in the most successful instances not a tenth of the suggestions, the hopes, the wishes, the preliminatory conclusions have been realised. (quoted in Beveridge 1957, p. 79)

Experimental studies have in fact shown how the most original, and hence the most potentially creative, responses to a given problem tend to come only after exhausting the initial pool of more obvious answers (e.g., Christensen, Guilford, & Wilson 1957; Parnes & Meadow 1963). Highly extroverted scientists will simply not have adequate time for this search process, and there are no shortcuts to originality. To paraphrase Euclid's response to Ptolemy I Soter of Egypt (who asked if there were an easier way to learn geometry), there is no royal road to creativity.

Furthermore, we must recognize the inherent superiority of intrinsic over extrinsic motivation. Amabile (1983) amply documented, with experimental and anecdotal evidence, how extrinsic motives – whether evoked by evaluation, social approval, or expectation of material rewards – tend to vitiate creativity; the creator must focus on the intrinsic properties of the task, not on potential rewards or criticisms that await the outcome. Indeed, extrinsic motivation should deflect any chance permutations toward the wrong goal. An individual might waste too much time generating chance permutations about the wrong things, such as fantasies about all the benefits of becoming rich and famous or worries about the adverse repercussions of failing to get tenure or a pay raise. Consequently, a creative scientist must retain an "internal locus of evaluation" (Rogers 1954, p. 254; see also Eiduson 1962). Recognition of the need to spurn extrinsic pressures toward conforming to social expectations may be partly responsible for the insistence on independence often displayed by creative persons (Cattell 1963; Chambers 1964; Razik 1967; Taylor & Ellison 1967). "The pervasive and unstereotyped unconventionality of thought which one finds consistently in creative individuals is related generically to a tendency to resist acculturation, where acculturation is seen as demanding surrender of one's personal, unique, fundamental nature" (Barron 1963, p. 151). This need also helps explain why a strong competitive motive is not necessarily conducive to effectiveness as a scientist (Helmreich et al. 1980; see also Knapp 1962; Thorndike 1950; cf. Matthews et al. 1980; Watson 1968).

Finally, social interaction may – in the case of truly extraordinary creativity – elicit a social interference effect, as would be predicted by Zajonc's (1965) theory of social facilitation. According to Zajonc, the mere presence of others tends to raise arousal, which in turn increases the likelihood that highly probable responses will be emitted at the expense of less probable responses. Because the chance permutation process demands access to low probability (infraconscious) associations, such socially induced arousal would necessarily inhibit creativity (Martindale & Greenough 1973; Simonton 1980a; see also Bastik 1982). In addition, to the extent that the presence of others implies the possibility of evaluation, this interference effect is heightened all the more. Creativity scores on a standard test (unusual uses) are actually lower under evaluative conditions than under more relaxed circumstances (Dentler & Mackler 1964; see also Amabile 1983).

To be sure, in this era of "big science," especially in such prestigious and heavily funded fields as high-energy physics and biomedical research, collaborative inquiries may be the norm, and thus papers with even dozens of coauthors are common. Price (1963) once forecast that the single-authored paper may soon become obsolete (see also Lawler 1963). Moreover, the quality of a paper, at least as gauged by the number of times it is cited in the professional literature, may actually correlate positively with the number of its authors (see, e.g., Beaver 1986; Lawani 1986; cf. Ashton & Oppenheim 1978; Smart & Bayer 1986). The financial repercussions of multiple authorship for researchers may even be better than those of single authorship, suggesting that more material value is placed on collaborative research (Diamond 1985). So perhaps in certain fields, groups of collaborators may become sufficiently well established that they can operate under more relaxed circumstances, with minimal concern for evaluation, thereby making negligible interference effect. It may even be feasible for such groups to "brainstorm," that is, to generate chance permutations via interpersonal interaction (cf. Abelson 1968; Osborn 1953).

Nevertheless, experimental studies suggest that solitary brainstorming is far more effective, in both quality and quantity of ideas, than is group brainstorming, this even when the evaluation apprehension is minimized (e.g., Bouchard & Hare 1970; Dillon, Graham, & Aidells 1972; Dunnette, Campbell, & Jaastad 1963). And field investigations have unearthed evidence that the per-capita output of research units declines as the number of coworkers increases, and hence that collaboration per se may not necessarily contribute to creative productivity (Andrews 1979). I would argue that the true breakthroughs in science – those that require unrestrained genius – emerge with higher odds from more solitary contemplation (cf. Pelz & Andrews 1976). Collaborators may contribute to the elaboration and verification of an initial creative idea, but that original concept normally arises from an entirely intrapsychic chance-permutation procedure. A scientist's productivity in a research laboratory is accordingly a positive function of how much influence that investigator has over the questions tackled by the group (Senter 1986). Inasmuch as this theory concentrates on explaining the highest-order genius, it is fitting that we quote Einstein's self-description: "I am a horse for a single harness, not cut out for tandem or teamwork; for well I know that in order to attain any definite goal, it is imperative that *one* person should do the thinking and commanding" (quoted in Sorokin 1963, p. 274). Descartes voiced a similar sentiment in Part II of his *Discourse on Method,* arguing that the products of a single meditative mind, whether artistic or scientific, are on the whole more coherent, more beautiful or true, than are collective contributions. The incessant necessity of having always to scan through a myriad of associative permutations dictates that any great scientist be, as William Wordsworth said of Newton, "a mind forever/ Voyaging through strange seas of thought, alone."

The foregoing points could be constructively subsumed under a broader view of motivation: We may say that the intrinsic motive to engage in scientific research for its own sake ensues from the more fundamental drive toward self-organization. Because a creative scientist has a mental structure lying closer to the intuitive genius end of the spectrum but instinctively seeks to attain the information-processing efficiency of the analytical genius, the successive discovery of chance configurations is accompanied by personal satisfaction, or subjective pleasure, that moves the scientist ahead toward order. So the quest for self-organization, or what Maslow (1962) would call "self-actualization," provides a powerful incentive that shoves aside other motives. Sociability, or a need for active social exchange, is probably one of the first conflicting motives to go. Elsewhere in this book I shall argue that this dependence of many personality traits on the degree of self-organization implies that the character of creative scientists should vary over the course of their careers, rather than serving as a permanent fixture in their personal makeup.

Discussion

We have just seen that the scientific genius may be distinguished by a particular cognitive style and motivational disposition. On the cognitive side, the highly creative scientist is extremely intelligent, but this intelligence is structured in a rather special way; besides possessing a cornucopia of mental elements, these elements must be profusely interconnected to optimize the effectiveness of the chance-permutation process. On the motivational side, the notable researcher exhibits a profound enthusiasm for scientific work, quite willingly assigning considerable time to that endeavor, even to the point of relinquishing the usual interest in social activities. Further, we have every reason to suspect that these personal attributes are applicable to all varieties of scientific genius, no matter what the discipline of application may be. Presumably, influential scientists project the same basic personality whether they go into mathematics, physics, chemistry, or biology. Indeed, the theory offers no basis for not supposing that this chapter has inadvertently sketched the picture of the "generic genius" who can make phenomenal contributions in any realm in the arts and sciences. The genius may pursue truth, or aspire to beauty, yet either quest requires the convergence of "high general abilities and continuous, energetic, highly personal effort over most of a lifetime" (Albert 1975, p. 143). We can even venture so far as to claim that a single set of traits supports achievement in any human activity, including those that emphasize leadership more than creativity. To exercise exceptional personal influence in a given domain demands that the individual hold a special collection of cognitive and motivational attributes. Galton (1869, p. 77) subsumed this cluster under the broader term of "natural ability":

I mean those qualities of intellect and disposition, which urge and qualify a man to perform acts that lead to reputation. I do not mean capacity without zeal, nor zeal without capacity, nor even a combination of both of them, without an adequate power of doing a great deal of very laborious work. But I mean a nature which, when left to itself, will, urged by an inherent stimulus, climb the path that leads to eminence, and has strength to reach the summit – one which, if hindered or thwarted, will fret and strive until the hindrance is overcome, and it is again free to follow its labour-loving instinct.

Galton here expressed in the most generalized form the personality requisite for history-making success as a creator or a leader.

Nonetheless, I do not want to be accused of overstating the case for a unified "genius personality" that transcends all realms of accomplishment. Empirical data do not favor the assumption of a generic characterization. Certainly, creators and leaders, even of the most momentous historical caliber, differ on some significant character traits. Thus, extraordinary intellectual power may assume a larger role in creativity than in leadership (Cox 1926; Simonton 1976a, 1985a, 1986f), and extroversion, dominance, and even aggressiveness may prove more prominent in successful leadership than in influential creativity (Knapp 1962; Simonton 1987e; Terman

1955; Thorndike 1950). Even if we concentrate on just creative personalities, scientific creators no doubt differ from artistic creators on a wide array of personal attributes, such as emotional stability (Cattell 1963; Cox 1926; Knapp 1962; Raskin 1936). Moreover, scientific creators may vary across disciplines on specific traits as well. In Roe's (1952a) examination of prominent investigators, the social scientists diverged from the natural scientists, the biologists contrasted with the physicists, and even in physics, the theoretical physicists displayed attributes that varied from those of the experimental physicists. Lastly, in any given discipline there may appear variations in creative styles; for instance, some may be "initiators," others "aestheticians," and yet others "methodologists," all contributing to the same domain of scientific knowledge (see, e.g., Katz 1984).

Such contrasts refer to the larger inventory of personality variables that lies outside the explanatory scope of the chance-configuration theory. There exist hundreds, maybe even thousands, of dimensions on which people may vary, dimensions both intellectual and dispositional, about which the theory is simply silent (see, e.g., Cox 1926; Simonton 1986f; Thorndike 1950). By the same token, these theoretically superfluous traits may be largely irrelevant as determinants of achievement. Instead, specific personality types may gravitate toward particular endeavors according to some matching of personal qualities and discipline requirements, yet what determines success in a selected field may lean most on the cognitive and motivational parameters emphasized by the theory (cf. Raskin 1936; Simonton 1986b). Hence, when we compare all scientists and all artists on every available personality trait and ignore the differential magnitudes of achievement reached within each domain, then scientists and artists will differ – just as physicists will differ from biologists and composers from painters. But if we focus only on the most distinguished contributors to each endeavor and limit our inspection to just those traits that are dictated by the theory, the similarities will loom larger than the contrasts. For example, Roe (1952a, p. 11) concluded from her extensive studies that "there are greater personality differences among artists than among scientists, but successful artists and successful scientists have one thing in common, – their intense devotion to their work." In a similar vein, Lehman (1953b, p. 192), after scrutinizing careers of virtually every kind, observed that "as compared with the average individual, our distinguished creative thinkers have usually possessed, among other things, an astonishing capacity for hard patient work." To state this argument in more concrete terms, Galileo and Michelangelo were probably more alike in fundamental cognitive style and motivational disposition than either were similar to those colleagues in the same creative enterprise who failed to leave a tangible mark on history.

The more momentous the accomplishment is, the less relevant, when anticipating personality, the consideration will be of where the contribution was made.

There still remains one crucial dimension, intrinsic to the theory, on which we should expect to be able to distinguish scientific and artistic genius: the intuitive versus analytical styles of information processing. Even though we predict that all outstanding creative minds, no matter what the field, will fall closer to the intuitive end of this spectrum than to the analytical end, creative scientists and artists probably will segregate themselves in placement. Artistic creators should gravitate toward intuition, the scientific creators toward analysis. This differentiation is consistent with the suggestion that artistic creativity requires more "divergent" thinking, whereas scientific creativity demands more "convergent" thinking (e.g., Hudson 1966). To illustrate how this differentiation might work in practice, scores on the Barron–Welsh Art Scale, which should correlate with placement along the analytical-intuitive dimension (Simonton 1975b), are higher for architects than for mathematicians, separating artistic from scientific modes of creativity. Nonetheless, among mathematicians alone, degree of distinction is positively associated with high scores, so that the more creative mathematicians are closer to the architects in cognitive style (Helson & Crutchfield 1970).

This contrast between scientific and artistic mentalities also fits in well with my speculation at the end of chapter 2 that artistic creativity dips more deeply into primary-process thought, and scientific creativity relies more on secondary-process thought. Hence, altered states of consciousness, such as dreams and drug-induced reverie, are more likely to contribute to artistic than to scientific originality. It is intriguing that the capacity to produce remote associations predicts scientific creativity only when the associations are moderately rare, whereas extremely bizarre associations are negatively related to success as a scientist (Gough 1976). Furthermore, this distinction may help account for why successful collaborative efforts (excluding master–disciple relationships) seem far more common in the sciences than in the arts – for which reason aesthetic collaborations are often far less successful than are scientific collaborations (see, e.g., Jackson & Padgett 1982). If artists use infraconscious associations more fully than do scientists, then a smaller proportion of the creative process in aesthetic endeavors will be accessible to interpersonal exchange, intercourse that requires conscious, cognitively mediated associations (see, e.g., Raskin 1936).

I do not wish to exaggerate the gap between scientific and artistic creativity, however. Not even considering the similarity of motivational profile in the two groups, an appreciable overlap between the two forms of creativity is expected on the dimension of cognitive style as well. Wilhelm Ostwald, the 1909 recipient of the Nobel Prize for Chemistry, distinguished between two varieties of scientific researchers, namely, the classicists, who are systematic perfectionists, and the romanticists, who have such a profundity of ideas that they fail to develop them fully. By the same token, artistic creators might be similarly differentiated, the classicists favoring precision, order, and stability, and the romantics, expression, richness, and novelty. Returning to Kuhn's (1963) distinction, which we pointed out in chapter 1, classicists are more traditionalist, romantics more iconoclast. The classicist artists could reasonably be more analytical than could the romantic scientists, thereby causing an overlap in the two distributions on this intellectual style.

With the minor qualification just offered, we may conclude that at the core of epoch-making achievement in any field is a single personality type. This special constellation of traits follows from the demands imposed on any individual who must depend on the chance-permutation process to arrive at valuable configurations. Alexander Bain put it in a nutshell over a century ago in his *The Senses and the Intellect* (1855, p. 596):

In the case of originality in all departments, whether science, practice, or fine art, there is a point of character that is worth specifying in this place, as being more obviously of value in practical inventions and in the conduct of business and affairs, I mean an active turn, or a profuseness of energy put forth in trials of all kinds on the chance of making lucky hits.

This essential character becomes most apparent in the phenomenon of productivity, the subject of the next chapter.

4 Productivity

The distinguishing characteristic of genius, scientific or otherwise, is immense productivity (Simonton 1984, chap. 5). The common misconception that phenomenal intellects contribute only a handful of selective masterworks, or even a single magnum opus, is plain wrong. Darwin could claim 119 publications at the close of his career, Einstein 248, and, in psychology, Galton 227, Binet 277, James 307, Freud 330, and Maslow 165 (Albert 1975). Edison may be best known for his incandescent light bulb and phonograph, but all told he held 1,093 patents – still the record at the United States Patent Office. Frank Barron (1963, p. 139) commented that

there is good reason for believing . . . that originality is almost habitual with persons who produce a really singular insight. The biography of the inventive genius commonly records a lifetime of original thinking, though only a few ideas survive and are remembered to fame. Voluminous productivity is the rule and not the exception among the individuals who have made some noteworthy contribution.

The chance-configuration theory helps explain three aspects of this feature of scientific creativity: (1) the distinctive cross-sectional distribution of productivity, (2) the relation between age and productive output, and (3) the association between quantity and quality. Moreover, at the close of this chapter I shall show how the theory clarifies three more issues of importance, namely, the Ortega hypothesis, the Yuasa phenomenon, and Planck's principle.

Cross-sectional distribution

The distribution of output in any scientific endeavor is highly élitist, with a small proportion of the total scientific community accounting for the majority of the published contributions. In a study of disciplines as diverse as linguistics, infantile paralysis, gerontology and geriatrics, geology, and chemistry, Wayne Dennis (1955) found that the top 10% most prolific contributors were responsible for about half of the total work, whereas the bottom 50% least productive can be credited with only about 15% of the contributions (see also Bloom 1963). Indeed, typically around half of those at all active contribute only one work each, meaning that the most prolific contributor is several times more productive than are the least productive contributors (Dennis 1955; see also Davis 1987; Shockley 1957). In psychology, for instance, the most prolific scientist can claim more titles than can 80 colleagues in the lower half of the distribution (Dennis 1954c). And as Dennis (1955) pointed out, these figures may tremendously underestimate the magnitude of élitism, as only those who have contributed at least one item to posterity are counted at all. Sometimes more than half of the young PhDs from a distinguished university may publish nothing beyond their doctoral dissertations (Bloom 1963). There is thus some justification for the prima facie preposterous claim of Cesare Lombroso, in his 1863 book *The Man of Genius,* that "the appearance of a single great genius is more than equivalent to the birth of a hundred mediocrities." Two laws have been proposed that describe the empirical distribution.

According to the Price law, if k represents the total number of contributors to a given field, then $\sqrt{k}$ will be the predicted number of contributors who will generate half of all contributions (Price 1963, chap. 2). Not only does this law imply a highly skewed distribution, but it also suggests a distribution that becomes ever more élitist as the discipline expands (Simonton 1984d, chap. 5). To illustrate, in a new discipline with only about a dozen investigators, around three, or one-fourth, will account for half of all contributions. But should the discipline grow to 100, the élite will consist of 10, or 10% of the whole field. This expanding hegemony of the few as a domain of inquiry gains practitioners has obtained empirical endorsement (e.g., Zhao & Jiang 1985), although the law probably does not hold for extreme values of k. If a discipline becomes extremely popular, recruiting an active membership of about 10,000, it seems unlikely that a mere 1%, or 100, would so dominate the creative enterprise.

The Lotka law attempts to describe in more detail the shape of this distribution, which is clearly monotonically decreasing at a decelerating rate, yielding a long upper tail (Lotka 1926). If n is the number of published papers and $f(n)$ is the number of scientists who publish n papers, then $f(n)$ will be inversely proportional to n^2, where the proportionality constant varies from discipline to discipline. It is interesting that this function is similar to Pareto's law of income distribution, in which wealth is allotted in inverse proportion to $n^{1.5}$ (Price 1963, chap. 2). If a leader is defined as a person whose influence over other group members far exceeds the norm, then clearly the most productive scientists will form an élite as dominating as that of the economic magnates who monopolize a nation's material resources.

These empirical findings and laws are extremely general, as they hold equally well for other kinds of creative productivity outside science. Dennis (1955) found the same productive élitism in the publication of secular music and in the books represented in the Library of Congress as he did in the scientific disciplines listed earlier. And the Price and Lotka laws are applicable to creative activities far broader than their authors claimed (Simonton 1984d, 1987b). For example, classical music: About 250 composers account for all the music heard in the repertoire, but a mere 16 can claim credit for creating half of those pieces ($16 \cong \sqrt{250}$) (Simonton 1984d, chap. 5; cf. Moles 1958). Bach's output alone fills 46 volumes (Albert 1975) – enough compositions, reportedly, to keep a copiest confined to regular working hours occupied a whole career merely copying the parts out by hand! Furthermore, the comparison between the Lotka and Pareto laws implies that the principle of productive élitism may apply to any domain of achievement, even those requiring leadership rather than creativity per se (Simonton 1984d, chap. 5). Thus the number of battles fought by generals, the number of laws written by legislators, the number of elections entered by politicians, and the amount of monetary assets accumulated by entrepreneurs all may be described by roughly the same skewed cross-sectional distribution.

Although there is some debate about whether the Price law can be derived from the Lotka law (Allison, Price, Griffin, Moravscik, & Stewart 1976), there is very little contention about the general applicability of these laws, at least as rough approximations. And certainly there is no disagreement about the broad form of the empirical distribution, however élitist it may be. The chance-configuration theory offers an explanation for this established fact. But before I present that account, let me briefly review some of the earlier attempts to clarify this phenomenon.

Previous interpretations

Even if all researchers concur on the skewed-right productivity distribution, there will be less consensus on the theoretical foundation for the observed curve. Indeed, at least three conceptually distinct interpretations have been offered, two more psychological and one more sociological in orientation.

Dennis (1954c) himself suggested that the observed distribution represents the upper tail of the normal distribution, a threshold operating to delete the lower portions of that standard distribution (cf. Nicholls 1972). This idea has immediate appeal, not just for its simplicity, but also for its compatibility with a long psychometric tradition – commencing with Francis Galton's classic *Hereditary Genius* (1869) – that has conceived exceptional intelligence in terms of the exclusive right-hand portion of the bell-shaped curve (see also Cattell 1903; Simonton 1985a). Yet the Nobel laureate Herbert Simon (1954) indicated that this will not do, because the tail of the productivity distribution is stretched out much farther than we would expect according to the normal curve (cf. Haitun 1983). Either some process must be activated that distorts the distribution in precisely the correct way, or else some entirely distinct mechanism is responsible for generating the skewed distribution. The remaining two interpretations pursue each of these possibilities.

Apropos of the first alternative, another laureate, William Shockley (1957), proposed the following route around the impasse: If we suppose that productivity is the *multiplicative* product of many factors all normally distributed, then the consequence will be a *lognormal* distribution, and hence one highly skewed right, with an appropriately elongated upper tail. This interpretation, too, is attractive. It is certainly plausible that several variables are requisite for creativity, that these variables contribute to creativity in a multiplicative manner, and that the variables are distributed normally in the population (Allison 1980b; Simonton 1987c). The main difficulty with Shockley's solution, however, is that the nature and number of the factors involved are neither theoretically nor empirically specified. Accordingly, his explanation must be considered incomplete.

Perhaps at the present time the majority view is that the cross-sectional distribution is the result of some accumulative advantage process whereby "the rich get richer and the poor get poorer" (e.g., Allison 1980a,b; Allison, Long, & Krauze 1982; Allison & Stewart 1974; Price 1976; Simon 1955). This mechanism is more sociological than psychological, depending as it does on the selective quality of the scientific reward system. Because access to research positions, journal space, grant money, and rewards or honors is severely restricted, those who succeed first obtain an edge that better enables them to succeed later, whereas those who start off on the wrong foot tend to establish a pattern of failure that eventually pushes them out of the competition for kudos. Success breeds further success; failure spawns failure.

Now we cannot really question whether this accumulative advantage (and disadvantage) phenomenon occurs for awards and honors in science. In this domain, what Merton (1968) styled the "Matthew effect" definitely applies. According to Matthew (25:29), "Unto every one that hath shall be given, and he shall have abundance: but from him that hath not shall be taken away even that which he hath." It is equally evident that once certain scientists attain high professional visibility or fame, their opportunities for publication are much better than are those of colleagues yet to establish a reputation at large. For example, eminent scientists receive more invitations to contribute chapters to books and articles to journals, thereby permitting them to bypass the frequently capricious decisions made by editors and their referees (Rodman & Mancini 1981). And finally, there is little doubt that the principle of accumulative advantage can explain many unique features of scientific influence and acclaim. But what is less apparent, in my mind, is whether this principle can account for the specific cross-sectional distribution of total lifetime output. It is telling that the distribution of publications is less élitist than is the distribution of citations or rewards (Allison 1980b; Allison et al. 1982; Allison & Stewart 1974; Davis 1987), a contrast that implies that some other process may be responsible for the skewed distribution of productivity across scientists, the Matthew effect operating merely to exaggerate this initial inequality yet further (cf. Allison & Stewart 1975; Faia 1975).

Although the first of these three explanations is plainly inadequate, I shall not assert that the second and third are just as wrong. I shall argue only that a fourth interpretation can be derived directly from the chance-configuration theory. Because the theory explains so many other facets of scientific creativity – as indicated in the previous and following chapters as well as the remainder of this chapter – this alternative account may be the most plausible overall.

Present interpretation

Like Shockley and Dennis, I posit that the basis for the productivity distribution is the normal curve, and like Shockley I propose some mechanism by which that curve can be distorted to yield a more skewed result. Let us suppose, in particular, that the number of mental elements available for chance permutations is proportional to an individual's intelligence and hence that this attribute is normally distributed in the population. According to this supposition, the total supply of potential chance permutations of those elements will be characterized by a highly skewed curve with an extremely stretched-out upper tail. This happens because the number of permutations of n items increases as an accelerating (nonlinear, concave upward) function of n. Unfortunately, we cannot specify what this function is. If we speak of combinations rather than permutations, there will be 2^n ways of taking n elements, a number that is both too large and too small. It is an overestimate inasmuch as it is improbable that all potential sets of n things will be considered (up to and including the set of all things!). And it is an underestimate insofar as 2^n refers to combinations not permutations. Therefore, we could use the combinatory formula for the number of permutations of n elements taken r at a time, where r represents the maximum number of elements that can be considered at any one time. Then $P_r^n = n! / (n + r)!$. The introduction of factorials yields a function that grows at an accelerating pace as a function of n. In fact, it probably increases too fast, indeed explosively, even when $n \gg r$ (for r may be somewhere near Miller's 1956 magical number 7 ± 2). Consequently, I shall offer, as a very rough guess, the more conservative exponential function. That is, if n is the number of mental elements, e^n will be the number of potential chance permutations, where e is the constant 2.718. . . . Even if n is normally distributed in the population of scientists, e^n definitely will not be. Indeed, the distribution will be decidedly lognormal rather than normal, with an immensely long upper tail.

To illustrate this point, I ran a simple Monte Carlo simulation (Simonton 1987b). The computer generated 10,000 random normal deviates to represent the distribution of the quantity of mental elements across individuals. A second set of random scores was created by taking the exponential of the first set. To make the comparisons more concrete, I standardized both sets of numbers to a mean of 100 and a standard deviation of 16, as if they were IQ-like scores, and then I truncated these standardized scores to integer values. The first set of scores, which is taken to reflect the supply of mental elements, ended up with a distribution not all that different from what is normally found for IQ. The minimum was 37, the maximum 155, for a range of 118 points, and the distribution was highly symmetric and normally peaked (skewness -0.02 and kurtosis -0.09). The second set of scores, in contrast, had a low of 87, a high of 341, for a spread of 254 points, and the distribution was highly skewed right, featuring a long flat upper tail (skewness 4.20 and kurtosis 31.37). The lowest score was much closer to the mean (100) than was the highest score, and the distribution monotonically decreased at a decelerating rate throughout almost the entire range of scores, making the outcome extremely élitist. The upper tail of the second curve, in fact, is indistinguishable from the distribution usually observed for scientific productivity. The two contrasting curves are shown in Figure 4.1.

Consequently, the chance-configuration theory can explain both the Lotka and Price laws according to the capacity for chance permutations to increase as a nonlinear and accelerating function of the repertoire of free mental elements. Again, although alternative interpretations of this phenomenon exist, the current explanation ensues from a larger theoretical framework that also handles many other data points. In addition, we have every reason to believe that this account fits lifetime output in creative endeavors outside science.

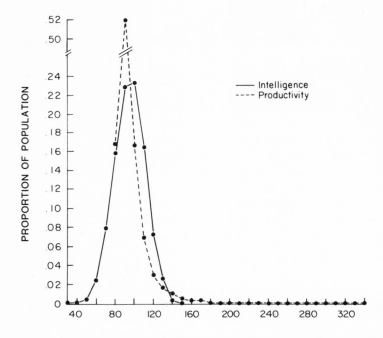

Figure 4.1. Theoretical distributions for intelligence and productivity (mean 100, standard deviation 16) by Monte Carlo simulation.

Age and output

Beginning with Beard's (1874), there has been a considerable amount of empirical work on the relation between age and productivity, culminating in Harvey C. Lehman's *Age and Achievement* (1953a). Here Lehman carefully and systematically examined numerous fields of creativity and leadership, including virtually every scientific discipline. His primary goal was to discern when productivity tends to begin, when it tends to end, and, most important, when productive output tends to attain a maximum. His principal inferences were twofold (see also Lehman 1962).

First, creative productivity within any field is a curvilinear, concave-downward function of age, with a shape approximating that of an inverted backward-J curve. Expressed in less abstract terms, creative output tends to increase relatively rapidly up to a definite peak productive age, after which there is a gradual decline. Typically, productivity begins somewhere in the 20s of a scientist's life, attains the high point sometime in the late 30s or early 40s, and thereafter turns downward.

Second, the specific form of the age curve–in particular the points defining the onset, maximum, and magnitude of the postpeak decline in productivity–varies in a predictable fashion from discipline to discipline (also see Cole 1979; Dennis 1966). In the biological sciences, for instance, the early 30s may be the optimal period for contributions to botany and classical descriptions of disease, whereas the late 30s may see more contributions to bacteriology, physiology, pathology, and general medicine. Likewise in the physical sciences, productivity apparently peaks in the late 20s for chemistry, the early 30s for mathematics and physics, and the late 30s for geology and astronomy (Lehman 1953a, chap. 20). The early peak for mathematics and theoretical physics is notorious (cf. Hardy 1940; Moulin 1955; Roe 1972b). This pervasive attitude is revealed in Einstein's words: "A person who has not made his great contribution to science before the age of thirty will never do so" (quoted in Brodetsky 1942, p. 699). This point is made more emphatically in the little poem of Paul Dirac, who won the Nobel Prize for Physics at the youthful age of 31, for work he had done when only 25:

> Age is, of course, a fever chill
> that every physicist must fear.
> He's better dead than living still
> when once he's past his thirtieth year.
> (quoted in Jungk 1958, p. 27)

These broad conclusions have been corroborated in many other investigations (see, e.g., Bayer & Dutton 1977; Blackburn et al. 1978; Davis 1954; Diemer 1974; Eagly 1974; Fulton & Trow 1974; Lehman 1953b, 1966a,b; Lyons 1968; Zhao & Jiang 1986; Zusne 1976). Nevertheless, Lehman's research has also been severely criticized on methodological grounds by Dennis (1956a,b, 1958, 1966) and by many sociologists (e.g., Cole 1979; Riley, Johnson, & Foner 1972; Zuckerman & Merton 1972). These critics' chief argument is that the downward turn in the tables showing aggregate output as a function of age is a mere artifact. First, Lehman is reputed to have failed to weigh the impact on his tabulations of including creators who did not live out their normal life span, thus introducing a spurious decline in the totals (the "compositional fallacy"). In addition, Lehman was accused of not controlling for the changes in competition as a creator's career advanced and the number of persons entering the same field expanded. Despite these complaints, Lehman's age curves were largely replicated in subsequent research that used more sophisticated analytical techniques (e.g., Diemer 1974; Horner, Rushton, & Vernon 1986; McDowell 1982; Oromaner 1981; Pelz & Andrews 1976, chap. 11; Simonton 1975a, 1977a, 1980b,d,e, 1984b,f; see also Lehman 1956, 1958, 1960, 1962, 1963, 1966a;

cf. Diamond 1986). Specifically, even though the optimal ages for output may sometimes differ slightly from what Lehman suggested (and often a bit later), the postpeak decline appears even after taking into account differential life span, secular trends in competition, and many other sources of potential methodological artifact. Indeed, there is ample justification for believing that the age curves may be transhistorically and cross-culturally invariant, for they have been replicated on samples of creators who lived in many different nations, even distant civilizations, and in different centuries, even separate millennia (e.g., Lehman 1962, 1963; Simonton 1975a, 1980e).

In my opinion, the primary drawback to Lehman's research, as well as that of his successors, is the near absence of a theoretical scheme for interpreting the key results. Why does the agewise distribution of output assume such a predictable form? For what reason does that form change from discipline to discipline? Lehman (1953a) himself, in the final chapter of his book, offered several post hoc interpretations, with an emphasis on physical health (see also Lehman 1962). Yet the age curves for creative output fail to correspond to those for physical fitness, nor would we expect that people in distinct fields feature comparable contrasts in vigor; and in any event, the decline in productivity materializes even when health is statistically separated out (Simonton 1977a). Over a century ago, Beard (1874) proposed a two-factor theory based on supposed changes in enthusiasm and experience over the course of a career, yet his theory lacks an a priori mathematical formulation, and it fails to handle all key findings (Simonton 1984b). Mumford (1984) put forward an alternative two-factor explanation based on the agewise distribution of two divergent adaptive styles, the accommodating and the controlling, with comparable limitations. Outside psychological accounts, some sociologists have attempted an interpretation based on the doctrine of accumulative advantage (e.g., Cole 1979), whereas some economists have tried to advance an explanation based on investment in "human capital" (e.g., Diamond 1984, 1986; McDowell 1982). Again, for various reasons, these offerings, however noteworthy, are unable to account for the full inventory of established results. More important, we can derive directly from the theory put forward here a model that treats the data comprehensively and precisely.

Information-processing model

We shall begin by observing that the chance-configuration theory maintains that creativity, on the intrapsychic level, involves a two-step cognitive process (cf. Wallas 1926). The first step is generating a configuration via the chance-permutation process; the second step converts this chance configuration into a communication configuration suitable for publication. Expressed in the scheme outlined in chapter 3, Step 1 engages more the infraconscious, primary-process associations accessible below the threshold of cognition, whereas Step 2 recruits more the conscious, secondary-process associations freely available at the cognitive level (cf. Suler 1980). In any event, the production of chance configurations depends on the supply of stray mental elements, that is, elements in a relatively disordered state in the mind, whereas the production of communication configurations depends on how many chance configurations have accumulated awaiting fuller articulation. This two-step conception of the chance-configuration theory dovetails nicely with a recent mathematical model of creative productivity (Simonton 1984b). It, too, is predicated on a two-step cognitive process: First, each creator begins with a supply of "creative potential" (i.e., the degree of rich associative interconnections among numerous elements) that, during the course of the creator's career, becomes actualized in the form of "creative ideations" (i.e., chance configurations); second, the ideas produced in the first step are progressively translated into actual "creative contributions" (i.e., communication configurations) for publication in the established disciplinary vehicles.

We can then derive a set of linear differential equations based on two rates. The first corresponds to Step 1 and is called the *ideation rate,* which assumes that a "law of mass action" operates so that the speed at which creative potential is converted into creative ideations is proportional to the size of that potential at a given time. In our theory, the velocity of ideation depends on the mass of still-disorganized mental elements. The more free mental elements there are, the more possible "collisions" there will be, to use Poincaré's molecular analogy, and thus the higher the speed will be at which stable permutations emerge. The second rate corresponds to Step 2 and is called the *elaboration rate,* which concerns the quantity of ideations that await articulation. In our terms, the speed at which communication configurations are generated is proportional to the existing backlog of chance configurations, assuming that creators work on more than one project at the same time (see Hargens 1978; Simon 1974). The solution to these differential equations yields the following equation:

$$p(t) = c(e^{-at} - e^{-bt}) \tag{4.1}$$

Here $p(t)$ is creative productivity (e.g., number of publications) at time t; a is the ideation rate; b is the elaboration rate; and e again is the exponential constant. The rate of ideation is assumed to be typically lower than that of elaboration (i.e., $a < b$), a reasonable assumption, as the proportion of chance permutations that make acceptable initial configurations is far smaller than the proportion of those configurations that can be converted into communication configurations. According to Wallas's (1926) four stages, the combined states of preparation, incubation, and illumination arrive at creative ideas less rapidly than the stage of verification can dispose of them. Or according to the associationist model presented in chapter 3, the speed of processing at the intuitive level is slower than that at the analytical level.

At any rate, the integration constant c, which scales the height of the predicted curve, is equal to $abm / (b - a)$, where m is the initial creative potential. That is, m represents the maximum number of contributions that a creator is theoretically capable of producing, given an infinite life span. Previously we affirmed that m should be roughly proportional to e^n, where n is the number of mental elements not yet tied down in a hierarchical structure of tightly consolidated configurations.

Significantly, t is taken to represent not chronological age, on which most research concentrates, but, rather, professional or "career age" (cf. Bayer & Dutton 1977; Lyons 1968), for this is an information-processing model in which $t = 0$ at the moment that the ideation (i.e., chance-permutation) process begins. Nonetheless, to validate the model, it is often necessary to translate career age into chronological age equivalents, a reasonable approximation, given that the two alternative measures tend to correlate .87 (Bayer & Dutton 1977; see also Andrews 1979). With that in mind, Figure 4.2 presents a typical age curve according to the model, assuming that $a = 0.04$, $b = 0.05$, and $c = 61$ (i.e., $m = 305$) and that $t = 0$ at chronological age 20.

In general, creative productivity increases rapidly (in a decelerating curve) up to a single peak in the early 40s – with a maximal output of about five contributions per annum – and soon thereafter begins a gradual decline, reaching the zero point asymptotically – yielding an inverted backward-J curve, as found in the empirical literature. Indeed, the average correlation between predicted and observed values is .95, and the equation even predicts data (see Cole 1979; Dennis 1966) claimed to contradict Lehman's age curve! It is significant that the longitudinal function exhibited in Figure 4.2 fits not only the overall form of agewise fluctuations in output but also the fine structure. For instance, a study of the careers of eminent psychologists indicated that the shape of the curve in the beginning is concave downward, in a decelerating curve, and that the closing portion of the curve is characterized by an asymptotic approach to the zero-output level (Simonton 1984b). Further, the model holds that a larger proportion of variance in the longitudinal fluctuations will be explained if the predic-

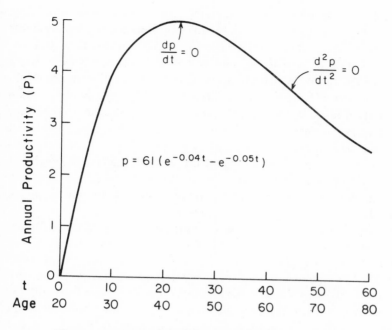

Figure 4.2. Predicted productivity as a function of age under typical parameters (from Simonton 1984b).

tions are defined according to career age rather than chronological age (Simonton 1984b). For example, the equation subsumes Zusne's (1976) empirical generalization that the age peak for any given career is located at the harmonic mean of the age of first and last contribution (Simonton 1984b). At the same time, the equation defines the circumstances when we would not expect Zusne's harmonic-mean model to hold, namely, when the values of *a* and *b* put the peak in the middle or latter portion of a career.

Nevertheless, the model's most important implications, besides accurately describing the typical age curve, concern interdisciplinary differences in the specific age function and the empirical association among precocity, longevity, and rate of output. After examining each of these subjects, I shall close this discussion of the information-processing model by outlining some useful qualifications.

Interdisciplinary differences

Any complete explanation of the age function for creative productivity must provide for the fact that the age curve alters systematically from one discipline to another. In the current model, this accommodation is accomplished by recognizing that the information-processing requirements for one field may be quite different from those for another field. That is, disciplines may differ in both the rate at which chance configurations are reached and the rate at which those configurations can be converted into communication configurations. This variation is registered by the ideation and elaboration rates, or the parameters a and b of Equation 4.1. To offer some examples, in theoretical physics and pure mathematics both the ideation and the elaboration rates may be rapid, resulting in a curve that peaks comparatively soon and drops off much more quickly (although not nearly so much as Dirac maintained). In geology and applied mathematics, both the ideation and elaboration rates are probably slower, generating an age curve that peaks later and then declines more gradually.

Let me illustrate how these two parameters may vary in practice. On the basis of a study of the careers of hundreds of creators, Dennis (1966) published tabulations of productivity rates across consecutive decades from the 20s to the 70s. Using a nonlinear estimation program (Wilkinson 1986), we obtain $a = 0.03$ and $b = 0.05$ for mathematicians, but $a = 0.02$ and $b = 0.04$ for geologists. Thus, both the ideation and elaboration rates are faster for mathematics than for geology. Granted, this contrast may not appear all that substantial, given how close the two pairs of parameters are. Even so, these small discrepancies translate into sizable gaps in predicted peak productive ages. With a little calculus we can show (Simonton 1984b) that the curve described by Equation 4.1 maximizes at

$$t_1 = \frac{1}{b - a} \ln \frac{b}{a} \qquad (4.2)$$

Substituting the parameter estimates into this formula, we find that the peaks for these two scientific disciplines are nearly a decade apart: Mathematicians tend to reach optimal output at career age 26, geologists at 35.

Not only can this model be adjusted to explain interdisciplinary contrasts in the age curves for the sciences, but the equations perform equally well in the arts and humanities. Fast ideation and elaboration are characteristic of lyric poetry, whereas writing novels requires more time both for isolating an original chance configuration and for transforming it into a polished communication configuration (cf. Lehman 1953a, p. 325) – a difference that holds for all the world's major literary traditions (Simonton 1975a). Moreover, in some creative activities, such as scholarship, it takes so much time to proceed from germinal idea to finished product that the elaboration rate becomes quite small, accordingly minimizing the amount of decline in the later years of the career (cf. Dennis 1966). For example, it took Gibbon practically his whole creative life to complete his *Decline and Fall of the Roman Empire*. To show again how such differences emerge in real data, we can once more use Dennis's (1966) longitudinal tabulations. The parameter estimates are $a = 0.04$ and $b = 0.07$ for poets, $a = 0.02$ and $b = 0.05$ for novelists, and $a = 0.02$ and $b = 0.03$ for historians. These estimated values yield predicted peaks, in terms of career age, of 19, 26, and 40, respectively (cf. Simonton 1975a). As we saw before, small changes in the two information-processing parameters can generate tremendous contrasts in expected productive peaks across disciplines.

Finally, by appropriately altering the two parameters, we can account for any observed historical trends in the optimal age for creative output. As a case in point, the peak age for contributing to science may have increased from around 25 years in 1500 to 37 years in 1960, an increment that cannot be adequately accounted for by corresponding enhancements in life expectancy over the same period (Zhao & Jiang 1986; cf. Roe 1972b). If we assume that the complexity of the problems faced by the scientific community enlarged over this time interval, then the ideation and elaboration rates would be expected to shrink in proportion.

Whatever the specific discipline or era, the same principles probably apply in determining the size of the two key information-processing parameters. If the mental elements entering the chance-permutation process are relatively simple and well consolidated, the configurations can be arrived at quite quickly, so that the creator will soon consume the initial creative potential. But if the elements are more rich and varied, the generation of stable permutations will slow down, and correspondingly more time will be needed to realize the full lifetime potential. Thus, because pure mathematics and theoretical physics deal with highly abstract conceptual entities, the peak age is younger than it is for those disciplines, such as geology, whose central ideas are more complex and concrete. The early productive peaks characteristic of lyric poets may be likewise explained (cf. Simonton 1975a, 1980e). Similarly, in certain fields the proper translation of chance configurations into intelligible and persuasive communication configurations is relatively straightforward, whereas in other fields much time may be consumed in verification, documentation, and calculation before the central idea has acquired presentable clothing. Again, in pure mathematics, once a theorem is conceived and its proof realized, the time necessary to ready a paper for submission to a professional journal may be negligible. As an example, Arthur Cayley, who wrote some 995 mathematical papers in his lifetime, averaged a paper every two weeks! On the other hand, in astronomy, especially before the advent of digital computers, many years were wasted in laborious calculations and observations, considerably delaying the time that a novel notion was in the right guise for publication. Indeed, it took Copernicus around 20 years to work out the details for his *On the Revolutions of the Celestial Spheres* (see also Abt 1983).

Even if this cognitive model features two central parameters, in many respects the ideation constant a is the most interesting, for this determines the rate at which creative potential is consumed, that is, the rate at which an intuitive genius is transformed into an analytical genius. We may define the typical "creative half-life" in any discipline as the natural logarithm of 2 divided by a. In mathematics, then, the half-life may be around 23 years, meaning that half of the initial creative potential is normally consumed in the production of chance configurations; so if the mathematician begins at, say, age 20, he or she will be midway between intuition and analysis by age 43. In more scholarly endeavors, the half-life may be about 35 years, signifying that a scholar still has half of a creative life ahead at age 55 if the career commenced at age 20. Creativity in other fields may fall between these two extremes. The half-life for creativity in poetry, for instance, may be around 17 years, the same half-life as in the prototypical case presented in Figure 4.2 (cf. Simonton 1984b).

As the Dirac poem quoted earlier suggests, creative persons themselves are all too aware of the loss of creative potential over time. In one study of eminent scholars in several disciplines, only 33% of the physicists with a mean age of 47 thought they had "more important contributions in the future," and only 17% of the mathematicians with a mean age of 53 expressed this hope (Simon 1974). For the social sciences and humanities these figures are 72% in political science, 50% in English, 38% in sociology, and 33% in philosophy (with mean ages of 55, 55, 58, and 64, respectively). Thus with the exception of the political scientists and philosophers, half or more of distinguished scholars believe they are "over the hill" when they reach their 50s.

Because of this pervasive attitude, we should stress that this cognitive model, rather than having pessimistic implications, projects an optimistic picture of the later years of a creator's life. Because we are dealing with a decay curve like that for radioactivity, creative potential is lost at a decelerating rate. Accordingly, in the typical case graphed in Figure 4.2, a creator who works for 60 years can still accomplish more in that last decade than was achieved in the first decade (see, e.g., Fulton & Trow 1974). Furthermore, at the end of that final career decade, about one-quarter of the initial creative potential will remain unrealized. The intuitive genius seldom completely self-organizes into an analytical genius. Moreover, not only will numerous creative ideations remain, but there also will be some backlog of ideations awaiting translation into creative contributions. It is worth noting that after a certain point in a career's postpeak portion, the decline in the generation of finished products ceases to be concave downward and instead becomes concave upward (Simonton 1984a). This inflection point occurs at

$$t_2 = \frac{1}{b - a} \ln \frac{b^2}{a^2} \tag{4.3}$$

Thus for the typical case, the inflection appears 45 years into the career, after which the loss in productivity begins to level off. Finally, as we shall discuss later, although the quantity in output may fall in the later years, the proportion of those products that are first-rate does not deteriorate in any way. Hence, a scientist of advanced age has grounds for considerable hope, even in fields in which youth seems to have all the advantages.

Precocity, longevity, and rate of output

The cognitive model just developed elucidates more than the longitudinal fluctuations in productivity within careers, for it accounts as well for the cross-sectional intercorrelation among the three independent components of lifetime output. At the beginning of this chapter we observed that scientists vary tremendously in the total number of communication configurations they offer to the world, but we said nothing then about how this distribution emerges in terms of the agewise progression of each scientist's career. To appreciate the time-related foundation for total productivity, we must start by recognizing that there are three principal ways that scientists can attain an impressive lifetime corpus of contributions.

First, prolific scientists can display creative *precocity* by beginning to produce at an exceptionally young age. Lehman (1953a, chap. 12) was among the first investigators to point out the strong connection between the age at which productivity commences and the final count in contributions at the career's close. He demonstrated that this relationship holds for disciplines as diverse as mathematics, physics, and chemistry, in the sciences, and philosophy, literature, painting, and classical music, in the arts and humanities. For mathematics, as an example, the correlation is $-.61$, signifying that the younger is the age at first contribution, the larger will be the final bibliography of contributions (p. 185). Subsequent investigators have repeatedly corroborated this conspicuous and reliable association: Early productivity is one of the single best predictors of later productivity in all domains of creativity (see, e.g., Blackburn et al. 1978; Clemente 1973; Cole 1979; Davis 1987; Dennis 1954a,b; Helson & Crutchfield 1970; Simonton 1977b). For the most part, major scientists begin productive output sometime in their middle 20s, and truly exceptional scientists may begin even earlier (Albert 1975; Helson & Crutchfield 1970; Horner, Rushton, & Vernon 1986; Lehman 1958; Raskin 1936; Roe 1972b). The classic case is Newton's *annus mirabilis,* during which before the age of 24, he had already begun to work out his ideas on universal gravitation, the theory of colors, the calculus (or "fluxions"), the binomial theorem, and the method of infinite series – his chief contributions to science. As this list implies, such precocity is particularly common in mathematics: Abel, Clairaut, Euler, Galois, Gauss, Hamilton, Lagrange, L'Hospital, Maxwell, Monge, Pascal, and Poisson all initiated their careers while still teenagers (Lehman 1953a, pp. 178–183), and mathematics is so much a "young man's game [that] the average age of election to the Royal Society is lowest in mathematics" (Hardy 1940, pp. 70–71). This precocity is also manifested in the fact that notable scientists tend to earn their PhDs – the supposed certificate of graduation into most scientific professions – at a comparatively young age, usually around the mid-20s (Roe 1952a; see also Helson & Crutchfield 1970). For instance, those psychologists who were later honored with the presidency of the American Psychological Association earned their doctorates, on the average, at about age 26 and were already highly visible researchers at around age 28 – all this when the mean age for receiving a doctorate in psychology was 31 years of age (Lyons 1968). As this example suggests, the odds that "late bloomers" will establish a scientific reputation are minuscule (cf. Busse & Mansfield 1981). Indeed, even scientists whose careers began at more ordinary ages tend to make only half as many "breakthroughs" as claimed by their precocious colleagues (Zhao & Jiang 1986). In summarizing his own data, Lehman quoted the words of Oliver Wendell Holmes, Jr.: "If you haven't cut your name on the door of fame by the time you've reached 40, you might just as well put up your jackknife" (1953a, pp. 185–186).

Second, productive scientists can exhibit extraordinary creative *longevity* by continuing to produce until quite late in life. Darwin, Freud, and Einstein, for example, not only started their creative careers in their early 20s, but they all continued to generate ideas for around half a century afterward. Generally, the truly eminent in any endeavor usually have careers spanning over a quarter-century, and careers a half-century long are not uncommon (Albert 1975; Davis 1987; Raskin 1936). The contributions of distinguished creators "are not 'one-shot' affairs. They are productive over many decades, and their most important contributions tend to be spread over many years" (Simon 1974, p. 335). Unlike their less illustrious colleagues, these workers retain an active enthusiasm for research until late in life (Blackburn et al. 1978) and refuse to acknowledge retirement as a limit on their activities. "Even after they have retired from regular academic or other positions, almost all of them continue to work long hours each day, most days of the year" (Simon 1974, p. 335). Indeed, the career of the high-caliber scientist is far more likely to be terminated by death or debilitating health than by a loss of intellectual fertility.

Third, prolific lifetime contributors can produce at high rates of output per unit of time. Harriet Zuckerman, in her *The Scientific Elite* (1977), compared Nobel laureates with a matched sample of scientists drawn from *American Men of Science,* finding that the former published at a rate over twice that of the latter: The laureates averaged 3.24 papers per year, the controls 1.48. Because the controls in her study could be clearly viewed as moderately successful scientists, it is not surprising that an inquiry into University of Chicago PhDs obtained an even more dramatic contrast; after a decade interval, the creative scholars yielded a mean of four publications per year, whereas the controls averaged fewer than one publication every two years (Bloom 1963). Those investigators who received the Distinguished Scientific Contribution Award from the American Psychological Association could boast a mean per annum of nearly three publications (Albert 1975). These figures, which are typical (see also Roe 1965), can be better appreciated when we observe that to obtain tenure at a major university in the United States normally requires about two publications per year. Hence, the prolific contributors are generating contributions at rates faster than needed for professional survival and advancement in academe. Indeed, security of employment has no impact whatsoever on the yearly output of those committed to the scientific enterprise (Bridgwater, Walsh, & Walkenbach 1982).

From a mathematical standpoint, these three components are quite distinct and can comprise orthogonal determinants of the final contribution count. If O represents total output at the end of the career, then obviously $O = R(E - S)$, where R is the mean rate of output per time unit, E is the age at which the career ended, and S is the age at which the career started. Clearly, R, E, and S may exhibit almost any arbitrary correlation, whether positive or negative, without changing their respective relationships with O. For example, we cannot rule out on mere a priori grounds the possibility that those who begin their careers earlier are disposed to end their careers earlier as well; if precocity were thus associated with "early burnout," the difference between E and S would be constant. Or those who have long careers may feature lower rates of production to compensate. Notwithstanding the mathematical independence of these three components, these three variables are empirically highly correlated with one another. Early productivity is strongly associated with high rates of output over a long career (e.g., Andrews 1979; Blackburn et al. 1978; Clemente 1973; Davis

1987; Dennis 1954a,b; Horner et al. 1986; Lehman 1953a, 1958; Lyons 1968; Roe 1952a; Segal, Busse, & Mansfield 1980; Simonton 1977b; Zuckerman 1977). As a consequence, highly productive scientists commence their careers well ahead of their less prolific associates, and this initial inequality between élite and hoi polloi only expands as their respective careers progress (Allison et al. 1974; Allison & Stewart 1974; Faia 1975; cf. Mulkay 1980). One comprehensive survey of university faculty concluded that

> those who will be productive over their full careers are the individuals who start early, receive their degrees when young, and take on the habit of regular output. These individuals are not affected by status changes (promotion, tenure) but rather continue to widen the productivity gap between themselves and their less productive colleagues as time passes. They are discernible early in their careers. (Blackburn et al. 1978, p. 140)

Dennis (1954b) published some instructive documentation of this generalization in an examination of notable 19th-century scientists, including mathematicians, astronomers, physicists, chemists, physiologists, naturalists, and geologists. Using the *Catalogue of Scientific Literature, 1800–1900,* Dennis tabulated the output in each consecutive career decade from the 20s to the 70s. Although the correlations in productivity were highest for adjacent decades (ranging from .49 to .84), the coefficients remained respectable for decades even far apart. The lowest correlation, namely, that between productivity in the 20s and in the 70s, remained an honorable .33 (see also Horner et al. 1986). In computing these correlation coefficients, Dennis used only those eminent scientists who lived into their 80s. This methodological choice was a wise one, for otherwise the link between precocity and longevity might be seriously underestimated. Data indicate that precocity is *negatively* related to life expectancy, and needless to say, the latter variable places an inescapable restriction on creative longevity (e.g., Simonton 1977b; Zhao & Jiang 1986). It is probably not so much that precocity *causes* an early death as that precocity *allows* a creator to die young and still place a name in the annals of history. As a case in point, Galois did not die in a duel at age 20 because he was an extremely precocious mathematician, but rather he was able to make a lasting contribution to mathematics, despite his tragic early death, because of his having become so prolific so early in his short life (cf. Simonton 1975a).

Significantly, the two-step cognitive model actually predicts a high positive relation among all three components. The source of this prediction is the integration constant c that we specified was a function of a, b, and m. The first two constants, the ideation and elaboration rates, are presumed to be characteristic of a given discipline, as discussed in the preceding section, but *m*, or the maximum number of potential contributions (i.e., configurations), directly gauges creative potential. With *a* and *b* fixed, *c* is directly proportional to *m* and accordingly stands for a scientist's potential output. Because all age curves are similar for a given field, *c* describes the height of the curve throughout the career. It immediately follows that the higher the creative potential is, the earlier output will begin, the higher the rate of productive flow, and the later the output will terminate (Simonton 1984b). Expressed in terms of our present theoretical schema, the more imposing is the inventory of potential chance permutations, the higher will be the probability of a scientist's arriving at a viable chance configuration early in his or her career; the higher will be the rate at which such configurations appear per annum; and the longer it will take for all possible configurations to be found.

On the other hand, the model predicts that the peak age for productive output – unlike precocity, longevity, and output rate – is independent of the final lifetime score (Simonton 1984b). That is, the maximum point on the curve shown in Figure 4.2, given in Equation 4.2, is a function solely of *a* and *b*, which reflect the information-processing needs of a given discipline, whereas creative potential, represented by *m*, is irrelevant. Although no study I know of has specifically tested this prediction, a number of investigators have inadvertently collected data that endorse it. Zusne (1976) showed that the correlation between the eminence of psychologists and the age at which they made their most outstanding contributions – which, as will be seen later, tends to be the optimal age for output – was virtually zero ($r = -.01$). No matter what the psychologist's fame, the maximum on the curve appeared around the 39th year, a point reinforced by data presented by Lehman (1953b) (cf. Horner, Rushton, & Vernon 1986). Zuckerman (1977) gave evidence that despite the higher rate of output exhibited by her laureates relative to her controls, the ratio of output for the two groups remained more or less constant over consecutive decades, something that would naturally follow from the assumption that the age curves were a function merely of the discipline and not of creative potential (see also Blackburn et al. 1978). Further, a cross-cultural and transhistorical survey of major figures in world literature suggests that the same prediction holds for the arts as well as the sciences. The peak age for creating a literary masterpiece is determined more by the nature of the composition than by the work's aesthetic success (Simonton 1975a). A similar dependence may hold for classical music (Lehman 1953a, chap. 20; Simonton 1977a,b). Lastly, a biographical analysis of 120 scientists and 123 literary figures from the 19th century found that in both domains eminence was positively associated with precocity but that the "age of greatest production" did not vary with the degree of distinction attained in either endeavor (Raskin 1936).

In any event, this prediction of the model is important, for it counters the claim, represented by the Dirac verse quoted earlier, that phenomenal scientists peak earlier and thus go "over the hill" faster. Because creative potential is associated with precocity, scientific geniuses will have an impact on their chosen fields much earlier than average, but that is the beginning, not the end, of their contributions. Einstein may have begun his career with a bang in 1905, yet he was publishing influential work for decades after that, and the peak of his career probably occurred at the normal time, in his late 30s, with the development of his general relativity theory. To generalize this point further, scientists who receive a Nobel Prize often make contributions subsequently that would earn them another prize if there were enough of them to go around (Zuckerman 1977). In fact, this practice of rewarding the *first* major contribution of an exceptional scientist may perform the disservice of exaggerating the creativity of youth (cf. Diemer 1974). Ironically, the earlier in their careers that scientists are so honored, the older they are likely to be before their production of prize-deserving work ceases.

To summarize, the chance-configuration theory, via the two-step cognitive model just developed, accounts for the age curves that distinguish various scientific disciplines; the empirical association among precocity, longevity, and rate of output; and the stability of the expected peak productive age with respect to individual differences in creative potential. Furthermore, we have every reason to believe at this time that the theory would be equally adequate in explaining the agewise distribution of contributions in esthetic endeavors.

Qualifications and emendations

To say that these implications arise from human information processing should not be taken as a dogmatic assertion that extrinsic events do not impinge on the intrinsic working out of creative potential. Chance-configuration theory implies, in fact, some of the ways that extraneous factors might interfere. Certainly anything that reduces the time invested in permutation generation would depress productivity, and thus it comes as no surprise that enlarged administrative duties may push productivity below the baseline expectation (Garvey & Tomita 1972; Roe 1972a; Stern 1978) or that poor physical health can have an adverse impact as well (Simonton 1977a). Likewise, increased parental responsibilities may cause creative output to be somewhat less than predicted by the model – a loss of almost one article per year (Hargens, McCann, & Reskin 1978; see also McDowell 1982). Apropos of this last point, Moses Gomberg, a chemist, never married and prohibited his students from marrying until after they finished their graduate work, believing that family life interfered with doing quality science. Furthermore, as we noted in chapter 3, because the chance-permutation process depends on having access to the network of infraconscious associations, any environmental stressor strong enough to raise appreciably the emotional level will inherently undermine creativity (Simonton 1980a). The dominant, high-probability responses will tend to be elicited instead, and these cannot effectively generate chance configurations. Therefore, it is perfectly consistent with the theory propounded here to find that major wars lower the probability of notable advances in science and technology (Price 1978; Roe 1972a; Simonton 1976e, 1980c; cf. Simonton 1976b).

Because the preceding remarks can be neatly integrated into the chance-configuration framework, they constitute more extensions than true qualifications. Nevertheless, other empirical findings apparently do not fit so easily into the given theory. In particular, there is some question concerning the supposed single-peak age curve for productive output. Occasionally investigators have observed a "saddle-shaped" function with two peaks, a noticeable sag appearing in the 40s or a bit later (e.g., Abt 1983; Andrews 1979; Blackburn et al. 1978; Dennis 1966; Diemer 1974; Pelz & Andrews 1976, chap. 10; Roe 1965; Stern 1978). On other occasions the bimodal curve consists of an age peak at the expected location, but with a secondary peak, small but still observable, around retirement age (e.g., Davis 1954; Haefele 1962, pp. 235–236). I can respond to these seeming discrepancies with the following four points.

First, the departures from the hypothesized single-peak function, when found, are seldom major. Higher-order polynomial terms beyond the linear and quadratic usually explain only a small proportion of additional variance, less than 7% (e.g., Bayer & Dutton 1977; Simonton 1977a, 1984b). It is for this reason that the predicted age curve still fits the data well even when some sort of momentary mid-career dip is evident.

Second, several of the reported aggregate tabulations may be guilty of the compositional fallacy warned against earlier; that is, productivity in two distinct disciplines with age peaks far apart may be summed across to yield a combined age curve with a spurious bimodal distribution (Simonton 1984b). For example, if agewise output is aggregated across both pure and applied mathematics, a saddle-shaped tabulation can emerge that fails to describe the real career trends in any of the mathematicians in the sample (cf. Dennis 1966; Stern 1978).

Third, in some cases the multiple peaks may not be artifacts but rather may represent mid-life career changes that entail a switch in the nature of creative output and hence a modification of information-processing requirements (cf. Pelz & Andrews 1976, chap. 11). For instance, it is common for scientists to shift from an emphasis on original theoretical or experimental research to more scholarly endeavors, such as history and philosophy. Because the age maxima are later for scholarship than for most scientific work – and such scientists have essentially launched a totally new career with a reset professional age – a secondary peak could naturally result. A similar phenomenon can occur in artistic creativity. For example, the age peaks for art songs, symphonies, and operas are separated by many years, and thus a composer who first created songs, then symphonies, and closed with operas could end up with a trimodel agewise distribution for contributions (cf. Lehman 1953a, chap. 20).

Fourth, we have already acknowledged that extrinsic factors may deflect the age curve insofar as they interfere in some way with the chance-permutation process. It is conceivable, therefore, that some supposed saddle-shaped age curves are in truth single-peak functions with a depression imposed by extraneous circumstances. Thus, a sag in the 40s may reveal more about the stresses associated with "mid-life crises" in creators' personal affairs than about bona fide shifts in the intrinsic ability to generate chance configurations. Or this same depression may result from a scientist's assuming administrative and "gatekeeping" roles, such as journal editorships or positions whose new responsibilities temporarily disrupt the research routine; scientists tend to assume these roles shortly after they reach their peak productive age (see Diemer 1974; Stern 1978; Zuckerman & Merton 1972; cf. Jernegan 1927). Similarly, the modest resurgence in output sometimes observed toward retirement age may betray changes in the time committed to research when an academic career is winding down (cf. Haefele 1962).

These four points affirm that this theory need not be drastically modified in order to explain the central findings on the connection between age and output. However, I would like to complete our discussion of this issue by introducing two potential amendments to the information-processing model.

First, the conception of creative potential so far given is likely too passive, even stagnant. Creative scientists are presumed to commence their careers with a fixed quantity of potential, conceived as the number of possible chance permutations they can realize, which thereafter is inexorably expended for the remainder of their lives. Yet without modifying the predictions of the model or the tenets of the theory, we can offer a more dynamic, more interactive version of this key idea. Certainly, a sizable portion of a scientist's creative potential stems from the responses he or she receives from colleagues in the scientific community *after* the career has already begun. Another researcher, even a stalwart opponent, may publish a theoretical, methodological, or empirical critique of one's work that implants new ideas, new elements in subsequent ideations. In addition, empirical researchers may receive further support from the hypothesis-disconfirming results they obtain in the laboratory, results that oblige them to rethink cherished ideas. Therefore, we may reformulate creative potential as the total number of conceivable chance permutations, taking into consideration the most probable array of responses from the creator's environment. Hence, two individuals may begin their careers with equivalent creative potential under the old definition but end up having disparate potential output by the new definition because of disparities in intellectual reactions from fellow scientists and in the magnitude of empirical reality testing. This altered conception of creative potential is now interpersonal and ecological, even sociocultural, rather than strictly psychological, but it does not appreciably alter the model's consequences. As long as we assume that the odds of receiving such stimulating recharges are more or less randomly distributed throughout the career, the same age curves and cross-sectional correlations will result.

In addition, we must reconsider the form of the predicted age curve in cases of extraordinary creative potential. We have up to this point postulated that the elaboration rate is proportional to the total supply of accumulated creative ideations – that the rate at which communication configurations emerge is proportional to the backlog of chance configurations. This assumption may be reasonable enough for those of low to moderate creative potential, but what about those whose capacity for chance permutations is far out on the right tail of the skewed distribution? Surely there is an upper bound in time and energy available for converting the initial germs into finished products. Accordingly, the most prolific scientists, the geniuses par excellence, will gather "works-in-progress" faster than they can dispose of them as publications. The result is a ceiling on the rate of contribution, an upper limit that will necessarily flatten out and extend the hypothesized age peak into a high plateau. In extreme cases, the peak is virtually nonexistent, as the scientist never succeeds in catching up with his or her imaginative powers and still has so much left undone when biological reality terminates the quest.

Gauss, a phenomenal mathematician, illustrates this possibility. Extremely precocious as well as exceptionally fluent in ideas, Gauss labored feverishly throughout his life to translate all his innovative notions into what he considered publishable form. Apparently he was told one day, while he was deeply enthralled by a problem, that his wife was dying, but he muttered, "Tell her to wait a moment till I'm through." Whether or not this is true, after he himself died, Gauss left piles of unpublished manuscripts containing ideas that anticipated much of the work of his contemporaries and successors. Thus, in cases of truly unusual scientific genius, the age curve may level off and decline only slightly in the last decades of the career. The predicted curve graphed in Figure 4.2 may be distorted not by extrinsic variables but by the fact that there are only 24 hours in a day.

Quantity and quality

Thus far we have been speaking of productivity rather than creativity per se, although at times I have hedged with the expression "creative productivity." Actually, on both empirical and theoretical grounds, these two concepts can be used almost interchangeably; productivity, or total quantity of output, is intertwined with creativity, or selective quality of output. Those scientists who claim the longest bibliographies also claim the longest lists of notable contributions, and hence the most impressive ultimate fame (Dennis 1954a,b; Helmreich et al. 1980; Segal et al. 1980; cf. Rubin 1978).

This link between quantity and quality is perhaps most thoroughly established in research that uses the *Science Citation Index* (*SCI*), a bibliographic tool devised by Eugene Garfield, founder of the Institute for Scientific Information (see Garfield 1979). From the *SCI* one can tabulate the number of times a scientist's published work is cited in the professional literature, at least as registered in the technical journals. Such citations exhibit two significant relationships. First, the number of citations that a scientist earns is the single most accurate predictor of scientific distinction, as gauged by such rare honors as the Nobel Prize (Ashton & Oppenheim 1978; Clark 1957; Cole & Cole 1967, 1971, 1973; Crandall 1978; Gaston 1978; Myers 1970; Rushton 1984; Rushton & Endler 1979; Simonton 1984h). Scientific acclaim requires that a researcher publish work that colleagues find useful or in some manner find impossible to ignore in their own work. Second, the primary predictor of the citation count is the scientist's total output (Busse & Mansfield 1984; Cole & Cole 1973; Davis 1987; Gaston 1978; Gupta, Gilbert, & Pierce 1983; Helmreich et al. 1980). Overall, the correlation between total productivity and citation counts ranges from .47 to .76, with a coefficient midway between these two values being fairly typical. Even when we restrict our attention to the citations received by the scientist's best work, that count is still a positive function of total output; the correlation between the number of citations of the three most-cited papers and the total number of papers published was .72 for a sample of physicists (Cole & Cole 1967). The connection between quantity and quality holds for larger units of analysis as well: Those academic departments that publish the most receive the most citations (e.g., Endler, Rushton, & Roediger 1978), and those nations that contribute the most total research also tend to make the most notable contributions (e.g., Lawani 1986).

Many critics of citation analysis have pointed out many problems with such bibliometric tabulations. For example, methodological papers usually are cited far more often than are theoretical or empirical papers (e.g., Folly, Hajtman, Nazy, & Ruff 1981; Peritz 1983); research papers become obsolete as their key findings are incorporated into the "common knowledge" of a discipline (e.g., Abt 1983; MacRae 1969; Price 1965); citation rates may be vulnerable to the effects of personal influence on students and colleagues, so that the rates change after the death of a particular investigator (Trimble 1986); papers originating in prestigious institutions may be cited more often even if those papers are equal in quality to papers coming out of less impressive laboratories (e.g., Cole 1970; cf. Stewart 1983); and citations practices make it possible for a scientist "to chalk up high citation counts by simply writing barely publishable papers on fashionable subjects which will then be cited as perfunctory, 'also ran' references" (Moravcsik & Murugesan 1975, p. 91)–not even considering such methodological difficulties as how to handle multiple authorship (e.g., Ashton & Oppenheim 1978; Lindsay 1980). Despite these complaints, citations remain one of the best objective and quantitative indicators of scientific worth (see also Cole & Cole 1971; Endler 1987; Folly et al. 1981; Rushton 1984; Shadish 1988; Simonton 1984h).

More important, the respectable covariation between quantity and quality can be demonstrated without resorting to citation data. Thus, the total number of published items that could be claimed by a 19th-century scientist correlates .46 with whether that same scientist was honored with an entry in the *Encyclopaedia Britannica* in the middle of the 20th century (Simonton 1981b); not a single scientist so honored published fewer than seven contributions (Dennis 1954a). Or to gauge success in more contemporary terms, those psychologists who were elected president of the American Psychological Association, became starred scientists in *American Men of Science,* or were invited to contribute autobiographies to *History of Psychology in Biography* almost invariably came from that upper crust of researchers in the top 10% in total output (Dennis 1954c). Similarly, mathematicians rated as extremely creative by colleagues published at over triple the pace of a matched group of less highly esteemed mathematicians (Helson & Crutchfield 1970). And total output in high-energy physics correlates .53

with recognition, the last defined as membership in honorary societies, editorships, and other professional acknowledgments of impact (Gaston 1973, p. 56). Even in the realm of obtaining extramural funding for research, the best predictor of having a grant proposal approved is the total number of proposals submitted (Cole, Cole, & Simon 1981). Hence, the positive cross-sectional association between quantity and quality is virtually universal, for it transcends indicator operationalization and unit definition.

After reviewing results such as these, Dennis (1954a, p. 182) concluded:

I submit that the correlation between fame and fecundity may be understood in part in terms of the proposition that the greater the number of pieces of scientific work done by a given man, the more of them will prove to be important. . . . Other things being equal, the greater the number of researches, the greater the likelihood of making an important discovery that will make the finder famous.

Hence "the likelihood of achieving a certain degree of eminence increases with the number of publications. In science, quantity and quality are correlated, although they are not identical" (p. 183). Actually, this idea was already nearly a century old by the time Dennis was writing, for the philosopher Alexander Bain (1855, p. 597) held that "the greatest practical inventions being so much dependent upon chance, the only hope of success is to multiply the chances by multiplying the experiments."

More recently this position was formally expressed as the "constant-probability-of-success model," which simply holds that the odds of making a contribution are a straightforward probabilistic consequence of total output (Simonton 1977a, 1984d, 1985b). Moreover, it has been argued that this model follows as an essential corollary of Campbell's (1960) blind-variation and selective-retention model. Accordingly, the covariation between quality and quantity can be derived from the chance-configuration theory as well. This derivation follows from the assumptions that any given chance configuration is but a random sample of all possible configurations obtainable from a given scientist's creative potential and that any one scientist's reservoir of potential chance configurations is likewise but a sample drawn from the larger pool of conceivable configurations in the larger scientific community. Therefore, whether any particular configuration will prove successful by winning social acceptance will depend in large measure on chance – on the luck of the draw. This tendency, of course, is analogous to what occurs in biological evolution, that those organisms within a species that produce the most offspring have the best odds of contributing to the population's gene pool.

To be sure, there apparently are exceptions regarding the close link between quantity and quality, for the correlation is by no means perfect.

To use the terminology introduced by the Coles, even if the majority of researchers in any discipline fall along the continuum connecting the "silent," who produce little and that of minimal worth, and the "prolific," who generate an impressive bibliography studded with significant contributions, two sorts of "outliers" appear in the graph as well: "perfectionists," who devote all their efforts to a handful of supreme contributions, and "mass producers," who churn out hundreds of worthless items (Cole & Cole 1973). Even so, the exceptions are nothing more than rare departures from a pervasive rule and would be expected anyway, according to theory. The more communication configurations that are made available for social selection, the higher will be the odds that one will earn acceptance, but those odds function only on the average or in the long run. If we compared samples of scientists with equal productivity levels, their contribution levels would not be exactly equal but rather would be probabilistically scattered around some central value. There will always be scientists who, by chance alone, will get a series of lucky hits, whereas other scientists will labor away without recognition in some cul de sac of science.

Furthermore, a portion of the scatter around the regression line can be ascribed to individual differences in the efficacy or application of variation generation. Many mass producers subject only a few mental elements to chance permutations, so that an entire corpus offers only a few choices to the selection process. Indeed, some mass producers do not use chance permutations at all but, rather, are engaged in routine research programs that apply unchanging techniques and heuristics to the same problems over and over. On the other hand, many perfectionists generate a few distinct configurations that cannot be considered merely as minor variations on the same theme. Some, such as the mathematician Gauss, apply extremely rigorous standards in determining which chance configurations will be given to the world for social selection, and thus their publications have been selected in advance. Sometimes this discretion is unfortunate, for society is not allowed even to see some potential landmark discoveries; for example, Gauss never gave the scientific community an opportunity to see the non-Euclidean geometry he had been working on.

These qualifications should not blind us to the fact that the proportion of hits to total shots remains more or less constant from one scientist to another. As a case in point, despite the substantial variation in both productivity and citations, the average citation rate per bibliographic item fluctuates relatively little from one scientist to another, and any individual differences fail to correlate with overt success (e.g., Davis 1987; Simonton 1985b). Further, the constant-probability-of-success model, and the chance-configuration theory from which it can be derived, has two additional implications concerning the nature of scientific creativity – implications that have received empirical endorsements. One consequence concerns how a scientist's odds of producing an influential work are distributed over the course of a career, and the other concerns the long-term impact of a scientist's body of work on his or her reputation.

The quantity–quality ratio within careers

The constant-probability-of-success model should apply not merely across careers but within careers as well (Simonton 1984d, chap. 6). That is, those periods in which a scientist is most productive should also be those in which the most exceptional contributions are made, thereby making quality a probabilistic result of quantity. If the sole generator of configurations is a chance-permutation procedure and if that procedure is truly as blind or haphazard as assumed in chapters 1 through 3, then the proportion of successful to failed ideas should not change systematically over a scientist's career. Again, the situation is analogous to biological evolution: Those periods in an organism's reproductive life in which the most offspring are produced are more likely, on the average, to be the same periods that produced offspring that survived and reproduced to continue the parental contribution to the gene pool – for organisms cannot through experience learn to improve the adaptive fitness of the genetic combinations they create each breeding season.

There is already ample evidence of this longitudinal extension of the model (e.g., Oromaner 1977; Simonton 1977a, 1984d, chap. 6, 1985b; cf. Lehman 1962). For instance, one study of eminent psychologists (Donald Campbell, curiously, among them) divided their entire output into major and minor items according to the frequency of citation in the professional literature (Simonton 1985b). Both major and minor works tended to covary within any given career even after separating out the overall age trend ($r = .23$). Further, the "quality ratio," or the ratio of major to total publications per time unit, exhibited no systematic change over time. The ratio neither improves nor deteriorates, nor does it adopt some curvilinear form. Rather, the proportion of successful communication configurations fluctuates randomly throughout the career. Some periods have more hits, others more misses, without any predictability, whether ascribable to time trends or autoregression. This result contradicts the suggestion that the cross-sectional nexus between quantity and quality is a mere consequence of the more prolific scientists' gradually learning what makes good science – the "practice makes perfect" hypothesis (cf. Lawani 1986). Researchers evidently cannot learn how to improve, by means of maturity and experience, the proportion of hits. At the same time, these data show that the scientist does not usually exhaust the best combinations at the beginning of his or her career, only to peter out as the career drags out (cf. Parnes & Meadow 1963). As we would expect from the assumption that creativity is founded on the haphazard collision of elements, success-ful combinations – in proportion to unsuccessful combinations – are ran-domly distributed throughout the career.

Moreover, the constant-probability-of-success model apparently applies just as accurately to artistic careers: One inquiry into the agewise output of classical composers arrived at the same conclusions as found for scientists (Simonton 1977a). In concrete terms, those career periods in which the most masterpieces were created were also mainly those that saw the most potboilers or *pièces d'occasion*. As was found for scientists, this linkage held whether we examined the overall age trend or the period-to-period fluctuations (in the latter case, r's between .32 and .45). It is as if even the greatest musical creators were unable to separate the grain from the chaff. Indeed, the favorite works of the most applauded composers are not neces-sarily the same as those most appreciated by audiences today. For example, Beethoven's personal favorites among his symphonies, quartets, and sona-tas are not identical with those that dominate the concert halls and record-ing studios – such as the Fifth Symphony and the Moonlight Sonata. This inability to identify one's "best" work also frequently appears in the sci-ences. In retrospect, Newton wasted a good deal of time on alchemical pursuits that contributed nothing to the advance of science, time that might have been better spent on further investigations in mathematics, mechan-ics, and optics.

In 1891 Helmholtz, upon reflecting on the similar lack of correspondence between his own appraisal of his work and the assessment of his contempo-raries, provided a plausible explanation for this discrepancy:

My colleagues, as well as the public at large, evaluate a scientific or artistic work on the basis of its utility, its instructiveness, or the pleasure which it affords. An author is more inclined to base his evaluation on the labor a work has cost him, and it is but rarely that both kinds of judgment agree. Indeed, we can see from occasional statements of some of the most celebrated men, especially artists, that they assign small value to achievements which seem to us inimitable, compared with others which were difficult for them and yet which appear much less successful to readers and observers. I need only mention Goethe, who once stated to Eckermann that he did not value his poetic works as highly as the work he had done in the theory of color. (Kahl 1971, p. 467)

Part of the disparity between personal effort and social effect may stem from the fact that some chance configurations are more easily transformed into communication configurations, but this ease of translation may not correlate with the value of the final product. More pertinent, perhaps, is the fact that the published communication configuration seldom conveys the difficulties that the investigator faced in creating it. Indeed, in the same speech Helmholtz later admitted:

But the pride which I might have felt about the final result in these cases was considerably lowered by my consciousness that I had only succeeded in solving such problems after many devious ways, by the gradually increasing generalisation of favourable examples, and by a series of fortunate guesses. I had to compare myself with an Alpine climber, who, not knowing the way, ascends slowly and with toil, and is often compelled to retrace his steps because his progress is stopped; sometimes by reasoning, and sometimes by accident, he hits upon traces of a fresh path, which again leads him a little further; and finally, when he has reached the goal, he finds to his annoyance a royal road on which he might have ridden up if he had been clever enough to find the right starting-point at the outset. In my memoirs I have, of course, not given the reader an account of my wanderings, but I have described the beaten path on which he can now reach the summit without trouble. (Helmholtz 1898, p. 282)

There is theoretical justification for scientists being so silent about their actual paths to their discoveries. The difficulties encountered en route to a solution are only partly connected with the problem's intrinsic complexity, for the road may be arduous or easy largely due to the whims of the chance-permutation procedure, as we documented in chapter 2. By deleting the narration of *how* an idea was finally reached, scientific colleagues are better able to judge contributions on their merits rather than on the basis of the contributor's luck. Even so, because the contributors themselves remember their hardships and frustrations, they will have very different favorites among their conceptions in comparison with those of their contemporaries. Creators are thus not the best judges of their own work.

But to return to the main point, a valuable implication can be deduced from the fact that the constant-probability-of-success model applies to within-career fluctuations, an implication that enhances our appreciation of how scientific creativity changes with age. The curve given in Figure 4.2 may look discouraging to those researchers already "past their prime." Yet we must repeat that this graph describes aggregate output. If instead we plotted the quality ratio – the proportion of hits to total tries – for single contributions as a function of age, a horizontal line would result. What this zero-slope linear function tells us is that contribution for contribution, or paper for paper, age becomes irrelevant as a predictor of scientific impact. To illustrate, one citational analysis of the fate of single sociological papers in the first decade after publication concluded that "there are no differences in the mean number of citations received by articles written by sociologists of various ages" (Oromaner 1977, p. 383). Hence, if we are reading an individual paper by some scientific colleague, any knowledge we have of the author's age will not help us determine whether that particular contribution will be dubbed "creative."

Admittedly, the colleague's age would, according to this theory, bear some strong connection with total output for a given year, information that would help us predict the odds of a hit for that year. Even so, productive quantity alone serves as the direct cause in this case, whereas age is solely an indirect factor behind quality output. In addition, despite the absence of a systematic change in the ratio of quality to age, that ratio is by no means constant over time but, rather, fluctuates randomly over a career. Consequently, even if we have a single paper written by an older colleague and we know that it represents that scientist's sole offering for that year, we have no special trick for determining whether or not this particular time is one of the author's lucky ones – when the success rate reaches 100%. The chance-configuration theory simply does not justify using age in a prejudicial manner to discount the worth of a scientific publication. And needless to say, this same silence applies equally to the novices whose productivity has yet to reach the peak rate. No matter where a scientist might be placed on the abscissa of Figure 4.2, each prospective contribution must be weighed on its own merits, leaving the author's age off the scales.

The durability of reputation

The constant-probability-of-success model also helps account for the notable durability of scientific reputation over time, even in the hindsight of centuries (Over 1982; Simonton 1984d, chap. 1). It is frequently observed that citation rates are extremely stable, that those authors who receive much attention in one year in the professional literature are largely those often referred to in consecutive years, with correlations typically in the upper .90s (see, e.g., Helmreich, Spence, & Thorbecke 1981; Rushton 1984). What is less often noted is that this reputation normally endures for generations. Notwithstanding occasional exceptions – Mendel offering the classic instance – scientists who attain fame in their own day tend also to be highly regarded by posterity, and the initially obscure remain so. One investigator concluded, for instance, that "in the case of psychology there was no individual who was markedly out of favor in 1903 but markedly in favor in 1966–1970, or vice versa" (Over 1982, p. 60); the "test–retest" reliability, or correlation across nearly three-fourths of a century, was .72. Scientists with enduring reputations are those who have staked their claims to eminence on a respectable body of varied contributions, and accordingly, their status does not rise or fall with the fate of single contributions. If one idea becomes outdated, another has high odds of picking up the slack. Newton's fame rests on far more than the *Principia Mathematica,* Darwin's on much more than the *Origin of Species;* Nobel laureate Max Born said that Einstein "would be one of the greatest theoretical physicists of all times even if he had not written a single line on relativity" (quoted in Hoffman 1972, p. 7). Often the contributions for which scientists are best known today are not identical with those that earned them renown in their own times. Einstein was honored with the Nobel Prize in 1921, 16 years after he began publishing on special relativity and 6 years after his work on general relativity began appearing in the journals. But the prize was not for relativity but, rather, was for his pioneer 1905 paper on the photoelectric effect and certain unspecified "services in theoretical physics."

It is worth pointing out that the same durability of reputation found in the sciences applies equally to the arts and humanities (e.g., Farnsworth 1969; Rosengren 1985; Simonton 1984d, chap. 1). Plato's reputation is not totally dependent on *The Republic,* nor Shakespeare's on just *Hamlet,* nor Michelangelo's solely on the Sistine Chapel ceiling, nor Beethoven's on the Fifth Symphony alone. No matter what creative endeavor we inspect, the stature of the individual creators is far more stable over time than is the status, epistemological or aesthetic, of the separate creative products on which their reputations rest (see also Simonton 1976a).

Nevertheless, if we can expect prolific scientists to enjoy high odds of success, they should also have fairly good opportunities to fail. Not all chance configurations, not even all those selected for conversion into communication configurations, will earn social acceptance, and some will even prove quite controversial. Sometimes an original notion will be controversial because it is revolutionary and thus difficult to assimilate without an exhaustive intellectual reorganization by potential acceptors. But an idea may also provoke debate because it is a spin-off from a mind on an off-hour and is plain wrong. That is, it is a myth to assert that genius is always in the right (Weisberg 1986). For example, Galileo insisted on circular orbits to the point of denying the cosmic reality of comets; Newton dogmatically maintained that an achromatic lens could not possibly be constructed; Darwin compromised his evolutionary theory with the doctrine of pangenesis; and Einstein persevered in advocating a totally deterministic unified theory that ignored the advances made by the Copenhagen school of quantum mechanics. It is virtually impossible to identify a prolific scientist who was right all the time – and some, such as Lord Kelvin (William Thomson), are nearly as famous for their errors as for their triumphs. Likewise, for any productive aesthetic creator we can easily list many compositional failures.

What W. H. Auden said of poets applies equally to creators in all domains: "The chances are that, in the course of his lifetime, the major poet will write more bad poems than the minor" simply because major poets "write a lot" (quoted in Bennett 1980, p. 15). We may style this tendency the principle of the "constant probability of failure."

This last principle, when coupled with what we noted earlier, again implies that creative scientists, even the highest-caliber geniuses, are not always the best judges of what their successes and failures are among the profusion of ideas that they thrust before the world. If the particular items on which a scientist's reputation is based may change over time, if even the most illustrious scientists can make big mistakes as well as milestones, and if scientists appear unable to improve their success rate with enhanced professional experience, then the expertise underlying scientific creativity seems largely restricted to the cognitive capacity and the motivational wherewithal for generating numerous and diverse intellectual variations. Nonetheless, it would be rash to surmise from this broad principle that productivity is sufficient to achieve success in science or any other creative endeavor. Distinction in any domain depends directly on the social acceptance of a large body of communication configurations, and mere productivity by no means ensures a hit; it only raises the odds. Stated differently, the proximate cause of acclaim is quality, not quantity, and quantity may have solely a probabilistic linkage with quality. Consequently, the direct impact of quantity on fame, after excluding its indirect effect by way of quality, should be tiny if not zero. Perhaps the mass producers may gain a little by impressing their colleagues with their energy and determination, but ultimately the laurels will go to those prolific creators who have persuaded members of the scientific community to restructure their thinking about the phenomena that define the discipline.

To illustrate this point, let me reanalyze some data reported by Cole and Cole (1973, p. 94) that they analyzed differently and, according to this theory, incorrectly. Taking a sample of physicists, the Coles showed that quantity and quality, or total publications and citations, correlated .60, whereas the correlations of these two measures with an index of scientific awards and honors were .45 and .57, respectively. With regard to honors, not only is the association for quantity less than that for quality, but much of this correlation may be the spurious upshot of the other two correlations. Therefore, we must determine what proportion of the variance in awards is determined by quantity, once we have taken out the variance directly attributable, on theoretical grounds, to quality. In other words, we should perform a hierarchical regression analysis (not a simultaneous analysis, as conducted by the Coles), in which quality is entered first as the independent variable and then quantity is added. Using this design, quality handles 32% of the variance in scientific kudos, whereas quantity increases this predictive power to only 34%, an almost trivial increment.

The lesson is manifest: Even if it may be more advantageous to be a mass producer than to be merely silent, it is far better still to be prolific in the positive sense. Scientists who labor hard at ballooning their "curriculum vitae" with pages of bibliography *may* also be prolific producers of high-quality efforts, but the possibility always remains, albeit with smaller odds, that such scientists may have done no more than build up long, almost autistic lists of unread and unappreciated titles. Quantity divorced of quality is indicative of little scientific creativity.

Discussion

This theory also has implications for three topics closely related to the issues discussed so far. Although all three of these topics were introduced solely in terms of scientific productivity and influence, I believe that they are more generally applicable, extending to artistic creativity definitely and to leadership possibly. These three topics are the Ortega hypothesis, the Yuasa phenomenon, and Planck's principle.

Ortega hypothesis

In *The Revolt of the Masses* (1957), the Spanish philosopher Ortega y Gassett asserted that

it is necessary to insist upon this extraordinary but undeniable fact: experimental science has progressed thanks in great part to the work of men astoundingly mediocre, and even less than mediocre. That is to say, modern science, the root and symbol of our actual civilization, finds a place for the intellectually commonplace man and allows him to work therein with success. (pp. 110–111)

This proclamation offers a very attractive idea insofar as it pictures scientific creativity as far more democratic than the image so far portrayed in this chapter. If Ortega is correct, then the élitism apparent in scientific productivity may be misleading, and even the term *scientific genius* may prove meaningless from the standpoint of the advancement of science. The scientific edifice is built piece by piece using small bricks mostly laid by undistinguished craftspersons. Hence, anyone with the appropriate training in the trade of science may participate in the construction of even the most impressive monuments (see also Spiller 1929).

Cole and Cole (1972) christened this intriguing notion the "Ortega hypothesis" and observed that practicing scientists, not just armchair philosophers, have subscribed to the same conception of scientific creativity. They gave the example of Howard Florey, who shared a Nobel Prize with Fleming and Chain for the development of penicillin. In his last presidential address before the Royal Society, Florey observed that

science is rarely advanced by what is known in current jargon as a "break-through," rather does our increasing knowledge depend on the activity of thousands of our colleagues throughout the world who add small points to what will eventually become a splendid picture much in the same way that the Pointillistes built up their extremely beautiful canvasses. (quoted in Crowther 1968, p. 363)

Newton may have said that he saw farther than his contemporaries because he stood on the shoulders of giants, but according to Ortega and Florey he more probably crouched on the backs of dwarfs – and may have been a dwarf himself!

Fortunately, the Coles subjected this hypothesis to empirical tests (Cole & Cole 1972). Looking at physics, they examined whether the classic contributions (i.e., the most frequently cited papers) leaned heavily on the publications of lesser-known figures in the field. Quite the opposite was found to be the case: Often cited papers tended to cite publications by often cited predecessors – thus reestablishing the élitism inherent in scientific creativity (see also Snizek 1986). Similar results have been obtained for other scientific fields, such as criminology (Green 1981) and sociology (Oromaner 1985). Indeed, if anything, the hard evidence seems to suggest that the mediocre scientists that Ortega so praises are largely ignored by their colleagues. In any given year, around 35% of all existing papers are cited not even once, another 49% just once, 9% twice, 3% three times, 2% four times, 1% five times, and the remaining 1% six times or more (Price 1965). Hence an extremely small proportion of the published papers are extensively used by others in the same discipline. In 1910, James McKeen Cattell, when listing some of the unanswered questions that must be addressed by a science of science, stated that "we do not know whether progress is in the main due to a large number of faithful workers or to the genius of a few" (p. 634). We now have evidence that this issue has been resolved in favor of the second alternative.

Looking at this problem solely from the standpoint of the chance-configuration theory, Ortega may have captured at best a partial truth. On the one hand, according to the constant-probability-of-success model, the odds of making a notable contribution to science is a function of the total number of attempts. Consequently, highly prolific scientists will tend, on the average, to exert more influence over the thoughts of their colleagues. Science is dominated by those intellectual leaders whom we may rightly call geniuses, making the enterprise more élitist than democratic, albeit a meritocratic élitism. On the other hand, as Campbell (1960, p. 393) noted, it is "likely that many important contributions will come from the relatively untalented, undiligent, and uneducated, even though on an average contribution per capita basis, they will contribute much less." After all, the connection between quantity and quality is far from perfect, with a wide dispersion around the regression line, readily enabling the existence of "outliers" consisting of relatively unproductive but nonetheless influential creators. And by the Lotka and Price laws we know that there are an immense number of mediocre scientists in the world, and so by chance alone a significant number will experience a stroke of phenomenal luck. Even so, these constitute true exceptions to a general rule. The odds are against an average scientist contributing to the advance of science. In this sense, then, the Ortega hypothesis is not just empirically inaccurate but also theoretically implausible.

We must be cautious about drawing policy recommendations from the rejection of the Ortega hypothesis. The Coles implied that the unpraised and unsung scientists of the world might be excluded from the profession without affecting the growth of scientific knowledge (Cole & Cole 1972). The condition of science could even be improved if scarce resources were transferred from the mediocre to the élite scientists. This suggestion has been criticized by those who speculate that members of the scientific élite are merely selected at random from the larger pool of talent and then are showered with citations and honors, not according to intrinsic merit, but by the luck of the draw. This alternative interpretation of the same data has been termed the "Ecclesiastes hypothesis" after the passage (9:11) that asserts, "The race is not to the swift, nor the battle to the strong, neither bread to the wise, nor yet riches to men of understanding, nor yet favor to men of skill; but time and chance happeneth to them all" (Turner & Chubin 1976, 1979).

The constant-probability-of-success model introduces a viewpoint somewhat more moderate than either of these two extremes. Let us posit that this model applies not just to individual creative products but to creative persons besides. Then an increase in the total number of scientists should correspondingly increase the number of scientists of quality. Even if according to the Price law, "the total number of scientists goes up as the square, more or less, of the number of good ones" (Price 1963, p. 53), we can still argue that reducing the number of mediocre scientists will *not* have a beneficial effect. To be sure, it seems reasonable to doubt the utility of these unsuccessful researchers for the whole scientific enterprise. But these supposed failures are actually performing an extremely useful if thankless task – they are being "unlucky."

This is where the Ecclesiastes hypothesis takes an ironic twist. Just as we cannot have winners of a race without having losers too, so we cannot really have successes in the absence of failures. What is required, according to the current theory, are many variations that are open to sociocultural selection. It would be dangerous, therefore, to decide to truncate artificially this individual variation just because some variations seem now to be unadaptive. Even though scientific reputation is largely consistent over historical time, there are enough exceptions to make the wise wary. Today's mass producers and nearly silent may turn out to be tomorrow's prolific and perfectionist scientists. Gregor Mendel is everyone's favorite example. Although there is some debate about how much Mendel was ignored by the 19th-century scientific community (Zirkle 1964), there is no doubt that his prominence in modern science well exceeds what he enjoyed in his own lifetime. Furthermore, scientists do not have to be vindicated posthumously in order to leave an impression on the advance of science, for some investigators succeed by failing. It is intriguing to note that many citations to other people's works are actually negative, criticizing or rejecting a conclusion posed in the cited reference (Moravcsik & Murugesan 1975). Unsuccessful researchers may document their scientific blind alleys by more informal means, too, such as professional conferences and graduate seminars. Of course, scientific failures become nonentities rather than celebrities, yet that does not lessen their role in the overall progression of science.

Hence, rejection of the Ortega hypothesis does not mean that we can deny resources to all but the currently fashionable élite without thereby retarding the advance of science. Rather, we should encourage all of those who have the intellectual and dispositional markings of scientific creators. Florey believed, despite his adherence to the Ortega hypothesis, that scientists may vary in creative potential, for "one thing that distinguishes the first-rate scientist from those absorbed in routine is that he very dearly loves to make discoveries – he burns to find out something new and he wants to be the first to do so" (quoted in Crowther 1968, p. 362). By distributing resources to all first-rate scientists without regard to outward success we give posterity the ideational diversity necessary for optimal sociocultural evolution.

Yuasa phenomenon

At the close of the preceding section we assumed that the constant-probability-of-success model is just as applicable to individual scientists as it is to separate scientific contributions. In both instances quality is a probabilistic function of quantity; the greater the number of scientists is, the better the chance will be that great scientists will be found among them. Actually, there already is supporting evidence on this point, not merely for science, but also for all creative activities (Simonton 1984d). Looking at transhistorical fluctuations in the number of creators per generation within a nation, culture, or civilization, we repeatedly discover that both prominent and obscure figures are contemporaries (e.g., Simonton 1974, 1975c; Sorokin & Merton 1935). Two aspects of these generational fluctuations attract our attention here. First, creators of all grades are not randomly distributed over historical time but, rather, cluster together, forming periods of potent activity (in both quantity and quality) separated by usually much longer periods of creative stagnation. This waxing and waning is not cyclical, only aperiodic, but nevertheless quite real. In regard to civilizations, Kroeber (1944) styled these historical gatherings of creators as "configurations." Second, the creative zenith of one nation (or civilization) normally does not correspond to the high point of another nation (or civilization). It is almost as if distinct cultural traditions take turns experiencing a golden age in a particular creative enterprise. However, it sometimes appears as if the flourishing of activity in one nation or civilization may stimulate a subsequent surge in a nearby nation or civilization. The center of creative activity accordingly may shift across both space and time, as the torch is passed on.

Yuasa (1974) was interested in this phenomenon in the case of science (see also Schneider 1937). In particular, he wanted to determine how and why the center of scientific activity in Western civilization has shifted from one nation to another since the Renaissance. Using archival data, including both a chronological table of scientific achievements and a biographical dictionary of outstanding scientists, Yuasa defined the "scientific prosperity" in which a nation was a major force in science "as the period in which the percentage of scientific achievements of a country exceeds 25% of that in the entire world in the same period" (p. 81). Under this definition the center of scientific activity has shifted as follows:

1540–1610   Italy (Florence, Venice, Padua): Galileo
1660–1730   England (London): Newton
1770–1830   France (Paris): Lavoisier, Laplace
1810–1920   Germany (Berlin): Gauss, Liebig, Helmholtz
1920–   United States (New England, California): Hubble, Lawrence

It is apparent that the main current of scientific activity lingers in a given center for an average of nearly 80 years, a point that Yuasa noted.

Although one may quibble over specific dates in Yuasa's periodization, his conclusions were predicated on the application of a precise definition to archival data of demonstrated reliability (see, e.g., Simonton 1976b; but also see Nye 1984). Thus, we should take his scheme seriously enough to ask: Why does one nation become a scientific center only to yield ground after a mere handful of generations to a rival? Yuasa's hypothesis (1974) was that "there seem to be necessary relations between political revolution and scientific revolution" (p. 95). To make his case, Yuasa analyzed the political foundation of French scientific prosperity. From 1750 to 1800 the French social structure was in a state of "anomy," as indicated by such events as the 1751–1772 *Encyclopedie* of Diderot and d'Alembert, the 1755 *Discourse on the Origin of Inequality* of Rousseau, and, most conspicuously, the 1789–1795 French Revolution that toppled the monarchy and aristocracy. These events helped create the conditions most conducive to the development of French scientific genius. Although Yuasa's discussion of this subject is strictly qualitative, historiometric inquiries partly support his speculations, as we shall discuss more fully in chapter 5.

But once the proper milieu is established for stimulating scientific growth and a nation becomes a hub of activity, a decline begins. Yuasa never fully explained why this happens, but we can offer a suggestion based on the present theory. Kroeber (1944), when discussing why cultural configurations come and go, referred to the phenomenon of "pattern exhaustion." That is, each cultural tradition commences its creative activities with a given pattern or paradigm that is developed to its fullest by successive generations of creators. A high point is reached after which the potentialities of the finite set of cultural premises lose their capacity to conjure up new ideas, and so the creative effervescence fades away after the splendor of the golden age. In science, the operation of this exhaustion process takes place when, in Bartlett's (1958, p. 136) words,

a mass of routine thinking belonging to an immediately preceding phase [of original work] has come near to wearing itself out by exploiting a limited range of technique to establish more and more minute and specialized detail. A stage has been reached in which finding out further details adds little or nothing to what is known already in the way of opening up unexplored relations.

To illustrate, toward the close of the last century, the physics section of the catalog of the University of Chicago–the department then chaired by Michelson–suggested that the laws of nature were so well established that little further research remained to be done except to determine to more decimal places the various fundamental constants–this on the eve of the quantum and relativity revolutions!

The remarkable fact about Kroeber's configurations, as well as Yuasa's centers, is that the timewise distribution is quite similar to the curve shown in Figure 4.2. Creativity tends to increase rather rapidly to a single peak and afterwards trail off slowly but usually irreversibly. To be sure, the initial portion of the curve tends to adopt a form like the logistic function, indicating exponential growth limited by an upper bound (Crane 1972, p. 172; Mulkay, p. 18; Price 1963, chap. 1). Even so, could the same process be responsible for both careers and centers? Let us suppose that each cultural tradition begins its creative life with a collection of cultural traits that, as mental elements, can then be recombined in diverse permutations to generate a large but finite number of configurations. Each creator in the tradition acquires a sample of this population of available elements, subjects them to chance permutations, and feeds the resulting communication configurations back into the system, there to become new elements to enter into permutations executed by subsequent generations of creators. If the creative potential of the sociocultural system is sufficiently high at the outset, these givens will at first encourage this activity, which will attain an acme and maybe even grant the system momentary status as a center of creative prosperity. Nevertheless, the number of worthwhile configurations yet to be derived from the initial cultural elements will invariably decline, causing a drop in output, and eventually the system will recede into the second rank and lower.

Analogies between entities at two levels of analysis are always risky, and so I do not wish to push the foregoing too far. We must not forget that there is no "group mind" that performs the chance permutations. Rather, the creative process dwells solely within individual members of the group. Accordingly, we may speak of the aggregate-level curve representing the ups and downs in creative activity as a sum of the individual-level curves representing the rise and fall in career output for the numerous careers spanning many generations. This modification in the account permits a logistic curve to describe the growth of a scientific field, even though the productivity age functions retain the same shape shown in Figure 4.2. Further, even this watered-down correspondence between the two levels implies that the analogy can be extended one step farther. Just as we expect productivity to ascend and descend with personal age, according to Equation 4.1, so we expect that the entrance into and exit from dominance enjoyed by a given sociocultural system would reflect a proportional shift in the age structure of its membership. In fact, Yuasa (1974) maintained that "one of the main causes in the decline of scientific activity appears to be the aging of the scientific community" (p. 102); "scientific activity will decrease gradually by the aging of the group of scientists" (p. 97). A follow-up investigation conducted by Zhao and Jiang (1985) provided additional evidence of this Yuasa phenomenon. Specifically they showed that "a country's science will decline if the average age of its outstanding scientists surpasses the border age of 50" (pp. 65–66), an age cutoff chosen because "the mean value of the terminal age at which the world's 1,228 noted scientists made their last contribution is exactly 50" (p. 66; cf. Fulton & Trow 1974; Lehman 1958; Raskin 1936). Yuasa may have failed to distinguish symptom from cause, for it seems more likely that the upward shift in mean age reflects the failure to recruit youthful replacements in the beginning ranks. Such an interpretation makes the Yuasa phenomenon a mere tautology, and thus Yuasa's proposed explanation begs the question. Nonetheless, any movement in the age spectrum away from the optimal age toward older mean ages should signal that a country has entered the downward path from glory.

Yuasa (1974, p. 100) was not afraid to indulge in prophesy, saying that "if this pattern holds true also for the U.S.A., then its scientific prosperity, which began in 1920, will end in the year 2000." Zhao and Jiang (1985) over a decade later apparently concurred. It is impossible at this time to prove this forecast right or wrong, but it cannot be simply dismissed as the envious and wishful proclamations of foreigners (Japanese and Chinese); even in the United States some people have expressed concern. Mark Oromaner, for instance, published an essay in 1981 ominously entitled "The Quality of Scientific Scholarship and the 'Graying' of the Academic Profession." Besides agreeing with the prediction that the output of truly significant scientific work may decline as the mean age of American scientists continues to grow older, Oromaner warned that the upward shift in age structure may make U.S. scientists, as a group, less receptive to innovative ideas. Without this openness, American science may soon be bypassed by the next scientific revolution and thereby lose its current world hegemony. Oromaner predicated this inference on Planck's principle.

Planck's principle

As a scientist's career advances, his or her mind moves along the cognitive continuum from intuitive to analytical genius. Besides expending creative potential in the process of self-organization, the scientist is also progressively changing his or her receptiveness to alternative ways of organizing mental elements. This means that during a career, a creative person should become increasingly unsympathetic to alternative approaches to structuring the same information. As a consequence, a truly revolutionary restructuring of knowledge may not be as well received. The younger members of the discipline, who have yet to finish organizing their scientific experience, should then display superior receptiveness to new ideas. Charles Darwin (1860, p. 240), in a passage that occurs a bit later than the quotation in chapter 1 from the *Origin,* said that he looked "with confidence to the future, – to the young and rising naturalists, who will be able to view both sides of the question with impartiality." Or as Max Planck (1949, pp. 33–34) put it, "a new scientific truth does not triumph by convincing its opponents and making them see the light, but rather because its opponents eventually die, and a new generation grows up that is familiar with it." Kuhn (1970) cited this idea as a constraint on scientific revolution, and various sociologists have agreed (e.g., Gouldner 1970, p. 377; Hagstrom 1965, p. 283). Barber (1961, p. 601) concluded his essay on the "resistance by scientists to scientific discovery" with the generalization that

as a scientist gets older he is more likely to be restricted to innovation by his substantive and methodological preconceptions and by his other cultural accumulations; he is more likely to have high professional standing, to have specialized interests, to be a member or official of an established organization, and to be associated with a "school."

There are many anecdotes that show how, with age, once-innovative scientists gradually become stalwart opponents of new ideas: Liebig strongly attacked the biological theory of fermentation advanced by Pasteur, his junior by almost 20 years; Magendie objected to the use of ether as an anesthetic; and Lord Rayleigh could not accept the quantum theory advanced by Planck. Some noted scientists have even admitted to the process by which a flexible and open-minded intellect becomes, with time, committed to only a single point of view. For instance, Sigmund Freud confessed in his *Civilization and Its Discontents,* written in 1929 at age 73 and toward the end of his life and career, that "the conceptions I have summarized here I first put forward only tentatively, but in the course of time they have won such a hold over me that I can no longer think in any other way" (p. 790). More significant than such anecdotes and testimonials is the fact that Planck's principle has been endorsed by some empirical research. Hull, Tessner, and Diamond (1978) showed that age bore some relation to the probability of accepting Darwin's theory, and Diamond (1980) demonstrated a comparable effect for the acceptance of cliometrics by historians. In both instances, around 6% of the variance in innovation acceptance may be attributed to the age of the potential acceptor. This principle seems to apply even to domains beyond pure science. For example, one inquiry into the "relationship between age and innovative behavior" indicated that "younger farmers were more likely than their older counterparts to adopt new agricultural practices" (Green, Rich, & Nesman 1985, p. 255). And in business enterprises, age is negatively correlated with managers' willingness to take risks (Vroom & Pahl 1971). Although I do not know of any specific research on the question, it is possible that Planck's principle intervenes in the dissemination of new ideas in the arts as well. Yesterday's artistic innovators may become tomorrow's defenders of the aesthetic status quo. Supporting this conjecture, scores on the Barron–Welsh Art Scale, which, as noted in chapter 3, record the preference for complexity, tend to decrease with age (Alpaugh & Birren 1977).

I must stress, nonetheless, that the size of the effect is not large enough to preclude many exceptions to the rule. Around 94% of the variance in the disposition to accept a novel concept has nothing to do with a person's age. Indeed, the chance-configuration theory leads us to expect that the reality underlying Planck's principle is far more complex than first meets the eye. Three considerations stand out in particular:

1. In chapter 1 we enumerated several constraints on the social acceptance of an offered communication configuration, constraints that have relatively little, if anything, to do with age. On the contrary, these factors mainly concern how representative the scientist is of the larger scientific community. Are the same mental elements being subjected to permutations? Are these elements in comparable states of cognitive disarray? Has the chance configuration been successfully encoded in a symbolic form that encourages an accurate decoding by potential acceptors? Answers to these questions may not necessarily entail considerations of age (see also Mahoney 1976).

2. If the decline in openness to the originality of others is truly coupled with the corresponding decline in one's own creative potential, then the agewise curve describing Planck's principle should be governed by the same function that, according to the theory, describes the loss in creative potential with increased age. This latter function is defined by the simple formula

$$x = ke^{-at} \qquad (4.4)$$

where x is the creative potential at time t (i.e., professional age), a is the ideation rate of Equation 4.1, and k is an integration constant (Simonton 1984b). If x at $t = 0$ is assumed to be the total number of potential contributions (e.g., publications), then $k = m$, where m is the maximum number of contributions possible in an unlimited life span. The curve defined by this equation is shown in Figure 4.3. The corresponding curve depicting how openness to new ideas varies as a function of age should parallel that shown in this figure (cf. Alpaugh & Birren 1977).

3. In calculating the relevance of Planck's principle, we must consider the initial level of creative potential at $t = 0$, or at the career onset. Many members of the younger generation (owing to factors that I shall discuss in the next chapter on developmental antecedents) will already have moved

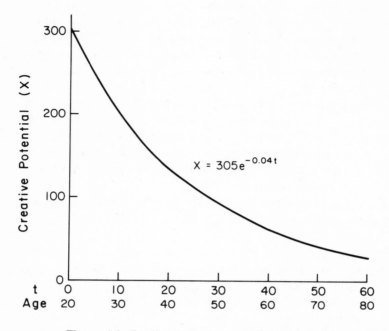

Figure 4.3. Predicted decline in creative potential as a function of age under typical parameters (from Simonton 1984b).

far along toward analytical genius, whereas many members of the older generation, owing to an impressive initial creative potential, will yet have a long way to travel before attaining maximal cognitive order. If the probability of accepting a novel idea is directly proportional to x in Equation 4.2, then it will also be proportional to m, or the given creative potential. We consequently will have a family of curves such as that shown in Figure 4.3, each with a different intercept on the vertical axis (i.e., $x = k = m$ at $t = 0$). It is this theoretical complication that permits highly creative scientists to appreciate the latest advances in the discipline even when they are old. To illustrate, Charles Lyell, though a dozen years older than Darwin, was still coordinating paleontological material when evolution by natural selection was announced. Not only did Lyell come around to Darwin's point of view, but he stood amazed that the idea had somehow escaped him.

The interpretation just derived from the chance-configuration theory clearly implies a number of empirically testable propositions. First, professional or career age is more important than is chronological age to determining the force of Planck's principle in a particular case. As an example, a scientist new to the field, even if of mature age, may be more responsive to the most imaginative suggestions. Moreover, when receptiveness to revolutionary ideas is plotted as a function of (professional) age, the resulting graph should not be linear but rather curvilinear – specifically, concave upward, as in Figure 4.3. This signifies that most of the change in openness takes place in the earlier portion of a career; indeed, half of the receptiveness will be lost in the same number of years as defines the half-life of creative potential [i.e., $(\ln 2) / a$]. Finally, any estimate of the variance accounted by Planck's principle must allow for individual differences in creative potential (e.g., as evidenced by a potential acceptor's productivity rate relative to that of others in the same discipline). Much of the longitudinal variation in receptiveness is probably swamped by the considerably larger cross-sectional variation.

When we recognize that all investigations published to date have used chronological age rather than professional age, have been based on linear statistics rather than testing for nonlinear functions, and have made no attempt to control for individual differences in intrinsic openness to the creativity of others, it is reasonable to conclude that the current estimates of the impact of Planck's principle may actually be biased downward.

Summary

We have examined how the chance-configuration theory elucidates the three most significant observations regarding scientific productivity. First, the theory accounts for the extremely skewed cross-sectional distribution: The upper tail of the normal curve for intellectual ability is highly distorted because of the accelerating increase in potential configurations as a function of the number of mental elements available for chance permutations. Second, the theory handles various aspects of the connection between productivity and a scientist's age. Specifically, the theory (1) yields an equation that precisely predicts the shape of the longitudinal curve, including the concave-downward onset, decelerating termination, and single peak; (2) explains interdisciplinary differences in the typical career course in terms of the information-processing demands of each discipline and also introduces the useful notion of the average creative half-life for a given discipline; (3) explains the predictive superiority of professional or career age over chronological age by emphasizing the intrinsic working out of creative potential via the chance-permutation process; and (4) makes theoretically necessary the empirical association among precocity, longevity, and productivity rate (as well as the dependence of the peak age on the discipline and not on the creative potential). Third and last, the chance-configuration theory subsumes the constant-probability-of-success model of the linkage between quantity and quality, a positive (albeit probabilistic) association that has been empirically demonstrated to hold both within and across careers.

After we established the theoretical basis for these core facets of productivity, we treated three subsidiary issues, namely, the Ortega hypothesis, the Yuasa phenomenon, and Planck's principle. We concluded that (1) despite the inherent élitism of scientific influence, the constant-probability-of-success model applies as well to individuals as to products, and therefore lesser scientists are not irrelevant to scientific advance; (2) the changing age structure of a scientific community provides a clue to the group's probable status as a center of science; and (3) the increased resistance to new ideas as a scientist ages is directly related to that scientist's progress in self-organization and is accordingly also related to initial creative potential. In addition, because the phenomenon of productivity operates no differently in the arts than in the sciences, the theory's explanatory and predictive successes may be quite broad and may even be applicable to domains of achievement that stress leadership more than creativity.

The unifying construct underlying most of the theoretical discussion of this chapter is the concept of creative potential. Consequently, our task in the next chapter is to examine the factors that contribute to the development of this potential.

5 Developmental antecedents

How does one acquire that creative potential that leads to a long and productive career as a scientist? Mach (1896, p. 171) again provided the start of an explanation when he said that "if the psychical life is subjected to the incessant influences of a powerful and rich experience, then every representative element in the mind is connected with so many others that the actual and natural course of the thoughts is easily influenced and determined by insignificant circumstances, which accidently are decisive." The mental elements of a scientific notable are profusely interconnected because the mind has been exposed to a supply of enriching experiences. The intellect is to some degree empirical; simple and predictable environments generate mental counterparts, whereas complex and unpredictable environments yield the opposite and thereby induce the need for the self-organization that is the hallmark of creative potential.

A sizable literature on creative development has accumulated that demonstrates the importance of diversified, enriching environments to individuals who attain eminence (e.g., Goertzel & Goertzel 1962; Goertzel, Goertzel, & Goertzel 1978; Simonton 1987a,c; Walberg et al. 1980; cf. Howe 1982). One noticeable drawback of this research, however, is that the diverse routes to achieving distinction are frequently lumped together: Leaders often rub shoulders with creators in the samples, and when creators are treated separately, artists and scientists are not always segregated. In addition, gaps in the literature on the development of scientific luminaries sometimes force us to extrapolate from investigations of other forms of outstanding creativity. All in all, the difficulties here are much the same as those we encountered in the chapter on personality. Nevertheless, I think that the chance-configuration theory is sufficiently well articulated at this point that we can tease out the applicable research findings. We thus shall review how creative potential in science may have five developmental antecedents, namely, family background, role models, formal education, marginality, and zeitgeist (cf. Fisch 1977).

107

Family background

The early childhood of the future scientific innovator is characterized by events or circumstances that should raise the eventual effectiveness of any chance-permutation mechanism. Anne Roe (1952b, p. 22) summarized the childhood of the "average eminent scientist" in this way:

> He was the first-born child of a middle-class family, the son of a professional man. He is likely to have been a sick child or to have lost a parent at an early age. He has a very high IQ and in boyhood began to do a great deal of reading. He tended to feel lonely and "different" and to be shy and aloof from his classmates. (See also Eiduson 1962)

We shall concentrate here on three core aspects of this description, namely, parental loss, birth order, and cultural enrichment (see also Goertzel & Goertzel 1962; Goertzel et al. 1978; Walberg et al. 1980).

Parental loss and orphanhood

Exceptionally achieving individuals in virtually every human endeavor are more likely to have lost a parent, and especially both, relative to any reasonable baseline (Albert 1971; Eiduson 1962; Eisenstadt 1978; Goertzel et al. 1978; Illingworth & Illingworth 1969; Martindale 1972; Walberg et al. 1980). Lenin was a teenager when his father died; Napoleon was around 15 when he lost his father; and Beethoven's mother died when he was 16, his father when he was 18. To show that these are not isolated instances, Eisenstadt (1978) examined 699 eminent personalities (about 14% of whom were scientists) from almost all eras and nationalities: 61% lost a parent before age 31, 52% before 26, and 45% before 21. Albert (1971) looked at the geniuses, both creators and leaders, who qualified for membership in the Cox (1926) sample and discovered that parental loss was characteristic of between 22 and 31%. Another investigation using a slightly overlapping sample of famous persons from all walks of life found that almost one-third of them had lost their fathers early in life (Walberg et al. 1980). This "orphanhood effect" has been most consistently demonstrated for literary creators: Martindale (1972) observed the absence of the father in 30% of a sample of poets, and more dramatically, Brown (1968) noted that 55% of his sample of writers had lost a parent before age 15.

This same effect may hold for distinguished scientists as well: Newton's father died before Newton was even born, and though not nearly so dramatic, Boyle, Huygens, Lavoisier, Count Rumford, Lord Kelvin, Maxwell, and Marie Curie all lost a parent early in their lives (Price 1963, p. 109).

Although the impact of parental loss may not be quite so great in the sciences as it is in the arts, there still is evidence supporting this effect (Silverman 1974; cf. Berry 1981; Eiduson 1962; Mansfield & Busse 1981; Woodward 1974). Roe (1952a) learned from her examination of notable contemporary scientists that 15% had lost a parent by death before age 10. Broken down by field, this happened to 25% of the biologists, 13% of the physical scientists, and 9% of the social scientists. To place this figure in perspective, Roe referred to data showing that only around 6% of college students lost a parent by age 10. Roe also mentioned Bell's (1937) work on illustrious mathematicians, in which around one-quarter had lost a parent before age 10 and nearly one-third before age 14.

Roe interpreted results such as these as proving that a scientist in-the-making needs to develop a capacity for independence – an interpretation in line with the current theory. It is evident that such a loss would seriously disrupt the usual socialization practices, producing a youth who may perceive the world in a less than fully conventional manner. Thus, scientifically creative adolescents tend to be less interested in sports than normal and to fit in less well socially with their peers (Eiduson 1962; Schaefer & Anastasi 1968; Terman 1955; cf. McCurdy 1960). It is interesting that prominent scientists were often sickly children in youth, for this also would interfere with more conventionalized socialization (Eiduson 1962; Roe 1952a; cf. Berry 1981). In any case, according to this view, it follows that the consequences of parental loss can occur by means other than orphanhood, such as alcoholism, abandonment, and divorce (Eiduson 1962; Silverman 1974; Simonton 1984d, chap. 2).

Birth order

In his *English Men of Science* (1874), Francis Galton was possibly the first investigator to maintain that firstborn and only sons are located in the ranks of the great in proportions well in excess of chance expectation. Thirty years later, Havelock Ellis (1904) showed that the prominence of the firstborns extends to other domains of achievement as well. At the present time, after over a century of research on this topic, the primacy of the firstborn child appears assured, not merely in science, but in almost all endeavors (e.g., Goertzel et al. 1978). In Roe's (1952a) classic study, 39 of her 64 distinguished scientists were firstborn (and 15 of these were only children), and 13 were second-born children in the family, leaving just a dozen to fill out the remaining ordinal positions up to the two seventh borns. Furthermore, Roe revealed that of the 25 who were not firstborn children, 5 were oldest sons, 2 had an older sibling who had died in infancy or early childhood, and many of the remainder were separated on the average of five years from their older sibling. Other recent investigations have replicated this preponderance: Firstborns usually represent half or more of the community of active scientists (Chambers 1964; Eiduson 1962; Gupta et al. 1983; Helmreich et al. 1980; cf. Datta 1968; West 1960). Significantly, too, the firstborns, relative to their later-born colleagues, have higher citation rates in the literature (Helmreich et al. 1980) and higher creativity ratings from experts (Helson & Crutchfield 1970). The birth-order advantage may even be stronger in the sciences than in the arts (Bliss 1970; Clark & Rice 1982; Eisenman 1964; cf. Schubert, Wagner, & Schubert 1977).

What is the meaning of this birth-order effect? We know that both intelligence and educational attainment are empirically associated with birth order (see, e.g., Adams 1972; Altus 1966), two variables that are clearly relevant to scientific achievement (cf. Schachter 1963). The fundamental factor, however, may be how birth order affects intellectual growth. According to Zajonc's (1976) "confluence model" of intellectual development, the ordinal position in the family determines the amount of environmental stimulation available during childhood. The firstborn child is exposed to social interactions defined by mature adults, whereas the later-born children are raised in an environment increasingly diluted by the rather more immature minds of older siblings. If valid, the confluence model would explain the preeminence of firstborns in science, for, as we discussed in chapter 3, an exceptional intelligence is likely necessary for the collection of richly interconnected mental elements (for further discussion, see Simonton 1987c). Furthermore, Zajonc's model explains why the later borns who do attain distinction will follow the pattern suggested in Roe's (1952a) investigation. That is, successful later borns will tend either to have lost an older sibling early or to have a much older sibling, with both situations lessening the intellectual disadvantage. The model explains, too, why eventual eminence in life is linked with early exposure to a great many adults (Walberg et al. 1980).

Nonetheless, the confluence model remains controversial, with some research confirming the logic and the predictions (e.g., Bernbaum, Markus, & Zajonc 1982; Zajonc 1983, 1986) and other research opposing this provocative idea (e.g., Brackbill & Nichols 1982; Galbraith 1982a,b). Some social scientists speculate that birth order is more germane to personality development than to intellectual growth (e.g., Albert 1980; Eisenman 1987; Stewart 1977). A few investigators have even challenged the conclusion that the birth-order effect exists at all (e.g., Schooler 1972). Although we cannot review here all the theoretical and methodological issues behind such debates (cf. Simonton 1987c), birth order does appear to be correlated with success as a scientist and this correlation may be due to the advantages that accrue to the firstborn child during intellectual maturation. This conclusion would hold even if it were demonstrated that it is simply because the first-born child, and especially the firstborn son, is the beneficiary of special family privileges, such as early independence training and full financial sup-port in college and university education. The birth-order phenomenon hence may be linked with the third and last family-background factor (see also McCurdy 1960).

Cultural enrichment

The household environment of a prospective creative talent is replete with intellectually and culturally stimulating materials (Goertzel & Goertzel 1962; Goertzel et al. 1978; Howe 1982; Schaefer & Anastasi 1968; Walberg et al. 1980). Parents are far more likely to have intellectual and cultural interests, as revealed by respectable home libraries, maga-zine subscriptions, and artistic or mechanical hobbies. These leisure activi-ties appear to rub off on their children, for quite early in life future achievers acquire numerous stimulating hobbies, including omnivorous reading. Indeed, George Bernard Shaw may have proclaimed that "read-ing rots the mind," but omnivorous reading in childhood and adolescence correlates positively with ultimate adulthood success (Simonton 1984d, chap. 4; see also Emery & Czikszentmihaly 1982; Schaefer & Anastasi 1968; Smith, Albright, Glennon, & Owens 1961; Taylor 1963). Moreover, parents of achievers are more likely to permit their children to explore actively the environment (Walberg et al. 1980). This picture of a stimulat-ing home environment holds for prospective scientists as well as for those attaining distinction in other domains of creativity or leadership (Roe 1952a; Schaefer & Anastasi 1968).

The family context that promotes creative development also has a few more properties that may be related to cultural enrichment. Although socioeconomic class is not always correlated with eventual achievement, it is true that noteworthy persons are particularly likely to come from the middle or professional classes (Raskin 1936; Simonton 1976a). This also holds in the case of science (Berry 1981; Chambers 1964; Eiduson 1962; Elliott 1975; Helson & Crutchfield 1970; Moulin 1955; Raskin 1936; Taylor 1963; West 1961). Over half of the distinguished researchers that Roe (1952a) studied were the sons of professional men; only 2 out of the 64 had fathers who were skilled laborers, and not a single one had a father who was an unskilled laborer. Roe's group also tended to avoid institutional religion, and most came from families that belonged to nondogmatic denominations if they had any religious upbringing at all (see also Berry 1981; Chambers 1964; Eiduson 1962; Helson & Crutchfield 1970; Lehman & Witty 1931; McClelland 1962; Simonton 1986b; Terman 1954).

Presumably, persons from professional families, on the average, are exposed to a richer array of cultural stimuli, because of both the parents' wider range of intellectual interests and their financial capacity to pursue those interests. Thus, children from middle-class backgrounds may be less traditionalist, and a bit more iconoclastic, than are those from lower-class settings. Furthermore, parents who subscribe to less rigid religious doctrines probably, again on the average, tolerate more diversity of opinion at home, which then contributes to an enriched home environment. This interpretation is compatible with Roe's interpretation of her own interview data, for she attributed the impact of these factors to the "love of learning" that generally was characteristic of such homes (cf. Datta 1967; West 1961).

But many of these research findings can be interpreted in more than one way (Simonton 1987a,c). On the one hand, parents who set up stimulating home environments are directly contributing to their children's intellectual growth – the traditional environmental or "nurture" account. The child's mind is a Lockean tabula rasa that reflects the diversity and intricacy of the surroundings. With such nurturing stimuli, the child grows up with an exceptional creative potential, a huge inventory of interassociated mental elements. On the other hand, some developmental psychologists have recently argued that many such supposed effects are actually spurious outcomes of underlying genotypic factors (e.g., Scarr & McCartney 1983). Parents with strong intellectual and cultural interests (1) construct corresponding home environments to satisfy these needs and (2) pass these genetic dispositions to their children via standard biological inheritance, therein creating the mere appearance of an environmental effect. If this "nature" position is more justified than is the nurture viewpoint, we have essentially returned to the stance advocated by Galton in his 1869 work, *Hereditary Genius*. Eminence then runs in families precisely as do the more obvious physical attributes (cf. Bramwell 1948; Simonton 1983b, 1984d, chap. 2). Roe (1952a) allowed for this possibility as well, but she favored an environmental explanation.

Although this alternative interpretation does have merit, its relevance to the present theory is minimized by two considerations. First, the genetic explanation fails to handle, with any elegance, the impact of certain developmental influences – such as orphanhood and birth order or the sociocultural effects to be discussed shortly – that lack an evident inheritable component (Simonton 1987c). Second, even if a portion of the relationship between family background variables and achievement can be ascribed to genetic endowment, the background variables at the very minimum serve as clues to which individuals are likely to have the intellectual capacity for creative science. At this point I am inclined to endorse a mixed account, in which intellectually bright parents may have comparably brilliant children (see, e.g., Simonton 1983b), but appreciable environmental input is required to convert this intrinsic intellectual power into creative potential (Simonton 1987c). To reiterate what chapter 3 stated, intelligence is a necessary, though not sufficient, condition for a repertoire of richly interassociated mental elements that can freely enter chance permutations.

Role models

Adulthood achievement in any given domain of creativity or leader-ship depends on the availability of role models during the early, formative years of a person's life (e.g., Simonton 1978a, 1987c; Walberg et al. 1980). Using generational time-series analysis (Simonton 1984c), the odds of an eminent figure emerging in generation g has been shown to increase with the number of illustrious figures in the same endeavor in generations $g - 1$ and $g - 2$, an autoregressive function that apparently holds for both creativity (Simonton 1975e) and leadership (Simonton 1983b). Another study showed that two-thirds or more of a sample of eminent personalities were exposed, in early development, to significant adults who worked in the field in which the eminence was later attained and to adults who themselves claimed some distinction in their chosen field (Walberg et al. 1980). More-over, these role models can be either impersonal "paragons" who are admired at a distance or personal "mentors" who affect the emerging ge-nius far more directly (e.g., Simonton 1984a). According to Erikson's (1951) theory of psychosocial development, adolescence may be the best period in a person's life for acquiring "models of leadership," for it is during this developmental interval that a person's identity is said to be established. In any case, the data collected to date support the generaliza-tion that somewhere between the teens and the 20s a young developing creator may be most susceptible to role-modeling effects.

Empirical research on scientific creativity has indicated that science likely operates no differently. Time series of aggregate scientific creativity display respectable autocorrelations that may betray the dependence of each generation on its predecessor (Simonton 1974, 1976b,e). On the indi-vidual level, the prospects for achieving acclaim appear to be enhanced by an apprenticeship under successful practitioners of science (Crane 1965; Goldstein 1979; Segal et al. 1980). For instance, the odds of winning the

Nobel Prize for scientific work are better for those who studied under past Nobel laureates (Zuckerman 1977). Indeed, it is this intergenerational linkage that is partly responsible for the clustering of creators into those Kroeberian "configurations" that we mentioned when discussing the Yuasa phenomenon in chapter 4 (Simonton 1981a; cf. Gray 1961).

Nonetheless, role models can have a negative rather than a purely positive consequence for creative development (Simonton 1976e,f, 1977b, 1984a), a possibility that has not received sufficient attention in the empirical work on scientific creativity. Even if the availability of role models improves the prospects of creative precocity (Simonton 1977b), for example, the long-term impact on lifetime productivity can be negative, perhaps because of the excessive imitation of models (Simonton 1987c). A fine line divides emulating one's predecessors and eventually surpassing them, and merely imitating them as virtually infallible models. Newton may have seen farther than all the rest by standing on the shoulders of giants, yet many of Newton's contemporaries (especially the Cartesians) were quite content to lie obscured in the shadows of giants. There are evidently at least three ways to augment the utility of models while concomitantly diminishing any tendency toward debilitating imitation (cf. Simonton 1984a).

1. The more models there are, the harder it will be to imitate any one. Thus, it is better to be the protégé of several mentors, and it is equally advantageous to depend on more than one standard of excellence.

2. In the instance of paragons, if one must admire just one or two predecessors, more benefit accrues from modeling oneself after those who are temporally most distant. The more historically removed the source of inspiration is, the less likely it is that the source can provide an exact template for guiding contemporary creativity. Einstein exemplified both of these patterns: The walls of his study contained the portraits of just three predecessors – Newton, Faraday, and Maxwell – whose careers terminated long before Einstein began his own (Maxwell, the closest in age, died the very year that Einstein was born).

3. In the case of mentors, it is probably more advantageous to study with a scientist still in the prime of his or her career rather than with someone in the later stages of self-organization (cf. Simonton 1984d, chap. 2). We proposed in previous chapters that over a career, the process of self-organization converts an intuitive genius into an analytical genius. A student studying under an intuitive genius will be exposed to a larger number of unresolved issues. In addition, mentors who have yet to organize themselves into analytical geniuses will be more accepting of original ideas generated by their protégés, in line with Planck's principle. In concrete terms, it seems optimal for the masters to be not much more than 20 years

older than their apprentices, yet not much less than 10 years older (see, e.g., Gupta et al. 1983; Zuckerman 1977, p. 119). So if apprentices are in their middle 20s, their mentors should be somewhere between 35 and 45 so as to maximize any beneficial effect.

From the perspective of chance-configuration theory, the equivocal influence of role models, whether paragons or mentors, illustrates the "essential tension" required for the scientific excellence of which Kuhn (1963) spoke (see chapter 1). On the one hand, the scientist must to some extent be a traditionalist, mastering the repertoire of problems, techniques, and standards. As noted before, whether or not an offered communication configuration proves successful in the competition for colleagues' attention hinges on whether the originator's mind contains the same body of mental elements, has those elements in a comparable condition of disorganization, and can effectively translate the initial chance configuration so that it can be understood by fellow members of the discipline. Insofar as identification with accomplished predecessors, especially distinguished mentors, provides this sort of expertise, some degree of exposure to suitable role models must be developmentally healthy.

On the other hand, to be truly influential, particularly to become a revolutionary who transforms the foundations of a science, demands that the scientist be an iconoclast. Otherwise, severe constraints will be placed on the chance-permutation process. First, the repertoire of mental elements that enter into the combinatory play will be more specialized, and the opportunity for truly novel permutations will be correspondingly truncated. Furthermore, the interconnections among these elements will be more limited, and what few linkages remain may be more firm, consequently undermining the basis for generating chance associations (an effect particularly likely if the disciple has studied under a single master sufficiently advanced in self-organization that most ideas have found their proper place in the intellectual hierarchy). In the extreme case of outright imitation, the protégés or admirers will be subjecting virtually the identical set of elements to permutations as had been recombined by their mentors or paragons, producing disciples who can advance science solely by, in effect, extending the careers of their masters beyond biological limitations.

This tension between traditionalists and iconoclasts implies a curvilinear, inverted-U curve between the magnitude of a role model's influence on a young scientist and that scientist's ultimate contribution to science. That is, the peak of the function represents the optimal trade-off point between these two conflicting forces. Just such a curve has been demonstrated to hold for artistic creativity (Simonton 1984a). The differential fame of 772 Western painters and sculptors was predicted by the formula

$$A = 16 + 12C + 0.15G + 0.23CG + 0.001G^2 - 0.001CG^2 \quad (5.1)$$

where A is the artist's eminence, C is the number of paragons admired by the given artist, and G is the average age gap between that artist and those paragons. If we take the partial derivative of A with respect to G for Equation 5.1, set the result equal to zero, and solve for G, we will get

$$G = \frac{75 + 115C}{C - 1} \quad (5.2)$$

This equation indicates the optimal age gap between creator and paragons, given a certain number of paragons. To illustrate, when rounded off, the average number of paragons across all artists sampled yields $C = 3$ as the typical case. By substitution, then $G = 210$ years. In different terms, among those artists who modeled themselves after three predecessors, the most famous were those whose models had been born over two centuries earlier. In line with the notion of a trade-off, when C increases, G decreases. Thus, the most paragons, or standards of excellence, claimed for any artist was 17 which, when put into Equation 5.2, yields a peak at 127 years. In contrast, if an artist has fewer sources of inspiration, then they must be historically more distant so as to avoid the temptation of imitation. In fact, in the extreme situation, when an artist relies on only one paragon from the past, Equation 5.1 degenerates into the linear equation $A = 28 + 0.38G$, and consequently, Equation 5.1 becomes undefined. The more extensive the age gap is, the better it will be. Figure 5.1 graphs the curve for the typical situation of three paragons.

Unhappily, few researchers have tried to indicate the existence of a more complex and ambivalent link between role models and scientific distinction, like that in the study of artistic creators. Sheldon (1979, 1980) proposed a complicated mathematical model of mentor–protégé influences that allows for adverse effects, but his empirical tests of these "hierarchical cybernets," although confirmatory, are rather oblique. Another investigation found that serving as a research assistant in graduate school was correlated negatively with the number of citations later received as a scientist, a correlation that has more than one interpretation (Segal et al. 1980; cf. Chambers 1964). Nevertheless, we have provided a theoretical rationale for believing that results similar to those found in the arts may be found in the sciences too, albeit the constants in the equations would probably differ. Assuming that scientific creativity demands more emphasis on traditionalism, whereas artistic creativity requires more iconoclasm, fewer paragons and shorter age gaps may prove more desirable in the sciences. Einstein's scientific idols may be close to the ideal. Despite our present lack

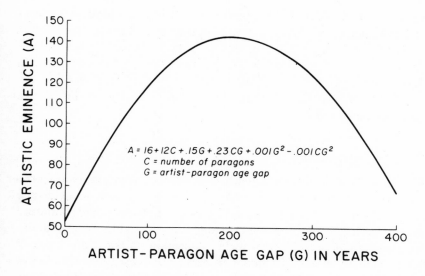

Figure 5.1. Predicted artistic eminence as a function of the number of paragons and the mean artist–paragon age gap for the typical case of three paragons (from Simonton 1984a).

of evidence on this point, the results reported in the next section seem corroborative, for a similar curvilinear relationship is found for the relation between creativity and formal education.

Formal education

Einstein is frequently cited to support the opinion that the development of scientific creativity is deterred by traditional education. At one time Einstein condemned education methods with the words: "One had to cram all this stuff into one's mind for the examinations, whether one liked it or not. This coercion had such a deterring effect on me that, after I passed the final examination, I found the consideration of any scientific problems distasteful to me for an entire year" (quoted in Hoffman 1972, p. 31). On another occasion, and on a broader scale, Einstein affirmed that

it is, in fact, nothing short of a miracle that the modern methods of instruction have not yet entirely strangled the holy curiosity of inquiry; for this delicate little plant, aside from stimulation, stands mostly in need of freedom; without this it goes to wreck and ruin without fail. It is a very grave mistake to think that the enjoyment of seeing and searching can be promoted by means of coercion and a sense of duty. (quoted in Schlipp 1951, p. 17)

To appraise the developmental repercussions of formal education we must address two questions: First, is there any correlation between how well a student performs academically and that student's eventual scientific accomplishments in later life? Second, what is the functional relationship between the level of formal education attained and the prospects for scientific success in maturity? After discussing these issues, I shall outline an integrative scheme based on the theory.

Scholastic success

Investigators have consistently shown that creativity is not necessarily correlated with high marks in school and college, such as registered by the grade point average (Baird 1968; Bednar & Parker 1965; Guilford 1959). This null effect has led some to infer that the educational system – whether primary or secondary or higher education – is not really designed with the talented or gifted student in mind (Bentley 1966; Haddon & Lytton 1968; Mahoney 1976, chap. 3; cf. Hudson 1966). High-IQ students (i.e., analytical geniuses) are often preferred to high-creativity students (i.e., intuitive geniuses) (Getzels & Jackson 1963; Hasan & Butcher 1966). That is, the capacity to master and organize the lessons as given is preferred to the ability to challenge conventional wisdom by speculating on alternatives to standard viewpoints. As a consequence, future creative individuals may not always be motivated to perform well in class work, becoming instead underachievers whose scholastic merits are uneven. MacKinnon (1962, p. 494) concluded from his studies of creative architects that in college "they were unwilling to accept anything on the mere say-so of their instructors. Nothing was to be accepted on faith or because it had behind it the voice of authority. Such matters might be accepted, but only after the student on his own had demonstrated their validity to himself."

Although granting that scholastic performance is definitely more germane to the development of scientific creativity, as compared with other kinds of creativity (Chambers 1964; Hudson 1966; Schaefer & Anastasi 1968), it remains true that high grades are not necessarily conducive to adulthood achievement in science (Gaston 1973, p. 51; Hoyt 1965; MacKinnon 1960; Razik 1967; Taylor, Smith, & Ghiselin 1963; Taylor 1963). Minkowsky said of his former pupil that "in his student days Einstein had been a lazy dog. He never bothered about mathematics at all" (quoted in Seelig 1956, p. 28). An investigation of fellows of the Royal Society indicated that their academic records as undergraduates were generally poor and certainly not superior to those scientists who failed to be elected fellows (Hudson 1958). Evidently, "much of our educational system seems designed to discourage any attempt at finding things out for oneself, but makes learning things others have found out, or think they have, the major goal. . . . Once a student has learned that he can find things out for himself, though, bad pedagogy is probably only an irritant" (Roe 1952a, p. 82). Before we consider these anecdotes, data, and speculations evidence that scholastic success damns a student as being devoid of scientific potential, we should weigh the following five facts:

1. Whether or not a scientifically talented student does well in formal course work is contingent in part on the structure and orientation of the instructional system (Torrance 1962). For example, colleges tend to produce fewer natural scientists if they emphasize conforming to social expectations, full involvement in collegiate activities, and, especially, dogmatic religious worship (Thistlethwaite 1963). A free-thinking iconoclast would clearly suffer under such oppressive circumstances, to the detriment of scholastic effort.

2. Regardless of the general atmosphere of the college or university, certain styles of teaching may encourage scientific talent to pursue formal requirements. In Roe's (1952a) study of eminent scientists, the best-liked teachers were those who let their students pursue personal interests, such as extensive outside reading (see also Schaefer & Anastasi 1968). For the most part, "the teachers who stimulate scientists tend to be non-directive in their teaching methods" (Thistlethwaite 1963, p. 275).

3. According to one criterion of scholastic accomplishment, at least, future scientific contributors do tend to distinguish themselves. As we briefly noted in chapter 4, those most likely to contribute to science as professionals usually earn their doctorates at a relatively early age – one of the most consistent predictors of scientific productivity and acclaim (Blackburn et al. 1978; Eagly 1974; Harmon 1963; Lyons 1968). Ironically, this relation may explain why prospective innovators may not do well by more formal standards, for they may focus more on pursuing their scientific curiosity than on winning respect from their teachers. Bloom (1963, p. 258), who studied the postdoctoral careers of University of Chicago PhDs, put it this way:

An individual who comes to a university with problems that he is really interested in, with some notion of himself as a research worker or scholar, and who is able to resist the student role of doing things because they are required or because he is told to do them is likely to be a most productive individual in his post graduate career.

4. It also has been repeatedly demonstrated that the most productive and most frequently cited scientists have usually completed their undergraduate and graduate education at the more prestigious institutions of

higher learning (Blackburn et al. 1978; Helmreich et al. 1980; Zuckerman 1977). This correlation may be interpreted as showing that entrance into the scientific élite requires attendance at élite institutions that provide the proper training, and yet it is no less plausible that this association represents a spurious effect. Those youths who hold the most promise of creative potential may select the better schools in the first place, as part of their quest for intellectual stimulation. If superior colleges and universities can also be presumed to offer more rigorous academic programs, it follows that just such a choice implies a lower grade point average, because of the higher standard of demonstrated competence in class work. To support this conjecture we mention the fact that the mean IQ for undergraduates ranges from 108 for the least selective institutions to 132 for the most selective, a spread of well over one standard deviation (Cronbach 1960).

5. Aside from the preceding considerations, the correlation between scholastic success and adulthood achievement is not necessarily negative, although it can be (Baird, 1968; Taylor et al. 1963; cf. Chambers 1964; Owens 1969; Taylor & Ellison 1967). For every notable scientist whose academic performance was noticeably below par, another scientist of roughly equivalent distinction can be named whose accomplishments in school would be a source of pride. Einstein may have been a mediocre student, as was evidently Charles Darwin, but Marie Curie, Sigmund Freud, and Max Planck were brilliant in their formal course work.

Before we can integrate these points into a larger framework, we first must discuss the connection between achieved eminence and the height a student climbs on the educational ladder of ever higher degrees.

Level of formal training

Because in this era of "big science," researchers almost always must have advanced degrees to obtain research positions – whether in academe, industry, or government – it is easy to assume that the process of earning a PhD actually nurtures creative potential. Yet this inference overlooks that many landmark contributions to science were contributed by investigators who lacked respectable academic credentials. Einstein did not obtain his doctorate by attending graduate seminars and working in the laboratories of professors, but rather he obtained his degree while engaged full time at a Swiss patent office. He once complained to a friend that "I shall not become a Ph.D. . . . The whole comedy has become a bore to me" (quoted in Hoffman 1972, p. 55), yet in the critical year of 1905 Einstein wrote four papers, the least important of which he sent off to the University of Zurich, which accepted the paper as a doctoral thesis (after

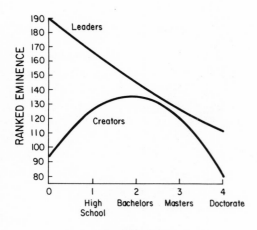

FORMAL EDUCATION

Figure 5.2. The relationship between level of formal education and the ranked eminence of the 192 creators and 109 leaders in the Cox sample (from Simonton 1983a).

having rejected a nearly identical paper four years earlier). Considering that his other papers of that year included the revolutionary papers on the photoelectric effect and the special relativity theory, it is clear that obtaining a doctorate contributed absolutely nothing to Einstein's capacity for doing creative science. Nor is Einstein atypical. Eminent scientists generally begin contributing to the store of objective knowledge *before* obtaining their doctorate (see, e.g., Helson & Crutchfield 1970; Roe 1972b).

This last tendency takes us to a more central generalization: A series of studies using diverse subject pools and operational definitions actually unearthed evidence that creativity may be a curvilinear, inverted-U function of the level of formal education (Simonton 1976a, 1981c, 1983a, 1984d, chap. 4; cf. Senter 1986; Taylor & Ellison 1967; Taylor et al. 1963). As educational level rises, the probability of achieved eminence in a creative endeavor also increases up to a certain optimum and thereafter declines so that further formal training diminishes the odds of achieving the highest eminence. For most historical periods and creative disciplines, the turnaround point appears somewhere between the junior and senior years of undergraduate education (Simonton 1983a). To illustrate, Figure 5.2 presents the curves observed for the 192 creators (and 109 leaders) who comprised the Cox (1926) sample. Considering that creativity is inversely related to dogmatism (i.e., idealistic inflexibility), it is also pertinent to report that there is a

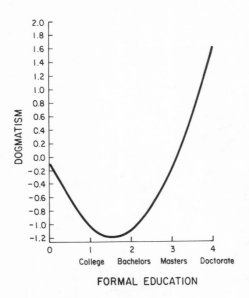

Figure 5.3. The relationship between level of formal education and the dogmatism of 33 American presidents (from Simonton 1983a).

mirror-image function for the relationship between formal educational level and dogmatism, as assessed for 33 past presidents of the United States. This reflection can be readily seen in Figure 5.3.

However, in the sciences this peak has, in recent years, moved toward the middle of graduate education (Simonton 1984d, chap. 4). That is, for scientists active in the 20th century, advanced training in graduate school appears to contribute to the development of creative potential (cf. Simonton 1986b). Even so, no shift in the optimal level of formal education has been spotted for creativity in the arts and humanities, the high point still appearing somewhere between the junior and senior years of undergraduate training (cf. Terman 1954).

As implied earlier, such nonmonotonic functions suggest that the essential tension that mediates the impact of role models also moderates the repercussion of formal education. On the one side, the traditionalist aspect of scientific creativity is reinforced by extensive formal training. Education, after all, is society's method of preserving and passing down to future generations the cultural variations that have had adaptive value in the past history of sociocultural evolution. The scientist-to-be must acquire the basic tools and concepts of the discipline in order to arrive at new communication configurations that enable social acceptance, for reasons given earlier.

On the other side, the iconoclastic facet of scientific creativity – the capacity to produce genuinely original chance configurations – obviously requires that the young scientist not be excessively socialized into a single, narrow-minded way of associating ideas. In this case, informal instruction, especially self-education, is far more conducive to creative development than is the highly formal, even rigid inculcation of cultural dogmas (cf. Haddon & Lytton 1968). Hence, the peak of the curve expressing achievement as a function of formal education may reveal the point at which the iconoclastic component begins to be sacrificed for the traditionalist component. Gains in the ability to compose comprehensible communication configurations cannot compensate for the losses in the capacity for generating chance configurations that depart significantly from the cultural givens.

General interpretation

To understand the theoretical meaning of the findings reviewed in the preceding two sections, we shall consider the following five points (cf. Simonton 1984d, chap. 4):

1. A person's native intellectual ability may have to be weighed when assessing the effects of both scholastic prowess and formal educational level. Let us suppose that intrinsic intelligence is correlated not only with the number of associations among mental elements that can be stored and retrieved but also with the relative speed with which such associations can be acquired. In other words, perhaps we can take somewhat literally the assertion that intelligent students are "quick" and unintelligent students are "slow." This supposition is consistent with the conception of IQ as the ratio of mental to chronological age (i.e., intelligence is associated with quicker intellectual advance). Then, highly intelligent students can complete their school work with minimal effort, leaving ample time to pursue those extra-curricular activities that may better support the development of an interconnected collection of ideas. Accordingly, if we first match students on inherent information-processing power, then we should expect a negative link between scholastic performance and creative potential. Holding intelligence constant, the requirements of formal education will directly compete with enriching self-education.

2. Even in controlling for intellectual ability, we must assume that the competition is really between educational demands and self-instruction. For example, some schools, colleges, and universities support special programs for the "gifted" that enable the student to earn academic credit for self-initiated courses of inquiry, thus making the education informal rather than formal (cf. Haddon & Lytton 1968; Mahoney 1976, chap. 3). More

significantly, there are many ways of becoming a poor student besides spending too much time on outside intellectual and cultural interests – such as having to cope with extraordinary economic, emotional, or social difficulties. Only when scholastic success is forced to give way to the demands of self-education, not these extraneous obstacles to study, does the negative correlation obtain between performance and creative potential (cf. Richards, Holland, & Lutz 1967). As noted earlier, gifted children and adolescents do seem dedicated to the independent pursuit of knowledge, as evinced by extensive independent reading and numerous intellectual hobbies (Goertzel & Goertzel 1962; Goertzel et al. 1978; Schaefer & Anastasi 1968; Segal et al. 1980; Walberg et al. 1980). As graduate students, particularly, creative scientists – in contrast with their unproductive peers – tend to devote far more time on research and study, over 50 hours per week (Chambers 1964). By one estimate, indeed, a full decade of preparation must transpire before a person's knowledge base becomes sufficiently rich to support creative output (Hayes 1981, pp. 209–214; Simon 1986). This intrinsically motivated mastery of a discipline is a sine qua non of success. "No man should dream of solving a great problem unless he is so thoroughly saturated with his subject that everything else sinks into comparative insignificance," said Mach (1896, pp. 170–171).

3. As one proceeds up the academic ladder, the effort that must be expended to achieve the maximal scholastic success, the highest grades, enlarges as well (cf. Taylor & Ellison 1967). The magnitude of competition from fellow students becomes more conspicuous. For instance, the average IQ of high school graduates in the United States is 110, an intellectual level that would give a student only a 50–50 chance of graduating from college and almost no chance of obtaining a PhD, for the mean IQ of a college graduate is 120 and that of a PhD 130 (Cronbach 1960). Aside from this intensified competition, the volume and difficulty of the material to be mastered become even more demanding. Consequently, even keeping intelligence constant and presuming the intrinsic motivation to seek out intellectual stimulation, the correlation between scholastic and scientific achievement should become more negative when advancing from primary through graduate education (see, e.g., Owens 1969).

4. Also to be taken into account is that there is more than one way to make a lasting contribution to science. First, one can be an *advancer,* a practitioner of what Kuhn (1970) styled "normal science." Advancers concentrate on "three classes of problems – determination of significant facts, matching facts with theory, and articulation of theory" (p. 34) in order to extend the explanatory power and precision of the prevailing paradigm. Because an advancer is thus more on the traditionalist side of the scale, both

high scholastic success and full progression along the formal education sequence are most beneficial. Robert Oppenheimer was an extremely remarkable student, but his contribution to science was limited to developing and enlarging the established views of his mentors and predecessors. Second, one can be a *revolutionary* scientist, which then places a bigger premium on becoming a more daring iconoclast, thus forcing the correlation between scholastic performance and attainment to become more negative and the function between formal educational level and final accomplishment more obviously nonmonotonic, concave downward. A revolutionary scientist must allow the chance-permutation process far more freedom in order to produce an original yet effective integration of scientific knowledge. Einstein, for instance, allowed himself to cut across traditional boundaries in classical physics, pondering simultaneously the phenomena behind both Newtonian mechanics and Maxwell's electromagnetic equations (Holton 1971–1972). Einstein took as fundamental problems what his predecessors took for granted as unquestionable premises.

5. Because revolutionaries – compared with advancers – are usually accorded more acclaim in posterity's eyes, one wonders why everyone with any ambition does not opt for the former path to posthumous glory. Herein emerges the final consideration, namely, the current state of the scientific zeitgeist. If the times are not ripe for a scientific revolution – if the elements necessary for an adaptive synthesis are not available and if the thoughts of the scientific community are sufficiently well structured around the traditional paradigm – it is improbable that chance configurations of revolutionary import can materialize, or, if they do, that the scientific world will be sympathetic to any attempt to fix what does not seem to require fixing. For instance, until such Kuhnian anomalies as black body radiation, the photoelectric effect, and the Michelson–Morley interferometer experiment became widely disseminated and debated, the zeitgeist was not ready for the revolutionary concepts of quantum and relativity theory. Hence one cannot always become a college dropout with the rational expectation of revamping the very core of science, for the times may hand all the creative opportunities to the advancers. Young scientists who strike out on novel paths despite the unfavorable setting can hope only to become mere precursors: · A *precursor* genius is a creator who follows an independent path rather than operating within the confines of the accepted paradigm but who, as a consequence, can often offer only incomplete anticipations of ideas that later will shake the foundations of science under the aegis of more notable names. Charles Darwin had several such precursors, the most striking among them, perhaps, being Patrick Matthew (Eiseley 1958, chap. 5; Zirkle 1941). Needless to say, precursors seldom earn as much credit as do

advancers in the annals of science, and uncountable potential precursors miss the mark altogether, becoming thereby merely eccentrics to contemporaries and nonentities to posterity.

To sum up, theoretical considerations suggest that Einstein's condemnation of education was far too simplistic. To gauge fairly the developmental influence on scientific creativity, we must know a student's native intelligence, the degree of personal involvement in self-education, the level of formal education presently demanding limited information-processing resources, whether that student aspires to revolutionizing rather than advancing science, and whether the zeitgeist is appropriately prepared for a scientific transformation rather than elaboration. These factors affect the optimal degree of scholastic success and formal educational level by determining the best trade-off between the traditionalist quest for immediately acceptable communication configurations and the iconoclastic search for original chance configurations.

Marginality

Campbell (1960, p. 391), in documenting his own model, noted that "persons who have been uprooted from traditional culture, or who have been thoroughly exposed to two or more cultures, seem to have an advantage in the range of hypotheses they are apt to consider, and through this means, in the frequency of creative innovation." To support this conclusion, Campbell cited such classic essays as Veblin's 1919 paper on the conspicuous intellectual prominence of Jews in Western civilization and Park's 1928 discussion of the "marginal man." This notion is compatible, too, with Toynbee's (1946) theory of a "creative minority" who advances human civilization through a process of "withdrawal and return." The Goertzels offered more contemporary endorsement by pointing to the respectable percentage of first- and second-generation immigrants among distinguished 20th-century personalities (Goertzel et al. 1978). A comparable advantage of immigration may hold for scientists as well, at least for mathematicians (Helson & Crutchfield 1970). Individuals raised in one culture but living in another are blessed with a heterogeneous array of mental elements, permitting combinatory variations unavailable to those who reside solely in one cultural world. The disproportional representation among notable scientists of those with Jewish backgrounds illustrates this point (Berry 1981; Hayes 1981, pp. 227–229).

Sociocultural marginality is not the only variety of marginality that may nurture the development of creative potential, because professional marginality can have much the same effect. Significant contributions to a given endeavor are frequently made by those who either switched fields or were self-taught (Hughes 1958), a circumstance that apparently holds specifically for science. Koestler (1964, p. 230) proclaimed that "all decisive advances in the history of scientific thought can be described in terms of mental cross-fertilization between different disciplines." Likewise, Bartlett (1958, p. 98) observed that "it has often happened that critical stages for advance are reached when what has been called one body of knowledge can be brought into close and effective relationship with what has been treated as a different, and a largely or wholly independent, scientific discipline." And finally, Kuhn (1970, p. 90) elaborated this point by asserting that

almost always the men who achieve these fundamental inventions of a new paradigm have been either very young or very new to the field whose paradigm they change. . . . [F]or obviously these are the men who, being little committed by prior practice to the traditional rules of normal science, are particularly likely to see that these rules no longer define a playable game and to conceive another set that can replace them.

In any event, a scientist exposed to more than one discipline can combine elements in a truly unique fashion, chancing upon original configurations that may revolutionize one or more disciplines.

There are many anecdotes illustrating the positive impact of professional marginality. As Bartlett noted, scientists will often be successful in one field precisely because they introduce ideas, techniques, or habits of thought that are practically standard in another domain. For example, Landsteiner's previous background in chemistry likely facilitated his isolation of blood groups, Kekulé's early ambition to become an architect may have nourished a thinking style conducive to his conceiving the structural basis of organic chemistry, and Helmholtz specifically acknowledged that his invention of the ophthalmoscope arose because he was obliged to pursue a medical career when his primary fascination was with physics, especially optics. At other times, in line with Kuhn's statement, the chief asset to be gained from professional marginality is an ignorance that allows the chance permutations to proceed afresh. Bessemer explained his success in devising an industrial process for steel production in this way: "I had an immense advantage over many others dealing with the problem inasmuch as I had no fixed ideas derived from long established practice to control and bias my mind, and did not suffer from the general belief that whatever is, is right" (quoted in Beveridge 1957, p. 5). Likewise, when chemist Pasteur was urged by his former teacher Dumas to tackle the disease that threatened the French silk industry, his protest "But I never worked with silkworms" was countered with "So much the better" (Asimov 1982, p. 423). Pasteur then advanced from one domain of ignorance to another, eventually propounding the germ theory of disease and introducing inoculation for rabies, among other feats that founded the basis for modern medicine.

Unfortunately, even if these stories make the concept plausible, little empirical work has been done to assess directly the role of professional marginality. Gieryn and Hirsh (1983) tried to gauge the association between marginality and innovation in X-ray astronomy. Even though they concluded that marginality bore little connection to innovativeness, a closer inspection of their data indicated that approximately 20% of the variation in innovation could be explained by their seven indicators of professional marginality (Simonton 1984e). In addition, Stewart (1986) conducted a quantitative inquiry into the early reception of Alfred Wegener's continental drift theory that found that (1) opponents were more likely to have published numerous articles in mainstream geology and that (2) proponents were more likely to have been scientists who were in some discipline other than the geosciences. Both of these results are in line with the hypothesized impact of professional marginality. So enough evidence exists to advise further research on this interesting issue. Nevertheless, the discussion offered earlier in this chapter also cautions future investigators to test for curvilinear as well as linear functions. When we examined the repercussions of role models and formal education on the development of creative potential, we surmised that the necessary compromise between traditionalism and iconoclasm implies a single-peaked, concave-downward curve. Plotting innovativeness as a function of professional marginality may yield parallel graphs. This possibility may apply to sociocultural marginality as well.

Thus, whatever the theoretical plausibility, there is little quantitative evidence for the conclusion that marginality, whether sociocultural or professional, enhances creative potential. Even so, some research has been carried out on yet a third kind of marginality, namely, geographic marginality, but this has been shown to have an adverse impact on creative development. That is, those creators born and raised far away from the cultural center of their day may face an uphill struggle for recognition, at least in aesthetic fields (Simonton 1977b, 1984a, 1986a). Although we cannot say for certain whether this negative relationship holds for the scientific enterprise equally well, the fact that the best scientists tend to study at the élite institutions (presumably at the current centers of creative activity) could be cited as possible support (see, e.g., Crane 1965; Eagly 1974; Zuckerman 1977). Also supportive is the finding that metropolitan areas produce a larger percentage per capita of distinguished scientists than do rural regions (Berry 1981). Further, the chance-configuration theory leads us to expect congruence. So-called provincials are likely deprived of the diversified and stimulating environments to be found in the capitals of civilization, with corresponding losses in the creative potential that can be developed (see Elliott 1975). Hence, further empirical studies on geographic marginality, focused on its linkage with scientific creativity, are needed.

Zeitgeist

In the section on formal education, we recognized how the scientific "spirit of the times" may mediate the developmental consequence of instruction. Several generational analyses have revealed, too, that the more broadly defined zeitgeist exerts an independent influence on creative development (Simonton 1978a). What transpires in generation *g* establishes the environmental context for the development of creators in generation *g* + 1 (Simonton 1984c). These cross-generational effects are of two primary types, sociocultural and political.

Sociocultural effects

The creative activity of one generation affects the probable creative output of the next in many ways. The impact of role-model availability that we discussed previously is one example. Because the quantity and quality of creative scientists depend on the supply of potential mentors and models in the preceding two generations, scientific geniuses tend to cluster together in time and space, as described by Kroeber (1944) and Yuasa (1974). Not only may the prior generation determine the opportunities for achievement in the following generation, but the content of the predecessors' contributions also may direct the course taken by their successors. For example, in the history of ideas, the prevalence of certain philosophical beliefs in one generation leads to the emergence of other beliefs in the succeeding generation, whether as reaction or as development (Simonton 1978c). The advent of empiricism tends to stimulate the appearance two decades later of materialism, individualism, conceptualism (i.e., universals are only mental constructs), and skepticism – intellectual trends that favor scientific growth (cf. Simonton 1976c). In turn, the prominence of empiricist thinkers in one generation has an ideational origin in the previous generation's preoccupation with nominalism, or the view that universals are but names.

Although many more examples can be given of intergenerational effects in the history of ideas, the main point is that the intellectual fascinations of one generation of intellectuals can inspire the ideas of the next generation. Thus the epistemological notion that immediate sensory experience is the source of all knowledge, or empiricism, becomes a natural component of other philosophical constructions, such as the awareness that knowledge ensues from a material process of physical stimuli striking physiological sense organs, that we as individuals are responsible for acquiring knowledge rather than receiving ideas more directly and infallibly via revelation, that abstractions are only mental creations used to coordinate the diversity of stimuli, and that our ability to know is vulnerable to the imperfections of sensation, as illustrated by the perceptual illusions (Simonton 1978c).

More directly relevant to understanding scientific innovation, however, are those studies that suggest how the discoveries and inventions of one discipline may insert the raw materials for contributions in neighboring disciplines after a one-generation delay (Simonton 1976e). The most interesting case is perhaps the finding that the chances for creative progress in biology are enhanced whenever the immediately preceding generations took major strides in medicine, geology, and chemistry. Specifically, the number of major discoveries in biology is a positive function of the number of landmark contributions that emerged about a quarter of a century earlier in these three disciplines. The development of creative potential in a future biologist is evidently nourished by the addition of new interdisciplinary ideas that enter into later chance permutations. The tremendous impression made by Lyell's *Principles of Geology* on the young naturalist on the *Beagle,* Charles Darwin, is one of numerous examples. Intergenerational effects such as these may equally represent at the aggregate level the role of professional marginality that supposedly operates at the individual level. The marginal scientists may be precisely the ones who carry over the key findings of one field into another field when those principles, facts, or techniques have interdisciplinary implications.

I confess that all these investigations are exploratory, and thus the generalizations are tenuous. But my remarks should stimulate more confirmatory research showing how one generation creates the mental elements used by the subsequent generation in its creative integrations.

Political effects

Far more intriguing than the sociocultural effects, in my view, are the instances in which the political milieu in generation g shapes the path taken by creativity in generation $g + 1$. It has been often speculated that nationalism is positively linked with creative development, whereas the emergence of large empires is antithetical to later creative fertility. Kroeber (1944) noted how rare it is for suppressed nationalities to make monumental contributions to human culture; Toynbee (1946) observed that the creative activity of a given civilization is negatively related to the expansion of "universal states"; and Sorokin (1947) said that many nation-alities reach the climax of their creativity right after their liberation from foreign domination. This historical generalization may be called the "Dani-levsky law," after the naturalist and philosophical historian who promul-gated it as his "second law of the dynamics of great cultures," namely, that "in order for civilization of a potentially creative group to be con-ceived and developed, the group and its subgroups must be politically independent" (quoted in Sorokin 1947, p. 543).

These theoretical speculations have been confirmed empirically, for cre-ativity in all domains, science included, increases whenever a multicultural civilization area is fragmented into a large number of sovereign nations, the growth of empire states signaling the decline of cultural innovation (Naroll et al. 1971; Schaefer, Babu, & Rao 1977; Simonton 1975e, 1976f; cf. Ting 1986). Such political fragmentation apparently augments cultural and ideo-logical diversity, a condition – via the influx of more variation in available elements – that promotes the emergence of individuals with exceptional cre-ative potential (Simonton 1976d). Political fragmentation also favors an ideological zeitgeist that may better shelter the developing scientist, namely, empiricism, materialism, nominalism, evolutionism, and individualism – characteristics, it may be argued, that give more free reign to an inquiring mind (Simonton 1976g). There are data that support the frequent conjecture that the collapse of controls during periods of political upheaval prepares the ground for fruitful creativity later (e.g., Barnett 1953). For example, revolts and rebellions directed against the hegemony of empires tend to increase creativity after a one-generation lag, an effect likely due to the resurgence of cultural heterogeneity (i.e., nationalism) against the homogenizing imposi-tions of imperial systems (Simonton 1975e). And civil disturbances generally tend to mix the cultural broth, thereby resuscitating the zeitgeist most friendly to creative growth (Simonton 1975e, 1976g).

In the preceding examples, political events may contribute to creative development by increasing the diversity of mental elements likely to enter chance permutations, in much the same way as does sociocultural and professional marginality. Nonetheless, not all violent or dramatic events in the political sphere have this pleasant outcome. Wars between states, for instance, tend to produce an ideological zeitgeist that may not welcome innovation (Simonton 1976g), and creativity is unlikely to come forth after a political system crumbles into total anarchy, as registered by military revolts, dynastic conflicts, political assassinations, coups d'état, and other examples of chaos among the power élite (Simonton 1975e, 1976f).

It is difficult to subsume these particular findings under the present theoretical scheme, but the essential tension between traditionalism and iconoclasm may once more offer an interpretative clue. On the one hand, wartime propaganda and patriotism may excessively reinforce traditionalism at the expense of iconoclasm; for instance, war indeed discourages the emergence of individualism and empiricism (Simonton 1976g). On the other hand, an era of political instability may instill in the forthcoming generation a debilitating iconoclasm, a distrust of tradition that may verge on nihilism. It is telling that the more rational and systematic endeavors, like science and philosophy, are more inhibited by political anarchy than are artistic activities, like painting and sculpture, for which iconoclasm is presumably more desirable (Simonton 1975e,f).

Conclusion

The goal of this chapter was to review some of the chief developmental factors that may contribute to the acquisition of creative potential. In the broadest terms, it should be clear that the several sets of developmental antecedents – family background, role models, formal education, marginality, and zeitgeist – influence the extent to which the child, adolescent, and young adult will possess an unusual number of profusely interassociated mental elements (Simonton 1987a,c). Though a few of these influences, such as birth order, may operate by augmenting the raw intellectual capacity for storing elements, most variables probably function as stimuli that nurture the cognitive style requisite for generating chance permutations. These inputs favor the emergence of an intuitive genius over an analytical genius. The intuitive genius can effectively appear only in a diversified and unconventional context, such as that nourished by parental loss, marginality, and a sociocultural milieu full of varied and novel events. Naturally, this picture contains a few complexities.

First, some of the observed relationships between environmental diversity and creative development may be the spurious result of genotype–environment effects. Thus, highly gifted parents may have highly gifted children and concomitantly construct a home environment filled with cultural stimuli that in fact make no direct contribution to their children's intellectual growth. And when talented youths reach a suitable age, they may actively shape their environments to be consistent with their genotypic disposition. This could include the selection of role models or educational experiences so as to produce the mere illusion of an environmental effect. Nevertheless, because the genetic interpretation can take us only so far in integrating all the data on creative development, at some point explanations in terms of nurture rather than nature become more plausible. It is certainly difficult to order all the results on parental loss, birth order, role models, education, marginality, and the sociocultural context to march under the banner of inherited personality.

Another complication regards the frequent intrusion of curvilinear functions. The research on role models and formal education, in particular, has come forth with nonmonotonic, concave-downward curves that indicate an ambivalence in how these developmental antecedents impinge on creative potential. These functions were interpreted as the essential tension between the iconoclasm necessary for uninhibited chance permutations and the traditionalism required to optimize the odds that any resulting configurations will earn social acceptance and thus prove influential. Furthermore, we predicted that similar curvilinear functions may be found elsewhere as well, as in the operation of professional marginality. In fact, we can speculate that such single-peak functions are more ubiquitous than so far indicated by the literature. As a case in point, we surmised that events that disrupt stereotyped socialization practices, such as parental loss, assist the development of creative potential, a point also repeatedly found in the research (e.g., Goertzel & Goertzel 1962; Simonton 1987c). Even so, we can readily imagine a family situation so troublesome, so chaotic, that entirely iconoclastic offspring emerge who, as adults, are mere nihilistic "rebels without a cause." Indeed, juvenile delinquents and suicidal depressed patients are two groups with incidences of orphanhood comparable to those observed for eminent personalities (Eisenstadt 1978; cf. Crook & Eliot 1980). Consequently, future research may find it profitable to calculate composite scores made up of the many ways of interjecting complexity and variety into cognitive development and then to test for curvilinearity when estimating the relationship between these aggregated scores and achieved eminence. Nonmonotonic functions may be found, too, for the sociocultural and political variables. A central point made by Arnold Toynbee in his *Study of History* (1946) is that the creative growth of a civilization requires a response to challenge, yet that challenge must lie at the "golden mean" between excessive adversity that arrests further advance and the easy life that encourages a culture to lapse into complacency. Although the few tests of this hypothesis have failed to confirm it (e.g., Naroll et al. 1971; Simonton 1975e; Ting 1986), the conjecture is well worth pursuing in additional inquiries (Hagen 1962).

A final nicety is related to the preceding: Any nonlinear equation expressing creative achievement as a function of a developmental variable would, according to theory, exhibit a single peak, yet the precise location of that optimal point is contingent on the specific endeavor under discussion. The best compromise between traditionalism and iconoclasm varies according to the nature of the contribution. Thus artistic creativity, which demands more intuitive or primary-process thought, is favored by more untoward environments, whereas scientific creativity, which mandates more analytical or secondary-process thought, especially in formulating effective communication configurations, has a peak that leans more toward the traditionalist end of the spectrum. In fact, artistic creators do tend, on the average, to come from more unstable and diversified environments, as compared with those of scientists (see, e.g., Berry 1981; Goertzel et al. 1978; Raskin 1936; Schaefer & Anastasi 1968; Simonton 1986b). Moreover, even when we concentrate solely on scientific creativity, we have plenty of reason for suspecting that the curves maximize at distinct locales corresponding to the scientist's specific contribution to exact, objective, and systematic knowledge. Precursors have their optima near the iconoclast end of the scale, advancers near the traditionalist end, whereas the revolutionaries fall somewhere between – another "golden mean" if we grant the most praise to the revolutionaries. These divergent maxima should immediately affect the particular manner in which the numerous developmental antecedents encourage or discourage the accumulation of creative potential. Still, more empirical work is needed to untangle this intricate web of suggested influences.

6   Multiple discovery and invention

The zeitgeist interpretation of multiples

In the last chapter we discussed how the sociocultural and political milieu may sway the course of creative development. We have evidence, too, that the zeitgeist can guide the adulthood realization of that creative potential. In fact, the situational context has been shown to affect the manifestation of all kinds of historical impact, whether political and military leadership (e.g., Simonton 1979b, 1980b, 1981c, 1984g, 1986e, 1987e) or the diverse guises of creativity (e.g., Simonton 1976f, 1980e, 1984a). In the case of scientific creativity, discoveries and inventions are more apt to appear in particular political, ideological, and cultural settings. For example, scientific advances are more likely to appear under peacetime, as compared with wartime, conditions (Simonton 1976e, 1980c) and under a cultural ideology that favors empiricism, materialism, nominalism, individualism, and determinism rather than mysticism, idealism, realism, statism, and the doctrine of free will (Simonton 1976c; cf. Sorokin 1937–1941). Economic prosperity may also contribute to the growth of scientific knowledge and the acquisition of technological expertise (cf. Rainoff 1929; Schmookler 1966, chap. 6). In addition, different extrinsic conditions may encourage distinctive types of creativity (Simonton 1975c), and various subdisciplines within science may be nurtured by a characteristic set of sociocultural circumstances (Simonton 1975d).

Nonetheless, one phenomenon has frequently been cited as the single best proof of the zeitgeist's participation – multiple discovery and invention. This phenomenon occurs whenever two or more scientists, working independently and often simultaneously, make the exact same contribution to science. Classic illustrations are the devising of calculus by Newton and Leibniz, the prediction of the planet Neptune by J. C. Adams and Le-Verrier, the formulation of the law of the conservation of energy by Mayer, Helmholtz, and Joule, the production of oxygen by Scheele and Priestley, the proposal of a theory of evolution through natural selection by Darwin and Wallace, the introduction of ether anesthesia in surgery by Long and Morton, and the invention of the telephone by Bell and Gray. Investigators have compiled extensive lists of such multiples, some running into the hundreds of separate cases: Ogburn and Thomas (1922) gleaned 148 from the annals of science, Merton (1961b) 264, and Simonton (1979a) 579 (see also Kroeber 1917; Lamb & Easton 1984; Stern 1927). Moreover, it has been argued on several grounds that such compilations, if anything, under-report the true incidence of multiples (Merton 1961b; Simonton 1978b). Indeed, so prevalent is this phenomenon that the existence of multiples was itself multiply discovered, a self-endorsing oddity that was in its turn noted by more than one independent scholar (Kroeber 1944; Merton 1961b).

The traditional interpretation of multiples was promulgated largely by sociologists and anthropologists (especially Kroeber 1917; Ogburn & Thomas 1922; Merton 1961a,b; White 1940, chap. 8), although a psychologist as eminent as E. G. Boring (1963) was enlisted in partial support (see Lamb & Easton 1984, chap. 1). Briefly, multiples are said to prove conclusively that the causal source of scientific advance lies outside the individual, for the sociocultural system, or the zeitgeist, determines the time for a given contribution. At a given moment in scientific history, particular discoveries or inventions become absolutely inevitable, in a supreme illustration of sociocultural determinism. Scientific progress, therefore, does not depend on acts of genius, for individual scientists are only interchangeable mouthpieces for their times, and correspondingly they are epiphenomenal to the course of history. Even the star scientists do not create or contribute but merely convey what the times have preordained to have a unity probability of appearing at an instant in history. Contributions are "in the air," which creators simply breathe. The anthropologist Alfred Kroeber (1917, p. 199) maintained with respect to the simultaneous and independent rediscovery of Mendel's laws by DeVries, Correns, and Tschermak, that "it was discovered in 1900 because it could have been discovered only then, and because it infallibly must have been discovered then." In broader terms, the sociologist Robert K. Merton (1961a, p. 306) asserted that "discoveries and inventions become virtually inevitable (1) as prerequisite kinds of knowledge accumulate in man's cultural store; (2) as the attention of a sufficient number of investigators is focused on a problem – by emerging social needs, or by developments internal to the particular science, or by both."

Notwithstanding that this traditional, zeitgeist interpretation has become widely accepted as near gospel (see, e.g., Whyte 1950), this position does have its critics (e.g., Schmookler 1966, chap. 19; Simonton 1987d). We cannot, nor should not, delve into all the logical and empirical objections that can be raised, for our main purpose here is to discuss how multiples can be explained according to the chance-configuration theory. Clearly, if the traditional explanation were valid, then the theoretical scheme offered in this book may be mistaken, because at some level the chance permutations must be predetermined to come out in a specified way–a seeming contradiction (Lamb & Easton 1984, chap. 2). Furthermore, as usually interpreted, the multiples phenomenon implies that scientific creativity functions on a different basis, compared with artistic creativity, despite all that we proposed in the preceding chapters. No lists have been compiled of multiples in music, literature, or the visual arts, nor has anyone yet claimed that the Fifth Symphony, *Hamlet,* and the Sistine Chapel ceiling would have entered our cultural heritage had Beethoven, Shakespeare, and Michelangelo all died in the crib. So it may be that the current theory is far more applicable to the arts than to the sciences. Perhaps discoveries and inventions, driven by impersonal and deterministic forces, are inevitable, whereas aesthetic creations alone emerge by chance (see also Lamb & Easton 1984, chap. 9; Stent 1972). That I am not setting up a false problem is revealed by Price (1963, p. 69), who stressed "the basic difference that exists between creative effort in the sciences and in the arts. If Michelangelo and Beethoven had not existed, their works would have been replaced by quite different contributions. If Copernicus or Fermi had never existed, essentially the same contributions would have had to come from other people."

Nevertheless, I shall show that multiples, far from providing convincing evidence of the zeitgeist hypothesis, actually offer some of the best evidence available for bolstering the chance-configuration theory. To make this case, let me review the definitional and empirical inadequacies of the traditional account and then sketch some Monte Carlo models that simulate the most salient properties of the multiples phenomenon (cf. Simonton 1987d). Along the way, the virtues of our alternative explanation will be made explicit. In particular, we should recognize the insight to be found in Donald Campbell's own germ of an interpretation: "If science is in part a trial-and-error process with many participants exploring variations upon the accepted body of science at any one time . . . then multiple independent discoveries of the same principle seem inevitable, given enough participants in the scientific process" (Campbell & Tauscher 1966, pp. 59–60).

Definitional issues

Assessment of the explanatory adequacy of the zeitgeist theory hinges on four distinctions: universal versus particular, independence versus antecedence, simultaneity versus rediscovery, and inevitability versus eventuality.

Universal versus particular

Merton (1961b, p. 477) was so convinced that multiples represent typical events that he maintained that "it is the singletons–discoveries made only once in the history of science–that are the residual cases, requiring special explanation" and that "all scientific discoveries are in principle multiples, including those that on the surface appear to be singletons." Even though Merton presented 10 overlapping reasons for adopting so extreme a stance (cf. Brannigan 1981, pp. 52–54), counterarguments are easily proposed that make multiples the exceptional events and singletons the normal state of affairs–just as our intuitions might have it (cf. Lamb & Easton 1984, chap. 5). Schmookler (1966, p. 191) scrutinized the standard list of nearly 150 multiples published by Ogburn and Thomas (1922) and concluded that this collection "is based on a failure to distinguish between the genus and the individual." For example, in the enumeration of technological multiples, generic terms such as *telegraph, steamboat,* and *airplane* are permitted to obscure the fact that the putative "duplicates" were often completely different conceptions. To offer my own example, the advent of photography is often credited to both Talbot, working in England, and Niépce and Daguerre, working in France, yet the inventions were quite distinct: The former made a negative image on paper, and the latter a positive image on metal, both using different photochemical processes. Likewise, a detailed study of both steam turbines and Pelton waterwheels demonstrated that neither can be counted as a multiple in any proper sense; each claimed duplicate turns out, on careful inspection, to have originated in combinations of different elements, even when convergent evolution interjected some superficial similarities in the final designs (Constant 1978). Schmookler (1966) pointed out, as well, that interference proceedings that emerge from applications at the United States Patent Office cannot be expropriated as evidence for the identity of rival patent claims. Each patent may normally list a large number of separate claims, sometimes over 100, whereas an interference proceeding may result if just one claim overlaps that of another patent application. And such proceedings arise for only 1 or 2% of the time anyhow.

Nor can Schmookler's objection be confined to just inventions: It is an oversimplification to say that "the" principle of energy conservation was discovered by several scientists (Kuhn 1977, chap. 4) or even that J. C. Adams and LeVerrier discovered the "same" planet Neptune, given how different their predicted orbits were (Simonton 1987d). One fascinating peculiarity about many hypothesized scientific multiples is that frequently two or more persons are said to have discovered the same abstract entity, even though the mental elements that were manipulated to arrive at the given conclusion were not the same: G. P. Thomson scattered cathode rays with a thin metallic film, and C. J. Davisson bombarded a nickel crystal with monokinetic electrons, but they shared the Nobel Prize for demonstrating the wave properties of electrons; both Scheele and Priestley may have generated oxygen, or rather "fire air" and "dephlogisticated air" (respectively), but in the former case by heating silver carbonate, manganese dioxide, and other substances that only loosely held onto contained oxygen, and in the latter case by heating mercuric oxide; Le Bel was trying to account for the molecular symmetry discovered by Pasteur, whereas Van't Hoff was more interested in the quadrivalent carbon atom advanced by Kekulé, although both ended up with similar ideas about how molecular structure is linked with optical activity; and J. Pecquet described the thoracic duct in dogs, Eustachio the same duct in horses, neither appreciating at the time the generality of this anatomical feature. Nuclear magnetic resonance was independently and simultaneously observed in 1946 by Purcell, Torrey, and Pound at Harvard, and by Bloch, Hansen, and Packard at Stanford, for which Block and Purcell shared the Nobel Prize 11 years later. Nonetheless, even though physicists "have come to look at the two experiments as practically identical," said Purcell, "when Hansen first showed up [at our lab] and started talking about it, it was about an hour before either of us understood how the other was trying to explain it" (quoted in Zuckerman 1977, p. 203). Such examples are often most reminiscent of biological evolution, in which distinct phylogenetic lines converged on analogous morphological features that may be mistaken for homologous features rooted in an ancestral prototype (see also Lamb & Easton 1984, pp. 67–69).

Furthermore, even if independent discoveries or inventions may have some components in common, very often one contribution is more fully developed than another (cf. Stent 1972). Ogburn and Thomas (1922, p. 93) themselves confessed, in a footnote, that "the most serious difficulty in making the list is the fact that the contribution of one person is in some cases more complete than that of another." They gave the example of the nebular hypothesis of the origin of the solar system, Laplace's treatment being far more advanced and sophisticated than Kant's earlier speculation – but many more illustrations may be culled from the lists of conjectured duplicates. Both Abel and Ruffini are recognized as originators of the "Abel-Ruffini theorem" in mathematics, but the former's proof was by far the more rigorous; Le Bel may be honored along with Van't Hoff for recognizing the connection between molecular structure and optical activity, but this is an act of generosity, given that the latter's analysis was appreciably more precise; Higgins protested Dalton's priority in introducing atomic theory into chemistry, yet Higgins did not fully develop his ideas and committed such big mistakes as assigning all atoms the same weight; and Cesalpino may have speculated on the greater circulation of the blood, but it was Harvey who transformed this germinal idea into an empirical demonstration that firmly planted it in subsequent medical science.

Patinkin (1983) persuasively argued that two scientists should not be credited with the same contribution unless the idea in question is the "central message" of both claimants (cf. Graber 1985; Patinkin 1985). Patinkin illustrated his point by scrutinizing and then rejecting the claims that both the Polish economist Micheł Kalecki and the Stockholm school of economics had participated in the multiple discovery of what now is called "Keynesian economics." Yet the same principle can be applied as a test for many other theoretical and empirical offerings in science. J. L. Meyer willingly admitted, for instance, the preeminence of Mendeléev in the establishment of the periodic law of the elements, for not only did the latter examine the relation between atomic weight and chemical valence (rather than atomic volume), but Mendeléev also was bold enough to stand by his theory to the point of placing elements out of order with regard to atomic weight and even to predict the existence of undiscovered elements where gaps appeared in his table (Kochen & Lansing 1985). For Mendeléev, unlike Meyer, the periodic law was a central message not just of a single paper, or his popular chemistry textbook, but of his entire career.

Any scientist capable of generating a massive corpus of publications will in all likelihood add many parenthetical remarks, incidental observations, or tangential speculations couched in digressive asides or hidden footnotes. To assign these ideational fragments the same status as completely elaborated and documented contributions is to trivialize the scientific enterprise. If Einstein's theory of relativity asserted nothing more than that "everything's relative" – as his revolutionary ideas are frequently encapsulated in popularized science – then, sure enough, Einstein had many, many anticipators! Likewise, numerous naturalists before Charles Darwin, from the Greeks on, casually referred to natural selection as an agent in the evolution of life, but only in the *Origin of Species* were the full ramifications of this ideational germ expounded in a convincing manner (Zirkle 1941). To say that neither Einstein nor Darwin proposed something original to human culture is to succumb to the error of what Merton (1961b, p. 474) styled "adumbrationism," or "the denigrating of new ideas by pretending to find them old."

According to the present theory, even when two contributions can be said to contain the same combinations of elements, their permutations may be different. That is, the various ideas composing the configuration may be assigned incongruent priorities, or divergent orders of emphasis. Wallace's theory of evolution had the same essential ingredients as did Darwin's, yet the underlining was at variance. As one example, for Darwin the evolution of the human species by natural selection became a central point, whereas for Wallace natural selection could not account for the emergence of the human brain (Eiseley, 1958, chap. 9). Curiously, there is reason to believe that Gregor Mendel may not deserve credit for discovering Mendelian genetics, for what 20th-century biologists found so significant in his 1865 papers was only a peripheral part of the main discussion, which concerned hybridization (Brannigan 1979). In a sense, DeVries, Correns, and Tschermak did not independently rediscover Mendel in 1900 but, rather, collectively distorted him (see also Olby 1979).

In fact, this last point intimates that many supposed multiples may better exemplify the tendency for historical hindsight to be myopic. That is, as events recede into the past, details are lost, and therefore crucial distinctions tend to become blurred. Evidence has been gathered that shows that the further back in time we go, the larger will be the number of separate scientists credited with the same contribution, and the longer will be the time span between the first and last duplications (Brannigan & Wanner 1983b). Although later in this chapter we shall give such findings a theoretical interpretation, these secular trends could just as well be considered methodological artifacts (Simonton 1987d). Historians may be less prone to assign excessively generic labels to more recent events, because of their greater awareness of how separate the contributions really are. This methodological possibility illustrates how precarious the identification of valid multiples is.

To summarize, by converting several distinct particulars into a single universal, those who compiled exhaustive lists of multiples too often overlooked critical contrasts in the content and organization of the elements defining each separate case. Of course, it may be too much to expect the duplication to be perfect, but frequently this supposed redundancy in scientific creativity is not even approximate. Those discoveries or inventions subsumed under one abstract label may have different elements, and when the same elements are present they may be configured in contrary ways. Herein arises the reason that artistic multiples are thought to be so rare, if any have been claimed to exist at all. More particularistic categories are assigned to artistic creations, more universalistic categories to scientific creations. Quite contrary results would obtain were we to reverse this order of affairs. On the scientific side, how many independent scientists wrote, or would have written, Newton's *Principia Mathematica* or Darwin's *Origin of Species*? These products are undoubtedly unique, not just in specific word order, but also in conceptual style and theoretical emphasis – and this uniqueness will remain no matter how long human civilization persists. On the other hand, how many artists can be credited with "a C-minor symphony," "a play about a son revenging his father's murder," or "a painting depicting scenes from *Genesis*?" Given such generic terms, the contributions of Beethoven, Shakespeare, and Michelangelo lose their uniqueness. Thus whether in art or science we can always gerrymander the dimension of universals versus particulars in order to maximize or minimize the odds of true multiples occurring. Scientific innovations are no more or less unique than are artistic innovations when we apply labels at roughly equal levels of abstraction (see also Stent 1972).

Independence versus antecedence

The excessive reliance on highly generic definitions in many compilations of multiples may betray a certain desperation by those advocating the traditional, zeitgeist interpretation. Why else would Ogburn and Thomas (1922) find Boerhaave and Hales as independently responsible for a contribution so vague and abstract as the "beginnings of modern organic chemistry"? This desperation – or at least this uncritical enthusiasm for spotting multiples almost anywhere – is revealed in yet another feature of so many enumerated multiples: In many cases the supposed participants in a putative duplication did not work in strict independence. A few examples illustrate: N. Abel and Jacobi both built on Legendre's earlier efforts, and therefore all three should not be credited with elliptic functions; Descartes may have known of Snell's law of refraction before publishing his own version; Galileo certainly did not conceive his own telescope until he had already heard of its invention by Dutch lens grinders; Dolland probably exploited without due credit C. M. Hall's ideas about devising an achromatic lens; Clausius, Rankine, and Waterston all should not have been honored for the independent development of the kinetic theory of gases when Rankine was aware of Waterston's prior work; and McCormick's own reaper was conceived in full cognizance of the machine already developed and demonstrated by P. Bell. It goes without saying that full independence is absolutely essential to the definition of a multiple if that term is to have any meaning whatsoever. Independence must be divorced from antecedence.

Of course, sometimes the scientists and inventors themselves are to blame for confusing the issue. The quest for fame and fortune often inspires the more unscrupulous to make unjustified claims to priority or independence. Lavoisier evidently had a special weakness in this respect, often repeating experiments conducted by others, such as Cavendish and

Priestley, and then demanding credit for the discovery, whether it be the composition of water or the element oxygen. Similarly, Morse failed to give proper recognition for the help he received from J. Henry in the invention of a workable telegraph. And DeVries may have come across Mendel's paper before completing his own experiments in genetics but dishonestly insisted otherwise (Brannigan 1979). Sometimes the process is reversed, as when Morton turned C. T. Jackson's mere suggestion of ether anesthesia into a demonstrated surgical practice, only to see Jackson assert his priority; Jackson protested that a similar misfortune happened to him with regard to the telegraph, Morse allegedly taking advantage of some conversations they had on a transAtlantic passenger ship. Naturally, often it is difficult to identify the direction and magnitude of influence, for the impact of one scientist on another may take indirect routes. Besides unknown access to unpublished manuscripts – as in Newton's unsubstantiated accusation that Leibniz plagiarized the calculus after seeing papers circulated among Newton's associates – one scientist can discover what another has accomplished through various intermediaries. Magendie may have found out through a student about C. Bell's ideas on the sensory and motor functions of spinal nerve-roots. Yet other times the lack of independence is so obvious that we are amazed that it was not noticed by the list makers. Fulton is placed along with Jouffroy, Rumsey, Stevens, Symington, and Fitch in the invention of the steamboat, yet Fulton specifically acknowledged the previous efforts of Jouffroy and even attended the trials of the ship constructed by Symington!

Again, I suspect that the proponents of the traditional interpretation got so carried away with documenting their thesis that their standards of evidence often lapsed. As a consequence, oddities are committed, such as crediting Clairaut, Euler, and d'Alembert all with the 1747 "solution of the problem of three bodies" when this problem has yet to be completely solved (Ogburn & Thomas 1922). But perhaps the prime example of this lapse is Kroeber's (1948) listing of Peary and Cook as multiple "discoverers" of the North Pole. He admitted that Cook's claim was probably fraudulent but stated nevertheless that the moment was ripe for a fake attempt, just as it was for a genuine discovery. Maybe so, yet Cook's assertion of priority was likely in response to Peary's much-publicized success and thus certainly cannot be counted as an independent effort!

Simultaneity versus rediscovery

The suspicion of interdependence becomes especially real when the separate contributions making up a multiple are divided by many years.

In Merton's (1961b) compilation of 264 multiples, 20% occurred within a one-year interval and another 18% within two years, whereas fully 34% required a decade or more to elapse before the last duplicate appeared. Indeed, in some instances supposed duplications may be divided by hundreds, even thousands of years, such as the discovery of the "Eustachian" tubes by Alcmaeon and Eustachio, the principles of hydrostatics by Archimedes and Stevinus, and the transit of Venus across the sun by al-Kindi and Horrocks. This magnitude of temporal separation not only raises doubts about the true independence of the participants, but it also casts a dark shadow over the traditional account as an explanation of scientific creativity. If at a given moment in history the laws of genetics had to be discovered, why did they have to be rediscovered? It is too glib to assert that Mendel was "ahead of his time"; if the time defines the generative mechanism, then such a circumstance is impossible!

The traditional interpretation obviously failed to distinguish between scientific creativity taking place within the individual mind and the social acceptance of an idea by the larger scientific community. The zeitgeist may influence which contributions are accepted but not necessarily which contributions are offered for colleagues' consideration. In the words of William James (1880, p. 448),

social evolution is a resultant of the interaction of two wholly distinct factors: the individual, deriving his peculiar gifts from the play of psychological and infra-social forces, but bearing all the power initiative and origination in his hands; and, second, the social environment, with its power of adopting or rejecting both him and his gifts.

Again in the present theoretical language, the chance-permutation process can generate many configurations without regard for the sociocultural milieu, yet whether those configurations can be converted into communication configurations that will succeed in the domain of interpersonal influence is altogether another matter.

In some instances a preoffered finding will be "premature" in the sense that "its implications cannot be connected by a series of simple logical steps to canonical, or generally accepted, knowledge" (Stent 1972, p. 84). Premature discoveries and inventions do not propel members of the scientific community toward augmented self-organization, toward enhanced information-processing efficiency. Indeed, if a finding or proposition is truly premature, it can only undermine the cognitive order of prospective acceptors and thereby provoke them, at worst, to attack or, at best, to ignore the obtrusive intellectual challenge. Only later, after new elements have been added to the mix, and especially after a scientific revolution has obliged a restructuring of those elements into a new pattern, will a niche emerge for the premature contribution to fit comfortably in the larger hierarchical scheme of knowledge. Hence, "the times were not ripe" for a mathematical theory of heredity in 1865, but the zeitgeist became more appreciative in 1900. The milieu did not, in any case, determine when Mendel would offer his theory and data to the world of science.

This discussion leads, I think, to two conclusions. First, the very occurrence of premature discoveries should force us to discount the traditional explication of multiples generation. The zeitgeist affects the social-acceptance process far more than the chance-permutation operation. Second, the inclusion of rediscoveries in the lists of multiples is of questionable validity, confounding as it does events with distinct etiologies and implications. A rediscovery reveals how the sociocultural milieu can allow an ideational combination to emerge without also permitting it to influence others in the scientific community.

Inevitability versus eventuality

A final definitional problem regards the doctrine of inevitability. Properly speaking, inevitability implies that at some designated time the probability of a specified event occurring becomes unity, or nearly so. Yet a closer inspection of how the word is used in practice reveals that the advocates of zeitgeist confuse necessary causes with necessary and sufficient clauses and thereby are nearly guilty of a malapropism: Rather than use the adverb *inevitably,* they should have used the far weaker word *eventually.* Contrary to what Merton (1961b) affirmed, the accumulation of prerequisite knowledge in the cultural repertoire does not *make* a discovery happen but only *allows* it to happen, eventually. Given all the mental elements needed for a given scientific synthesis and granted sufficient time, chance permutations will eventually generate all possible configurations of those elements, including the desired synthesis – but that is not equivalent to saying that such an outcome is inevitable, except in the loosest sense. Scientific history is replete with discoveries that could have just as well been created much earlier than they were, in regard to prerequisites (Simonton 1987d). A. J. P. Martin, who shared the 1952 Nobel Prize for Chemistry with his colleague R. Synge for their development of paper chromatography, dismissed the value of this contribution by saying that "all the ideas are simple and had peoples' minds been directed that way the method would have flourished perhaps a century earlier" (quoted in Daintith, Mitchell, & Tootill 1981, p. 531).

The common occurrence of rediscoveries establishes the generality of this last remark. If a contribution can truly be proven to amount to nothing more than a rediscovery of an idea promulgated decades, if not centuries, earlier, then obviously the presence of the hypothesized necessary conditions cannot ensure the immediate realization of the corresponding concept. The requisite elements for a given synthesis may be "in the air" for generations without necessarily coalescing in the mind of a single scientist. The advent of the telescope did not mean that the sunspots would be noticed at once, despite the apparent lapse of only about a year and its multiple discovery to boot (by Galileo, Scheiner, Fabricius, and others all within a year of one another). The Chinese had observed sunspots over a millennium earlier *without* a telescope. And on the other side of the coin, the microscope had been around long before Leeuwenhoek decided to use it to look at a sundry collection of everyday objects – to discover protozoa, bacteria, spermatozoa, blood corpuscles, and the like. Hence, a plus or minus of decades or more intervenes between the fulfillment of the supposed prerequisites and the accomplished realization of the notion implicit in those prerequisites. The chance-configuration theory, naturally, accommodates such temporal slippage with ease: Given a set of elements, haphazard permutations will eventually generate stable combinations, but whether a particular configuration appears earlier or later in the sequence of ideational trials is ruled solely by chance. A hit may, by good luck, emerge early in the series or, by bad luck, suffer a seemingly "inexplicable" delay. The stochastic variation in the duration of incubation that occurs at the individual level, which we discussed in chapter 2, has its proper counterpart on the sociocultural plane.

In addition, Merton's (1961a) second basis for inevitability – that enough researchers have concentrated on a given problem – again merely specifies more a necessary than a sufficient condition. Provided there are enough scientists with the demanded mental elements and assuming that all can ruminate indefinitely, chance permutations will eventually discover the right configuration, even by two or more researchers. Yet this condition by no means ensures inevitability – no more than it is sensible to maintain that it is inevitable that a room full of monkeys typing randomly will reproduce all the lines of Shakespeare. When the Royal Society announced a prize for work on the laws of the mutual impact of bodies, it inspired enough scientists to labor away on a readily solvable problem that soon a multiple discovery emerged – at the hands of Huygens, Wallis, and Wren – but many other prizes have been publicized by numerous scientific organizations before and since without so dramatic a consequence, yielding either no response or that of a solitary winner. At the time of this writing, immense human and financial resources are being devoted to discovering a practical means of exploiting nuclear fusion. But despite all the manifest social need, the breakthrough is far from inevitable. To be sure, it may be that a necessary component is missing, but even were all the pieces of the puzzle accessible, the large number of researchers would only increase the probability that the crucial discovery will occur sooner rather than later, in either case only eventually.

These definitional difficulties should cause us to question the traditional view that scientific history unfolds in a foreordained sequence of events. If discoveries and inventions, even when the prerequisite elements are present and the social need is manifest, take place only eventually rather than inevitably, the course of subsequent events for which those contributions are required will depend on chance. Social determinism becomes indeterminism (see Schmookler 1966). Further, the unique character of so-called duplicates signifies that it is important which particular scientist succeeds first in making a given contribution. Gunter Stent (1972), a molecular geneticist, developed this point at length with regard to the discovery of the structure of deoxyribonucleic acid (DNA) by Watson and Crick in 1953. After granting that the chemical organization of DNA would have been worked out eventually, Stent nonetheless maintained that it was by no means inevitable that it would have been discovered in precisely the same way. Instead, he speculated that

if Watson and Crick had not existed, the insights they provided in one single package would have come out much more gradually over a period of many months or years. Dr. *B* might have seen that DNA is a double-strand helix, and Dr. *C* might later have recognized the hydrogen bonding between the strands. Dr. *D* later yet might have proposed a complementary purine–pyrimidine bonding, with Dr. *E* in a subsequent paper proposing the specific adenine–thymine and guanine–cytosine nucleotide pairs. Finally, we might have had to wait for Dr. *G* to propose the replication mechanism of DNA based on the complementary nature of the two strands. All the while Drs. *H, I, J, K* and *L* would have been confusing the issue by publishing incorrect structures and proposals. (p. 90)

The single paper published by Watson and Crick in *Nature* was distinguished for a completeness that foreclosed such a piecemeal and confused revelation at the hands of numerous researchers and for a finality that obviated any need for further amendments and glosses. With one stroke, the upshot of a potentially long and haphazard research tradition was encapsulated (see also Watson 1968).

The same lack of social determinism obtains for the mathematical sciences. The advent of calculus is an example. Zeitgeist theorists would have us believe that it is irrelevant who actually introduced the differential calculus, Newton or Leibniz; the calculus would in any case have become one of the techniques used by subsequent generations of scientists. But this interpretation ignores that the specific communication configurations offered by these two men contain different elements, these ordered in distinct ways. Newton's notation, for instance, was far more cumbersome than that introduced by Leibniz, the one in current use, and each was fascinated with a different set of substantive problems for which the calculus provided the means of solution. As a consequence, the direction that the mathematical sciences might have taken would have depended on which version of the calculus had been established. We often forget how much of a scientist's own personality individualizes a contribution, even in so objective an endeavor as mathematics. Boltzmann said that "a mathematician will recognize Cauchy, Gauss, Jacobi, or Helmholtz, after reading a few pages, just as musicians recognize, from the first few bars, Mozart, Beethoven, or Schubert" (quoted in Koestler 1964, p. 265). When Newton once sent an anonymous solution to a mathematical challenge posed to the international community, the recipient immediately recognized "the claw of the lion."

In broad terms, the set of elements that supply the creative potential for each scientist is idiosyncratic, especially in revolutionary scientists whose marginal backgrounds place them outside the mainstream. The creative process, noted Carl Rogers (1954, p. 251), grows "out of the uniqueness of the individual on the one hand, and the materials, events, people, or circumstances of his life on the other." Thus, chance configurations mirror a scientist's personal makeup, with noticeable consequences for the course of science (see also Holton 1982). It is highly unlikely that the theory of evolution by natural selection would have enjoyed such wide acceptance had Wallace been its chief proponent in the latter half of the 19th century. That is, Wallace's proclivities toward spiritualism would have helped discredit an otherwise coherent scientific argument (Eiseley 1958, chap. 9).

This discussion leads us to surmise that scientific contributions are no more inevitable than are artistic creations. Stent (1972) observed in his excellent essay on this issue that once we adduce the essential qualities of a given masterwork in music, literature, or the visual arts, we must admit that creations having those same attributes will eventually appear. Whether we consider aesthetic form, emotional content, or another abstract property, there are qualities belonging to Beethoven's Fifth Symphony, Shakespeare's *Hamlet,* and Michelangelo's Sistine Chapel fresco that most certainly would have emerged at some time or another, albeit under different names and with contrasting particulars. Hence we have another reason to suspect that one theory of creativity may account for significant contributions in both the arts and the sciences.

Empirical questions

If the preceding remarks are insufficient to overthrow the social deterministic account, the empirical data should, for the facts lend far more support to the inference that multiples ensue from stochastic processes (Simonton 1986g). To establish this conclusion, let us simply accept the compilations of multiples on face value, or at the minimum assume that some of the candidates for multiples status are indeed legitimate – that two or more scientists have independently contributed virtually identical configurations. Then we must address four empirical issues, namely, multiple grades, simultaneity, participation, and necessary conditions.

Multiple grades

First we must recognize that hypothesized multiples can be distinguished according to their "grade" (Simonton 1978b). A multiple's grade is simply the number of independent investigators who are reputed to have independently made a given discovery or invention. Thus we can talk of multiples of grades 2 (doublets), 3 (triplets), 4 (quadruplets), 5 (quintuplets), 6 (sextuplets), and so on. To illustrate, according to Ogburn and Thomas (1922, pp. 93–98) the "law of inverse squares" was a grade 2 multiple (Newton, 1666, and Halley, 1684); the "law of quadratic reciprocity" was a grade 3 (Gauss, 1788–1796, Euler, 1737, and Legendre, 1830); the "mechanical equivalent of heat" was a grade 4 (Mayer, 1842, Carnot, 1830, Seguin 1839, and Joule, 1840); the "solution of the problem of respiration" was a grade 5 (Priestley, Scheele, Lavoisier, Spallanzani, and Davy, all 1777 [sic]); the "self-exciting dynamo" was a grade 6 (Hjorth, Varley, Siemens, Wheatstone, Ladd, and Wilde, all between 1863 and 1867); and the "cellular basis of both animal and vegetable tissue" was a grade 7 (Schwann, Henle, Turpin, Dumortier, Purkinje, Muller, and Valentin, all around 1839). We can also speak, albeit loosely, of multiples having grades of 1 (singletons) and even zero (nulltons). Einstein's general theory of relativity was a grade 1 multiple, and the *perpetuum mobile* or the squaring of the circle or the trisection of an angle was a grade zero.

The advocates of the traditional interpretation are fond of citing the appearance of the high-grade multiples as the coup de grâce of any genius theory, but they almost invariably fail to note that the frequency distribution of grades for true multiples displays a distinctive pattern: The lower the grade is, the higher the frequency will be. This monotonically decreasing, concave-upward function can be seen in Table 6.1, which shows the

Table 6.1. *Observed multiple grades and predicted Poisson values for three data sets*

Grade	Ogburn–Thomas		Merton		Simonton	
	Observed	Predicted	Observed	Predicted	Observed	Predicted
0	–	(132)	–	(159)	–	(1,361)
1	–	(158)	–	(223)	–	(1,088)
2	90	95	179	156	449	435
3	36	38	51	73	104	116
4	9	11	17	26	18	23
5	7	3	6	7	7	4
6	2	1	8	2	0	0
7	2	0	1	0	0	0
8	1	0	0	0	1	0
9	1	0	2	0	0	0
μ	1.2		1.4		0.82	

Source: Adapted from Simonton 1986g.

grade frequencies for the three most extensive tabulations of multiples (Merton 1961b; Ogburn & Thomas 1922; Simonton, 1979a).

Derek Price (1963, chap. 3) was the first to suggest that the empirical distribution of multiple grades could be interpreted as the consequence of a Poisson probability process. Expected values for the observed distribution can then be calculated according to the formula

$$P(i) = \frac{\mu^{i}e^{-\mu}}{i!}, \qquad \text{where} \quad i = 0, 1, 2, \ldots, n \qquad (6.1)$$

Here $P(i)$ is the probability of obtaining a multiple of grade i, e is again the exponential constant, and μ is the mean of the distribution. What makes this suggestion especially provocative is that the Poisson distribution applies best to events that are extremely rare, events so unlikely that an unusual number of trials must be undergone before those events have any reasonable opportunity of occurrence. A famous case in point is that the number of Prussian military officers to die from a horse kick in a given time interval during the 19th century follows a Poisson distribution. To comprehend the relationship between the Poisson and improbable events, it is sometimes useful to conceive the single parameter of the Poisson distribution, μ, in terms of the two parameters of the binomial distribution, namely, the probability that a single trial will successfully generate the event (p) and the number of attempts assigned to achieving that same event (*n*) (Simonton 1978b). The Poisson distribution then becomes the exponential limit of the binomial distribution as *p* approaches zero and *n* approaches infinity, in which $\mu = np$ (and therein both the mean and the variance σ^2). Plausible parameters probably fall somewhere between $p = 0.1, n = 10$, and $p = 0.01, n = 100$ (Simonton 1978b, 1979a).

Whatever the specific binomial parameters, this conception of multiples origination dovetails more closely with a chance-configuration theory than it does with the traditional viewpoint. In the chance permutation of elements, a huge succession of unstable mental aggregates must be sifted through before a stable permutation can emerge, and there is no guarantee that the desired chance configuration will appear at all, given how improbable such stable permutations are. Thus, the isolation of a chance configuration requires many trials, each with a minuscule probability of success.

To appreciate the compatibility of the observed distribution of grades with the current theory, we may inspect Figure 6.1, which offers an admittedly schematic representation of the expected distributions under the three alternative interpretations. According to the chance account, many trials are required to arrive at a sound result, and each attempt enjoys only low odds of success, yielding the skewed-right distribution in which the probability of occurrence declines monotonically with multiple grade. In contrast, the romantic conception of genius (not favored by the current theory) holds that each potential discovery or invention has only a single corresponding contributor, but fortunately, that individual has such a prodigious intellect that only one attempt is required, as the original idea appears in a sudden "flash of insight." This idealized case yields a degenerative distribution consisting merely of singletons, with no nulltons (for genius always wins out) and no multiples (for the gifts of true genius are inherently unique). Last, we have the zeitgeist interpretation in which many scientists are capable of making a discovery and each has fairly high odds of success, producing a distribution in which high-grade multiples are considerably more common than are low-grade multiples, singletons, and certainly nulltons (for virtually all contributions are inevitable). In truth, a stronger form of the story's traditional version would yield an even more unrealistic expected distribution. If we wish to rid ourselves of the nulltons, we could make the number of scientists and their odds of success far larger (say, $p = 0.9$ and $n = 20$), but we would end up with a distribution skewed extremely on the left – quite opposed to empirical reality.

Besides the close fit between the present theory and the hypothesized stochastic mechanism, the Poisson distribution yields expected frequencies for multiple grades that match the observed values almost perfectly, as is also apparent in Table 6.1. Chi-square goodness-of-fit tests reveal that any

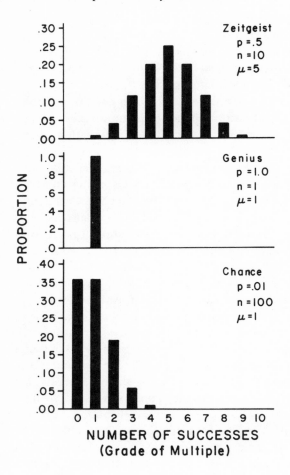

Figure 6.1. Predicted probability distributions obtained by interpreting the three alternative theories in terms of the binomial distribution with different values for *n* and *p* (from Simonton 1979a).

discrepancies between the observed and expected frequencies can be ascribed to sampling error (Simonton 1978b, 1979a). Moreover, the congruence between data and theory persists even when the tests are confined to only the most secure cases of multiples (Simonton 1979a) or when the samples of multiples are broken down by discipline (Simonton 1978b, 1979a). To demonstrate the congruence in the latter case, Table 6.2 shows the fit of the Poisson distribution to subsets of the multiples published by Ogburn and Thomas (1922). In some instances, principally in astronomy, the agreement between prediction and observation is perfect or nearly so.

Table 6.2. *Observed (O) and predicted (P) grade frequencies: Ogburn–Thomas subgrouped sample*

Grade	Astronomy O	P	Mathematics O	P	Chemistry O	P	Physics O	P	Electricity O	P	Biology O	P	Technology O	P
2	11	11	15	16	15	14	18	19	9	9	16	18	6	5
3	4	4	7	7	6	6	7	8	5	5	2	4	5	4
4	1	1	2	3	1	2	1	2	2	2	1	1	1	2
5	0	0	2	1	0	0	2	1	0	1	2	0	1	1
6	0	0	0	0	0	0	0	0	2	0	0	0	0	0
7	0	0	1	0	0	0	0	0	0	0	1	0	0	0
8	0	0	0	0	0	0	1	0	0	0	0	0	0	0
9	0	0	0	0	0	0	1	0	0	0	0	0	0	0
μ	1.1		1.4		1.2		1.2		1.7		0.6		2.5	

Source: Adapted from Simonton 1978b.

It is rather striking that the estimated values of μ (using the two-moments method for truncated samples) have an apparent central tendency of around unity, which is consistent with the conjectured ranges of *p* and *n*. Given this value, just about one-third of all potential contributions become multiples, whereas another third become only singletons, and yet another third become nulltons. Thus, the existence of multiples cannot disprove that some discoveries and inventions are never made! In addition, this startling implication would still hold even if the inventory of multiples were considerably expanded. Indeed, the model actually predicts that the absolute number of multiples is tremendously underestimated in all the published lists, for the expected frequencies must be multiplied in order to force the predicted number of singletons to match the observed number of grade 1 discoveries and inventions, which is far greater than the parenthetical figures seen in Table 6.1. By one estimate, there may be at least around *6,000* more multiples than contained in the compilations gathered thus far (Simonton 1978b). A collection of multiples therefore may be expanded 10-fold over the largest list so far put together, without imposing even the slightest qualification on a stochastic interpretation.

The only way that the identification of missing multiples can work against our argument is if the proportion of high-grade multiples expands at the expense of low-grade multiples, to the point that the most common grade is not a doublet or triplet but, rather, some higher grade, such as a sextuplet, septuplet, octet, or nonet. A change like this in the shape of the probability distribution would result in a picture more consistent with the zeitgeist than the chance theory, as interpreted in Figure 6.1. Nevertheless, both reason and reality suggest that something quite the opposite would result if we could capture more fugitive examples. Common sense dictates that the higher the multiple grade is, the more dramatic the occasion will be, and so the larger the chance will be that the event will be reported in the annals of history. The incidence of publicity-attracting priority disputes and litigations may also be greater when the number of independent participants in the multiple is larger. And the facts show that the more inclusive the multiple list is, the more the lower-grade multiples tend to predominate. Returning to Table 6.1, we see that the ratio of doublets and triplets to total multiples increases as the number of multiples expands, from 85% to 96%. If this empirical trend persists, the unearthing of still more multiples is likely only to aggravate the lopsided representation of low-grade multiples relative to high-grade multiples. So the case for the traditional viewpoint is probably worse than the data suggest.

Multiples can be produced by a process of scientific creativity that interjects an appreciable amount of indeterminacy into scientific history. The multiples phenomenon certainly does not mean that contributions are inevitable, as Schmookler (1966) also argued from an alternative but compatible mathematical analysis. The extrapolation of the Poisson distribution to nulltons can be criticized, of course (Brannigan & Wanner 1983a). Nonetheless, if this aspect of the model is disliked, the distribution can perhaps be renormalized to remove all nulltons (Simonton 1986g). That maneuver would be congruent with the notion that all potential contributions must be made eventually, requiring that trials continue until the pool of conceivable stable permutations is exhausted. Monte Carlo simulations that introduce this principle of exhaustion still reproduce the observed frequency distribution of multiple grades, as we shall see at the end of this chapter (Simonton 1986c).

Degree of simultaneity

A far more serious objection to the simple Poisson model is that it cannot account for the commonplace near simultaneity of multiples (Simonton 1984d, app. D). Bell and Gray announced their independent invention of a telephone to the U.S. patent office just hours apart on the same day, for example, and W. C. Bond and W. Lassell observed Hyperion, the seventh satellite of Saturn, on the same night. To account for this empirical facet of multiples, some variety of communication mechanism must be added. Brannigan and Wanner (1983a) put forward the negative contagious Poisson process as a more acceptable mechanism for generating multiples (cf. Simonton 1984d, app. D). In essence, this stochastic process assumes that once a trial is successful, the probability that another trial will generate the same event declines with time (a negative contagion). The corresponding equation is

$$P(i) = \frac{\alpha\,(\alpha + \beta)\,\ldots\,(\alpha + [i - 1]\,\beta)\,e^{-\alpha}(1 - e^{-\beta})\,i}{i!\beta^i} \tag{6.2}$$

This equation looks rather different from Equation 6.1, but it belongs to the same family. The parameter α has much the same role as does μ in the previous formula, whereas β merely gauges the magnitude of the contagion, in which β should be negative for the Brannigan–Wanner model. In fact, as β approaches zero in the limit, Equation 6.2 becomes Equation 6.1, α becoming equivalent to μ. This takes place whenever the mean and variance of the observed distribution are identical, just as we assumed in the simple Poisson (for β equals the natural logarithm of the ratio of the variance σ^2 to the mean μ). In any case, this more elaborate Poisson model does not predict the observed distribution of multiple grades substantially better than does the simple Poisson (Simonton 1986d), but it does favor simultaneous multiples over rediscoveries, predicting that the probability of a given temporal separation decreases with the size of that separation between duplicates.

Although Brannigan and Wanner (1983a) believed that a negative contagious Poisson can be subsumed under a version of the traditional position (their "maturation hypothesis"), this process is far better conceived of in terms of the chance-configuration theory (Simonton 1984d, app. D; 1986d). We postulated that for the act of scientific creativity to be counted as complete, the original chance configuration must pass through a series of selection processes, including the process of social acceptance. When a certain contribution has been successfully used by scientific colleagues in their own endeavors at cognitive self-organization, further efforts in that direction will be precluded. Neither the original creator nor the acceptors of the creative product will even be in the intellectual state to generate chance permutations in that specific domain, for the constituting mental elements will have become consolidated sufficiently so as to function as a unit in thought – and thus enter subsequent chance permutations as a single psychological entity. Once the wheel has been invented and widely disseminated, it becomes literally inconceivable for an inventor to reinvent it. The wheel, instead, has become a well-consolidated element that may be involved in further permutations to yield other configurations, such as the wheelbarrow, chariot, wagon, and automobile as well as the pulley, gear, turbine, fan, and propeller.

But the real issue is that the sequence of intrapsychic and interpersonal events connecting the initial chance configuration with its final assimilation by the scientific community is a long one, each step consuming time. Time must pass to convert the stable chance permutation into a communication configuration, and further delays intervene between the articulated idea and the moment when it becomes part of how colleagues perceive the natural world – even if only as a deliberately rejected hypothesis. Nonetheless, as time advances, the odds that some other scientist will remain ignorant of the contribution must decline as well, making multiples even more unlikely. In this interpretation, simultaneous multiples are not remarkable at all, because they merely reflect inefficiencies in the exchange of scientific knowledge. As scientific communication increases in effectiveness, multiples must become more simultaneous, and the grade of those multiples must decline as well. Brannigan and Wanner (1983b), in reanalyzing my data (1979a), confirmed this expectation. For instance, the average interval between duplicates declined steadily from around 86 years in the 16th century to a bit more than 2 years in the 20th century. Moreover, the efficiency of scientific exchange probably varies across different disciplines and nationalities, with a corresponding variation in the typical delay between first and last contribution to a multiple, and this expectation, too, has empirical endorsement (Brannigan & Wanner 1983b). For instance, chemistry has the shortest mean interval, whereas mathematics has the longest, a contrast that likely reflects different attitudes between chemists and mathematicians toward rushing into print. Mathematicians, in particular, are far more apt to circulate derivations or proofs for some time in manuscript rather than hastily publishing what turns out to contain a fatal error in their logic.

Consequently, rediscoveries become the truly intriguing events, for they imply that a worthy chance configuration cannot jump all the hurdles to ultimate acceptance and utilization by the scientific community, thereby permitting subsequent investigators to repeat the permutation process to reach the same end. Sometimes scientists, to their own regret, fail to follow the competitive norm of publishing results quickly, and accordingly see themselves preempted by others. Newton's procrastination in this regard gave Leibniz the opportunity to announce the calculus first, just as J. Henry saw Faraday proclaim the discovery of electromagnetic induction, when both Newton and Henry had priority. Such delays may not even be the scientist's fault: Scheele lost priority for some of his chemical discoveries because of his publisher's negligence; J. C. Adams saw his priority in predicting a planet beyond Uranus evaporate when Airy failed to respond as quickly as did Galle to LeVerrier's somewhat later prediction; and Couper's claim to have introduced structural theory into chemistry was usurped by Kekulé because of a delay caused by Couper's mentor, Wurtz.

Of course, sometimes a scientist neglects to publish at all, leaving the gates open for another entrant in the race to discovery: Fermat, Cavendish, and Gauss were especially notorious in this. Fermat, for example, devised an analytical geometry but left it unpublished, granting Descartes free rein to claim fame for the (re)discovery. On the other hand, even when scientists rush their latest ideas into print, there is no assurance that their offering will disseminate properly so as to avoid duplication. Occasionally scientists fail to compose a broadly intelligible communication configuration. Lomonosov is a classic example, for many ideas that he anticipated made others famous years later, because of his decision to publish in Russian, a language outside the 18th-century mainstream, even in Russia. When the language imposes no obstacles, the choice of the appropriate vehicle for publication may prove crucial to winning quick acceptance. It has been often conjectured that Mendel's impact was compromised owing to his having published in the rather obscure *Transactions of the Brünn Natural*

History Society and that Gibbs's influence was thwarted because his key papers on chemical thermodynamics appeared in the similarly provincial *Transactions of the Connecticut Academy of Sciences*. Finally, rediscovery may always result when the first attempt to promulgate an idea proves premature. Presumably a discovery is premature when there is no congruence between the originator's and colleagues' cognitive constitution in regard to the organization of mental elements in the discipline. A premature discovery cannot inspire a restructuring of thought because it does not yet have a place in the hierarchical arrangement of scientific knowledge.

Multiples participation

It is worth pointing out that the chance-configuration theory explains more than can the observed distribution of multiple grades and the manifest occurrence of simultaneous multiples. The constant-probability-of-success model that we derived from the theory applies just as well to multiples as it does to singletons. Merton (1961b, p. 484), in providing some latitude in his theory for the operation of individual creators, said that "men of great scientific genius will have been repeatedly involved in multiples . . . because the genius will have made many scientific discoveries altogether." Assuming that we have an "invisible college" of scientists all subjecting more or less the same collection of mental elements to chance permutations, it follows that those who produce the most total configurations will be more prone to generate the most configurations that are similar to those conceived by colleagues. By comparison, less prolific scientists will be responsible for fewer total configurations and thus participate in multiples less often. Hence, as Merton noted,

men of scientific genius are precisely those men whose work in the end would be eventually rediscovered. These rediscoveries would be made, not by a single scientist, but by an entire corps of scientists. On this view, the individual man of scientific genius is the functional equivalent of a considerable array of other scientists of varying degrees of talent. (p. 484)

This position echoes Lombroso's, as quoted in chapter 4, with the proviso that although a single genius may be worth a hundred lesser intellects, in the long run the total number of contributions to the advance of science would not change, no matter whether geniuses or mediocrities made the contributions.

In line with this constant-probability-of-multiple model, evidence arrives from two quarters that the more distinguished scientists are in fact more apt to become involved in multiples. Warren O. Hagstrom (1974) surveyed almost 2,000 mathematicians, statisticians, physicists, chemists, and biologists in order to determine the consequence of scientific competition. All were presented with this query: "Scientists are sometimes anticipated by others in the presentation of research findings. That is, after they have started work on a problem, another scientist publishes its solution. How often has this happened to you in your career?" (p. 2). Over 60% of his respondents reported that at least once in their careers some other scientist had preceded them in the publication of a finding, and approximately one-third admitted some worry that credit for their current work would likewise be preempted by others quicker on the draw. Those who have been superseded in the past are especially likely to be concerned about being superseded in the future, and some scientists become so worried about the possibility of their work's being wasted without credit that they consider such maneuvers as becoming more secretive about their research activities, publishing their results more quickly, or changing their specialty area. An instance of this last, most drastic action was revealed by a noted mathematician:

The scientist may be and often is discouraged from studying such and such a problem not by the knowledge that it has been solved, but by the fear that it has been solved without his knowing it, a fact which would render his work useless. . . . I even add that, after having started a certain set of questions and seeing that several other authors had begun to follow that same line, I happened to drop it and investigate something else. (Hadamard 1945, p. 132)

Though the prospects of being at the losing end of a multiple thus seem very real, the chances were not evenly distributed throughout the survey's respondents. On the contrary, "individuals are likely to be anticipated if they publish much and have their publications cited often" (Hagstrom 1974, p. 1). Of these two predictors, publication rate is the more important, as both a zero-order correlation and a standardized coefficient in a regression equation. Indeed, when Hagstrom tested for the Publication X Citation Interaction, citation no longer had a main effect on the frequency of anticipation, whereas publication still did so (1974, Table 3). This interaction effect reveals that the relationship between being prolific and experiencing anticipation becomes more likely with the frequency of citation of the researcher's earlier works. This result can be interpreted in terms of the present theory if we assume that the citation rate reveals whether the researcher is in a mainstream specialty harboring numerous potential competitors (cf. Cole & Cole 1971). With many possible rivals all subjecting more or less the same elements to permutation, the odds of duplication are great, especially for those scientists who are most prolific. In contrast, in a less populous specialty with fewer rivals, productivity would not be associated with the likelihood of anticipation, for hardly anyone else is working with the same intellectual material. This relationship between the number of workers in a specialty and the threat of duplication, when coupled with each scientist's desire to escape involvement in multiples, may help propel the fragmentation of the scientific enterprise into ever more specialized domains. In other words, when a research area becomes too big and the competition too oppressive, specialties may split and separate, or bud off, to return the invisible college to a more manageable size, thereby reducing the danger of futile efforts.

Whatever the case, Hagstrom's survey results can be interpreted as showing how the opportunities for multiple participation are distributed across scientists in direct proportion to the total number of each scientist's attempted contributions and to the total number of scientists working in the same research area. In regard to historical stars in science, comparable conclusions obtain (Simonton 1979a). A sample of 789 scientists and inventors born between the 16th and 19th centuries was drawn from standard biographical dictionaries and then gauged on three attributes: (1) eminence, as determined by prominence in encyclopedias, (2) creative productivity, as measured by the number of contributions listed in chronologies of scientific and technological events, and (3) multiples participation, as indicated by how many of 579 different multiples each scientist was participating in. The eminence of a scientist was correlated with multiples participation, a result not unlike that Hagstrom observed between citation and anticipation (if we suppose that historical eminence is roughly associated with the size of a field). Still, the number of multiples was even more closely related to the count of notable contributions, the creative productivity index. Further, given what we found in chapter 4, eminence and creative productivity should be positively correlated, which in fact they are. This latter correlation raises the specter of spuriousness; that is, the association between eminence and multiples participation may be largely ascribable to their common dependence on creative productivity. If we examine the partial correlation between eminence and participation, while controlling for productivity, the coefficient will be reduced to a trivial size. This analysis also parallels Hagstrom's, who found that controlling for publications shrank the impact of citations on anticipation. The conclusion is then that as predicted by the theory, the probability of becoming involved in a multiple discovery or invention is mostly a positive function of total output. The more prolific is the scientist or inventor, the greater will be the odds of duplication, whether anticipation or rediscovery.

Needless to say, when two or more researchers become entangled in a multiple, a dispute over priority often results (Lamb & Easton 1984, chap. 10). The scientific consensus is that the scientist who publishes first obtains the credit, and hence arise various protective practices, such as dating manuscript submissions in technical journals, submitting abstracts of works in progress, and the like. However, what happens when the participants are ensnared in a simultaneous multiple? Sometimes the most famous scientist involved will usurp most of the glory (see Merton 1968), and this may even happen when the less eminent participants had priority with respect to time (Simonton 1979a). This stealing of credit from a less illustrious predecessor is particularly likely when a scientific genius composes a massive and impressive synthesis that contains many elements already anticipated by others (cf. Simonton 1976f). The exceptional success of Cartesian analytical geometry was largely due to its completeness, a trait that rendered almost impertinent any assertion by predecessors that they had already anticipated this or that separate idea.

On the other hand, under some circumstances the scientist of lesser renown will be the one to receive the honors. Campbell and Tauscher (1966) illustrated how this may come about in a specific type of eponymy – when a scientist's name becomes a label for a particular law or principle. They demonstrated how the multiple "relating the apparent size of an afterimage to the distance of the surface upon which it is projected" (p. 58) came to be known as Emmert's law of 1881 when Emmert had several, and often far more illustrious, rival claimants, namely, Séguin, Lubinoff, Zehender, and maybe Schopenhauer. The basis for honoring Emmert, even though his discovery came at least a quarter-century after the first claim, was that he wrote the most comprehensive treatment of the subject; his article covered this topic alone; he himself provided no convenient designation for the law; and most significantly, he "contributed nothing else to the field" (p. 61). Thus, assigning Emmert eponymic status avoided the confusion that might have arisen from taking a name associated with many more distinct contributions. According to Campbell and Tauscher, "the names of one-time contributors are more efficient than the names of the great who contribute many principles to science" (p. 62). They suggested that the relationship between greatness and eponymy might actually be curvilinear: "The total nonentities would be omitted, the multiply great rarely represented, while the bulk of instances would come from that intermediate echelon of one-shot contributors to science" (p. 62).

Although the current theory provides no guidance on this particular issue, the Campbell-Tauscher principle of eponymy does exemplify a key assumption of the theory. In chapter 1 we assumed that the scientific enterprise is driven by the personal quest for self-organization, for enhanced information-processing efficiency. By carefully selecting the names that tag central laws, principles, and effects, scientists optimize the effectiveness of their cognitive functioning. Of all the labels that could be assigned, the one chosen is the most precise, complete, and unambiguous – which often means that it is the one-shot scientist who receives the eponymic laurels. This consequence of the search for maximal cognitive order adds a peculiar twist to the Ortega hypothesis treated in chapter 4. If the Campbell–Tauscher principle applies to enough instances of multiples, then the apparent role of the more "mediocre" scientists in scientific advance may be unduly overemphasized at the expense of the truly great scientists whose contributions are far too many for them to provide useful eponyms for single efforts. To be sure, the frequency of multiples relative to that of singletons may be too small for this discriminatory effect to have any consequence, yet the accumulation of numerous laws, principles, and effects attributed to obscure names may project the illusion that scientific genius is irrelevant to the course of science, as Ortega maintained.

But to return to the main point of this section, the chance-configuration theory leads us to the following generalization about multiples involvement: Scientists are most likely to become unwitting participants in multiples when (1) they are highly prolific themselves and (2) they are active in research areas with a large number of competitors. By comparison, scientists who are nearly silent or who explore a new domain alone have the least to fear from the standpoint of anticipation or rediscovery. This generalization ensues from one unifying principle, namely, the more independent trials there are, the higher the odds of duplication will be, a probabilistic association that operates on two levels, products and creators.

Necessary conditions

The anthropologist Leslie White (1949), although an advocate of the "science of culture" and an antagonist of the genius interpretation of history, began his analysis of scientific creativity with ideas that are not unfriendly to the current theory. He started by defining a scientific contribution: "An invention or discovery is a synthesis of already existing cultural elements, or the assimilation of a new element into a cultural system" (p. 204). The "culturological definition of genius" then becomes "a person in whose organism a significant synthesis of cultural elements has occurred" (p. 212). In our terms, *cultural* elements become *mental* elements within an individual mind (whether through exploration, socialization, or education), and these cognitions, when recombined, form novel configurations, a genius being one in whom such configurations happen to emerge. In addition, White hinted that something tantamount to chance permutations takes place, for he maintained that "the rate of occurrence of inventions and

discoveries at any given time is determined . . . by the number of elements . . . *and* the velocity of their interaction. . . . The greater the number of traits, or the greater the velocity of their interaction, or both, the
greater the number of cultural syntheses" (p. 227). If we view this jostling
about of elements as occurring within single intellects, which we must, this
conception will be consistent with our theoretical notions of creative potential, as developed in chapters 3 through 5. White's language even recalls the
imagery of randomly colliding molecules that Poincaré used in the introspections quoted in chapter 2. A final similarity is White's rejection of a
purely intrapsychic definition of genius in favor of a sociocultural definition, just as we put forward in chapter 1: "A genius will be defined as a
person who is regarded as a genius; there is no point in saying that many a
genius is born, lives and dies unrecognized" (pp. 201–202). The exertion of
exceptional personal influence is an inescapable prerequisite for genius.

But at this juncture the culturological and chance-configuration theories
diverge. White emphasizes that a potent intellectual power is irrelevant to
the cultural synthesis. That is, the elements will array themselves in almost
any human mind, including one of rather mundane ability, in the same way
that a gumbo soup will taste the same whether made in a pot or in a
caldron. "A consideration of many significant inventions and discoveries
does not lead to the conclusion that great ability, native or acquired, is
always necessary. On the contrary, many seem to need only mediocre
talents at best" (p. 212). White then developed this extreme view – which
has certain obvious affinities with the Ortega hypothesis – by belittling the
cognitive capacity underlying several inventions and discoveries. Typical of
this sometimes nearly insulting diatribe is White's assessment of how easy it
is to devise a workable steamboat: "Is great intelligence required to put one
and one – a boat and an engine – together? An ape can do this" (p. 212).

To clinch his point, White noted that creative genius is geographically and
historically clustered, whereas genetic endowment for superior intelligence
is probably evenly distributed across space and time. This is no doubt true
(cf. Simonton 1984d, chap. 2), but it is a non sequitur to conclude that a
better-than-average intellectual endowment is not needed to become a cruci-
ble for cultural synthesis. Intelligence, as we discussed earlier, is a necessary
but not sufficient factor behind genius, and other variables – these largely
environmental – are responsible for structuring exceptional intellect in the
proper way for generating successful configurations. This exceptional cognitive style and motivational disposition also facilitate the exploitation of serendipitous discoveries, or inventions that White would no doubt disparage as
not demanding more than a mediocre mind. Serendipity tends not to happen
to just anyone but, rather, to those singular personalities that evince a

"curiosity about many things, persistence, willingness to experiment and to explore" (Austin 1978, p. 78).

Most important, White (1949) summoned the multiples phenomenon on behalf of his argument, and it is here that his theory departs most conspicuously from mine. He articulated the difference in no uncertain terms:

(1) No invention or discovery can take place until the accumulation of culture has provided the elements – the materials and ideas – necessary for the synthesis, and, (2) When the requisite materials have been made available by the process of cultural growth or diffusion, and given normal conditions of cultural interaction, the invention or discovery is bound to take place. (pp. 204–205)

This quotation shows that the traditional interpretation of scientific creativity actually consists of two separate claims, what may be styled the "weak" and the "strong" forms of the theory. According to the weak form, the requisite ingredients must exist before a given discovery or invention is even possible. No genius, no matter what the magnitude, can conceive new ideas from nothing, but rather, all creativity originates in a cultural matrix. According to the strong form, the provision of the cultural substratum is both necessary and sufficient – that what *can* happen *will* happen. Proponents of this strong position mean that discoveries and inventions will appear inevitably, not just eventually. What empirical evidence is there for these two facets of the culturological, or zeitgeist, interpretation?

The theory's weak form certainly contains some truth, with stipulations appended. The chance-configuration theory does not refute the claim that the spirit of the times is nothing more than the provision of the mental elements essential to the sought-for configuration. Clearly, certain discoveries or inventions must be contributed before other contributions are conceivable, forming an a priori ordering of (at least a subset of possible) events according to necessary conditions. It may be impossible to imagine a calculus without an algebra, an algebra without an arithmetic, and an arithmetic without a number system; and most of the landmark achievements in the natural sciences are inconceivable without these mathematical prerequisites. Newton needed the calculus, and even Mendel used basic probability theory.

The plausibility of some a priori temporal ordering notwithstanding, no empirical studies actually assess the extent to which these ordinal constraints intervene in science and technology. Several anthropologists have argued for consistent sequences in the evolution of human cultures, certain traits being added to a society in a fixed progression that allows us to gauge a society's degree of sociocultural advancement (e.g., Carneiro 1970; Lomax & Berkowitz 1972). Carneiro (1970), for instance, applied Guttman scale analysis to hundreds of cultural traits. Many of these traits, albeit a minority, are scientific, or at least technological, in nature, such as the animal-drawn plow, astronomical observation, calendrical system, canals, casting, coined money, forging, glass, lock and key, metal armor, number system, ore smelting, papermaking, paved streets, pottery, sailboats, scales or balances, stone lintels, surgery, watercraft, wheeled vehicles, and writing. Because nearly 100 of the entire collection of cultural traits form a scalogram (with a respectable coefficient of reproducibility), we have here an empirical illustration of the potential existence of predetermined sequences predicated on necessary causality, orderings that appear to be cross-culturally and transhistorically invariant.

I do not wish to participate in the controversy surrounding the problems of linear evolution and scales of advancement, a debate that has not yet been resolved for either sociocultural or biological systems (see, e.g., Capitanio & Leger 1979; Granovetter 1979; Nolan 1982; Yarczower & Hazlett 1977). I shall point out only that this research falls far short of a full-fledged proof of the weak form. Insofar as discoveries and inventions are even present in the evolutionary scale, these are rather primitive achievements differentiated only in extremely generic categories. As such, these scalograms have not restricted the advance of modern science since the Renaissance. What we need are more finely differentiated classifications of appreciably more sophisticated technoscientific traits, and then we must determine how well these traits can be scaled. An obstacle to performing this inquiry, however, is that very few civilizations evolved an advanced science and technology, and most of these civilizations borrowed quite freely from one another. Probably the best that we can do is compare the sequence of discoveries and inventions in European and Chinese traditions. But even here our analysis would be stymied by the arrested development of Chinese science compared with that of European science.

Granting that we lack an empirical demonstration now, the weak form enjoys enough prima facie plausibility that we may accept it merely as a matter of faith. Even so, we must qualify this acceptance. First, not every element that enters into a configuration will come directly from the culture in which the creator acts. White appears to admit as much in his own definition of a scientific contribution, which implies that an innovator may introduce new elements from outside the sociocultural system. One external source was discussed in chapter 5, namely, that a creator marginal to the system may introduce elements from another system, whether a neighboring discipline or an alien culture. In the history of science and technology, examples of such cultural diffusion (through *individuals,* I stress) are numerous, including the cipher, paper, gunpowder, and variolization, just to cite a few cases in which the West borrowed from the East. These elements originated not within a given zeitgeist but, rather, from outside that milieu.

Another potential source of new elements is more interesting: The element may be an observation, fact, or datum adopted immediately "from nature," from empirical inspection of "raw reality." For example, Jupiter's moons, spermatozoa, and X-rays were introduced as conceptual entities into science by Galileo, Leeuwenhoek and Röntgen, respectively, from experiences mostly external to the system, although these experiences could not have taken place without using provided elements, whether the telescope, microscope, or cathode ray tube. Hence, the sociocultural system can be enriched with new elements extraneous to that system, elements that expand the wealth of possible stable permutations that can arise out of the given "culture pattern." But the introduction of these outside entities also may disrupt the expected flow of a particular system, by inserting components for discoveries and inventions that would not have emerged otherwise. Therefore, even if scientific creativity depends on the cultural store of elements, creative scientists can add to that store elements that are not obvious permutations of old elements already embedded in the culture.

A second qualification pertains to the extent of ordering imposed on the sequence of contributions by the existence of necessary prerequisites. First, a configuration may consist of prerequisite elements, yet many of those elements may have one or more substitute elements, and so a configuration with equivalent function may arise if the requisites are not met. For example, although algebra seems to be essential to calculus, a usable calculus could have arisen solely in terms of geometry, as an extension of the protocalculus of Archimedes. Indeed, Newton composed his entire *Principia* in the classic geometric style of the Greeks, without referring to the calculus that he had already devised. What we said earlier about the dissimilarities separating many supposed duplicates shows that such substitutions are common. Moreover, even if we admit that certain elements must exist before a configuration can appear that is composed of those said elements, each configuration will contain only a few of all the elements available. Carneiro (1970) observed, with respect to the scaling of cultural traits, that although economic traits follow a particular order, and political traits are temporally ordered, the ordinal position of the economic traits relative to the political traits is far less fixed. Likewise, discoveries in physics lean mainly on earlier discoveries in physics, seldom on previous discoveries in biology, and so the progression of events in either discipline can run largely without reference to what transpires in the other. As a consequence, although certain contributions must appear in a fixed a priori temporal order, science as a whole has no single ordinal positioning in historical time. Rather, an almost infinite number of temporal orderings are permissible. For instance, although some ideas of Copernicus probably had to appear before Kepler could offer some of his ideas, and Vesalius similarly provided a necessary foundation for Harvey, the order of Copernicus with respect to Vesalius or Kepler relative to Harvey is free of determination. A priori impositions on event orderings are quite soft.

The very occurrence of rediscoveries proves that many orderings are possible. Whether Mendelian genetics was established in 1865 or 1900 makes a dramatic difference in the ordinal position of that contribution with respect to the hundreds of discoveries and inventions that occurred within the 35-year interval. Given the infinity of perfectly feasible orderings, the weak form of the zeitgeist theory imposes hardly any constraints on the chance-permutation process. Chance still makes the final decision as to which realization of event ordering will be transcribed in the annals of science. Indeed, as we shall show later when we discuss some Monte Carlo simulations, in some ways the imposition of prerequisites gives chance a more decisive role that it would have otherwise.

To be fair, White (1949) claimed to "predict the course of evolution but not of history" (p. 230). That is, his culturology aims only to anticipate the broad flow of human culture rather than the details. Even so, this prediction of general movements has meaning only if the strong form of the thesis is accepted. The existence of specified elements must cause the expected synthesis to take place. And if the strong form were justified, then the present theory would be seriously challenged, as we pointed out earlier when discussing the doctrine of inevitability. Fortunately, the evidence for necessary *and* sufficient causality is extremely meager. White himself allowed that "it is not quite so obvious, perhaps, that when the elements necessary for a given synthesis *are* present in a process of interaction that the synthesis *will* take place" (p. 208). To assuage any skepticism on this assertion, White tried to gain as much as possible from the existence of high-grade and simultaneous multiples, by leaning heavily on the Ogburn–Thomas list and Kroeber's logic. Yet we saw in earlier sections of this chapter that this proof will not go very far. Multiples of the highest grade so far detected in history can easily be generated from a stochastic mechanism, without presupposing sufficient or necessary causes. In addition, the telltale shape of the probability distribution of multiple grades is more consistent with a stochastic than a deterministic process. These same stochastic models, furthermore, can account for the characteristic of simultaneity by adding a single simple postulate – that no one will strive to contribute what they know has already been contributed.

Consequently, the occurrence of simultaneous multiples does not oblige us to accept the zeitgeist as a productive process. Events are not chained in rigid sequences of necessary and sufficient causes. All contributions could be produced at any time in any sequence throughout history and still have simultaneous multiples appear under the sole assumption of negative contagion. Gray would not have dreamed of working on the electronic transmission of speech were a Bell telephone already in his office. Particularly today, when the efficiency of scientific communication is so high – indeed, when a science of such information exchange has emerged – contributions usually must be nearly simultaneous for multiples to occur at all.

So the facts advise us to reject the strong form of the traditional interpretation of multiples and accept the weak form only with reservations. Necessary conditions may constrain what can be created, but there is no reason to maintain that contributions are beaded together on a string of necessary and sufficient causes. This point will be elaborated in the next section, when I try to expand my explanation of the multiples phenomenon.

Monte Carlo simulations

One of the difficulties of treating multiples in terms of the theory is that the phenomenon is so complex that the mathematics easily becomes intractable. Equations 6.1 and 6.2 are predicated on assumptions that are simplistic, yet to complicate matters would yield differential equations that are not easily solved. So let us take a different approach – Monte Carlo simulation models (Simonton 1986c). If the process underlying multiples is stochastic, then we should be able to use a random-number generator to mimic the phenomenon's main characteristics, especially the distinctive distribution of multiple grades and the common appearance of simultaneity. All told, six Monte Carlo models were developed, each incorporating some new principle or factor that illustrates some special aspect of a theoretical interpretation. Each simulation started with the assumption that there were 100 contributions to be made, an arbitrary number selected merely so that the frequency of various multiple grades would translate immediately into percentages. The purpose of each simulation was to "discover" or "invent" these 100 potential contributions over a series of trials. To obtain stable estimates of the percentages, each of the six models was run on the same set of 10 random-number sequences (i.e., same 10 "seeds") and an average taken. The outcome can be summarized as follows:

1. *Model A* embodies what Price (1963) styled the "ripe apple" model: There are 100 apples in the tree, and 100 apple pickers all blindly reach up at the same time, some apples touched by more than one hand (multiples),

Table 6.3. *Grade percentages for Poisson and six Monte Carlo simulations*

Grade	Poisson ($\mu = 1.0$)	Model					
		A	B	C	D	E	F
0	36.8	36.3	36.9	00.0	00.0	30.7	13.4
1	36.8	37.3	37.8	46.1	45.6	32.5	45.5
2	18.4	18.9	17.5	37.2	36.3	24.2	25.4
3	6.1	5.7	6.3	13.0	15.1	10.3	11.2
4	1.5	1.3	1.2	3.2	2.3	1.7	3.6
5	0.3	0.4	0.2	0.5	0.5	0.5	0.8
6	0.1	0.1	0.1	0.0	0.1	0.1	0.1
7	0.0	0.0	0.0	0.0	0.1	0.0	0.0
Trials		100.0	1000.0	487.4	4474.5	2011.5	1746.8

Source: Adapted from Simonton 1986c.

some apples picked by one hand alone (singletons), and others left on the tree (nulltons). To simulate this most rudimentary stochastic mechanism, the computer program generated 100 two-digit random integers (from 00 to 99) and then counted the number of times that each integer appeared. The average of 10 experiments is shown in Table 6.3. Also given for comparison are the Poisson expected frequencies for $\mu = 1.0$, as implied by the Price model. The congruence is quite close and would be perfect were the simulations to run indefinitely. Even so, this model is obviously an unrealistic portrayal of how multiples may arise.

2. Instead of assuming that there are just 100 random attempts to make 100 potential discoveries or inventions, for *Model B* we expand the number of total trials to 1,000. On the average, therefore, for each potential discovery there will be 10 potential discoverers. In a certain sense, this model satisfies one facet of the zeitgeist theory, namely, that no contribution must wait for a single contributor in order to be realized. No one scientist can be considered indispensable to the advance of science if there are nearly a dozen researchers for every would-be contribution. As it currently stands, however, this model cannot reproduce the conspicuous distribution of multiples grades consistently found for empirical data. Rather, high-grade multiples will outnumber low-grade multiples in a manner not in keeping with "Poisson-like" frequencies. Accordingly, we must posit that the probability of success is not 1.0 for each scientist, but rather, each potential contributor has a probability of only 0.1 of attaining the goal. This specification is clearly more in keeping with the present theory, for it now parallels the binomial model discussed earlier, where $p = 0.1$ and $n = 10$, approximating

a Poisson distribution with $\mu = 1.0$. So the result remains a Poisson process, as can be seen in Table 6.3. Any frequency differences between Models A and B may be ascribed to sampling error persisting after aggregating across 10 experiments.

3. The first models generate a sizable proportion of nulltons; as in the Poisson distribution, some 37% of the potential contributions result in "nondiscoveries" or "uninventions"–contributions that could have been made but were not and will not because of persistent bad luck. Although this outcome, as we have seen, has intriguing consequences for the doctrine of inevitability, it is an idea not free of criticism either (Brannigan & Wanner 1983a,b). Whether or not we accept the existence of nulltons is more a matter of theoretical bias than conclusive demonstration; if our world civilization were to encounter the science of an alien planet we might be able to establish an inventory of missed opportunities in our own history. So let us now pursue some simulations that convert all potential discoveries and inventions into outright contributions. In *Model C* the probability of success for any given trial is returned to unity, and most important, the trials continue until all potential discoveries have been made–the principle of *exhaustion*. Nevertheless, some constraint must be added to this process if we want a realistic representation of the empirical distribution of multiple grades. Otherwise the outcome will be a distribution in which high-grade multiples vastly outnumber doublets and triplets, the only grades that are truly commonplace. This incongruence can be avoided by using the factor of *communication*, such as advanced by Brannigan and Wanner (1983a,b). In the simulation model, once a particular contribution has been made, only so many trials are allowed to pass before the opportunities for duplication are curtailed. After that "last chance" cutoff, the initial contribution is assumed to have been so effectively diffused throughout the scientific community that a multiple is no longer likely. Because we must have an outcome that convincingly mimics the observed distribution of multiple grades, the number of permitted trials was varied in the Monte Carlo experiment until a reasonable approximation emerged, and a 75-trial limit proved adequate. The averaged results from the 10 experiments is displayed in Table 6.3.

It took 487 trials, on the average, to generate all 100 contributions at least once, and thus scientific history would still have appreciable indeterminacy under Model C. Moreover, the pattern remains fairly Poisson-like despite the decision to exclude the nulltons outright via exhaustion. Because the absent nulltons have been redistributed over the singletons and multiples, thereby inflating the proportions for grades 1 and up, this correspondence may not be self-evident. As a consequence, the percentages for

Table 6.4. *Grade percentages for multiples only: Theoretical and empirical distributions*

Grade	Poisson ($\mu = 1.0$)	Model						Empirical		
		A	B	C	D	E	F	Ogburn	Merton	Simonton
2	70	72	69	69	67	66	62	61	68	78
3	23	22	25	24	28	28	27	24	19	18
4	6	5	5	6	4	5	9	6	6	3
5	1	2	1	1	1	1	2	5	2	1
6	0	0	0	0	0	0	0	1	3	0
7	0	0	0	0	0	0	0	1	0	0
8	0	0	0	0	0	0	0	1	0	0
9	0	0	0	0	0	0	0	1	1	0

Source: Adapted from Simonton 1986c.

the multiples only, excluding both nulltons and singletons, are offered in Table 6.4. It now becomes clear that Model C supports a distribution of grades that departs in no crucial way from that of the two strictly Poisson models. No matter which simulation we examine, doublets account for about 70% of the true multiples, triplets a bit less than 25%, quadruplets slightly more than 5%, and quintuplets somewhat over 1%.

4. Despite the similarities, Model C has one advantage over the first pair of models, namely, that it can account for the common near simultaneity of so many multiples. If the advent of a multiple entails a race between the independent duplication of a contribution and the successful communication and acceptance of the first contribution, then the various participants in a multiple must clearly make their respective claims within a narrow time frame. Even so, one aspect of the model requires qualification, namely, its insistence that the probability of success is 1.0 for any given trial. The history of science is full of instances of failed attempts, and such cases are, if anything, immensely underreported. Faraday tried to establish a link between magnetism and light, a discovery that had to await Zeeman. And of course, the chance-configuration theory itself demands that the odds of a hit be rather small, as observed under Model B. Accordingly, we shall combine the last two Monte Carlo models into a single stochastic mechanism named *Model D*. Like Model B, the probability of a hit in any given trial is set at only 0.1, yet the exhaustion mechanism and communication restriction operate just as in Model C. To realize a predicted distribution that still accords with the data, the maximum number of trials before ending the accumulation of duplicates must be multiplied 10-fold – a 750-

trial cutoff. Inspection of the summary results in Tables 6.3 and 6.4 reveals the same fundamental distribution as seen three times before, especially when we ignore the nulltons and singletons. The only real departure from the preceding model is that it takes many more trials to exhaust all the possibilities. To remove all nulltons, 4,474 trials were required, on the average, again making scientific progress less inevitable than before.

5. Even if the last pair of models were specifically designed to prohibit the appearance of nulltons, the dissemination of scientific information itself could also work to produce them. Besides the communication of successes, scientific exchange spreads awareness among practitioners of failures – of research cul-de-sacs in which precious effort has been expended in vain. In some instances these dead ends prove very real: Squaring the circle, changing base metals into gold, and constructing *perpetuum mobile* are a few well-authenticated blind alleys in the history of science and technology. Nonetheless, a portion of any scientific tradition may include a list of futile topics that are actually capable of solution, and so these outcast subjects of inquiry contribute to the stock of nulltons that are potentially true contributions. To incorporate this notion, *Model E* was modified from the preceding model by instituting a running count of the number of failed attempts for each potential contribution. When 10 failures occurred without any interrupting success, then a permanent nullton resulted. Word presumably spread that these consistently elusive targets marked questions that ruin promising careers. As the outcome in the two tables demonstrates, Model E still leads to the same expected proportions for multiple grades, only now nulltons are allowed once more. Because the scientific enterprise is permitted to turn away from recalcitrant problems, the number of trials necessary to attain exhaustion is reduced from the situation in Model D. Naturally, by adjusting the length of the sequence of consecutive failures to qualify a nullton, we can manipulate the proportion of nulltons at will. Model E thus defines the most general simulation, for we can vary the percentage of nulltons from zero, as in Models C and D, to over one-third, as in Models A and B.

6. Without exception, the foregoing models implicitly postulate that every scientist or inventor has the same odds of success (cf. Brannigan & Wanner 1983a). Sometimes the probability of a hit was fixed at 0.1, other times at 1.0, but in every model the chances were held constant across trials. Different researchers will use contrasting success probabilities. A scientific genius may be one whose chances are particularly high owing to an extraordinary creative potential that produces many permutations. Accordingly, *Model F* postulates that the success probabilities are distributed in rectilinear manner, ranging from 0.0 (the silent scientists) to 0.9 (the

prolific scientists). To be sure, a more complex formulation might have been used, such as introducing the sort of skewed distribution seen in Figure 4.1, yet this simple version should suffice to make the key point of this exercise. Because the average probability was increased, however, the maximum trial separation for the communication constraint had to be shrunk proportionately. Model F consequently entails a rectilinear distribution of probabilities with a limit of 150 trials for multiple collection and 10 trials for fixing permanent failures. The mean outcome of 10 Monte Carlo experiments appears in Tables 6.3 and 6.4. The predicted percentages remain in line with what transpired before. The proportion of nulltons falls about midway between the two Poisson models and the two communication models, whereas the number of trials to exhaustion is most like that observed in Model E. Like the latter model, too, we can fine-tune Model F to generate any proportion of nulltons we believe is plausible, including zero. Hence, this last model represents an even more general simulation, one that can, by appropriate adjustments, reduce to any one of the preceding models as a special case.

To help evaluate the compatibility between empirical reality and the simulations, Table 6.4 adds the percentages of the several multiple grades for the three published distributions of Ogburn and Thomas (1922), Merton (1961b), and Simonton (1979a). The only striking peculiarity in these patterns is that Merton's data fail to exhibit a monotonically declining distribution, grade 6 multiples outnumbering those of grade 5, and grade 9 multiples exceeding the frequencies for either grade 7 or grade 8. Nevertheless, these discrepancies can be easily attributed to sampling error. As previously noted, none of these distributions differs significantly from a Poisson distribution according to the accepted goodness-of-fit tests (Simonton 1978b, 1979a). Further, comparable discrepancies emerged in single Monte Carlo runs, a fact obscured in the tabular averages. Thus, one Model A experiment obtained a distribution much like the Ogburn–Thomas data, and one Model D experiment yielded results like the Merton data. The empirical distributions nonetheless are only samples from a larger population of multiples, the overwhelming majority of which have not been detected. More significantly, the population of scientific multiples is only one random sample from an infinite number of permissible realizations of the same stochastic process. The whole of Western science constitutes merely a single experiment, as is evident from the fact that the histories of science in other civilizations, most notably the Chinese, have pursued contrasting event sequences.

The six Monte Carlo models yield results close enough to the facts that they can serve as a basis for further Gedanken experiments that clarify additional facets of the present theoretical interpretation. For instance, let us think about the repercussions of accommodating a weak form of the zeitgeist theory in which certain discoveries or inventions are prerequisites for subsequent contributions. None of the models imposes an ordinal sequence defined by necessary (even if not sufficient) causes, but rather, all trials are randomly generated. Still, no obstacle stands in the way of subsuming an intrinsic causal ordering as part of a stochastic model (Simonton 1984d, 1986c). For these simulations, as a case in point, we can easily demand that the two-digit numbers appear in a specified order. The random-number generator could be compelled, for instance, to count from 00 to 99 so that any number that turns up out of sequence is automatically rejected as a possible success. This requirement would be analogous to what takes place when an investigator tries to discover or invent something before the necessary basis has been laid in past research (i.e., the elements essential to the configuration are as yet unavailable).

Inserting this further test would not alter the predicted distributions of the multiple grades shown in Tables 6.3 and 6.4. On the contrary, inserting an a priori ordering that symbolizes necessary conditions would serve only to expand astronomically the number of trials necessary to reach those same percentages. The probability of success per trial would be effectively reduced, and thus far more trials would be necessary to exhaust the supply of potential contributions. Appending the weak form of the traditional view, consequently, makes the outcomes more uncertain, thereby making chance a more conspicuous agent in realizing scientific history. The record will be riddled with casualties—scientists out of step with their times and thus thwarted by insurmountable obstacles. The numerous and sometimes humorous attempts to invent an airplane, from Leonardo da Vinci onward, best illustrate this contingency.

We can therefore introduce necessary causality without compromising the claim that the fundamental process underlying multiples is stochastic, as the chance-configuration interpretation dictates. But what about the strong form of the zeitgeist theory? Can we insert causes both necessary and sufficient? The response is negative, for this doctrine means that we must dispense with the random-number generator. Instead we must substitute a preformationist sequence of numbers representing the socially determined course of scientific events. On empirical grounds, nonetheless, this change will not do, for such a deterministic model would not reconstruct the observed data regarding multiples. A stochastic component must be reintroduced in some form. As an example, we might take the number of scientists capable of making a contribution (at the instant that it becomes "inevitable") subject to a Poisson process, as in Models A and B. Alternatively, we could posit that the number of potential discoverers is large but that the communication factor operates according to a stochastic mechanism, thus coming forth with another rendition of Model C. In the last analysis, a strong form of the traditional explanation simply appears untenable. Moreover, the simulations demonstrate that the involvement of the zeitgeist is definitely not required to explain multiples emergence. Probability models can reproduce the chief empirical features of the multiples phenomenon without postulating that scientific history is powered by sufficient or even necessary conditions. From this I conclude that the chance-configuration theory provides a more elegant and precise account of multiples than can be offered by the traditional approaches.

Summary

Let me recapitulate the argument of this chapter. The occurrence of multiples, if we accept the received tradition at face value, seriously challenges the plausibility of the chance-configuration theory. Multiples suggest that scientific creativity is subject to sociocultural determinism, which is hard to reconcile with a theory that places so much stress on chance. A corollary of this implication is that scientific creativity is worlds apart from artistic creativity, for multiples are not claimed to occur in music, literature, or the visual arts. Nevertheless, we have presented several analyses that seem to question the accepted wisdom and instead endorse the alternative theory developed in this book.

First, numerous logical problems interfere with the uncritical acceptance of the data cited on behalf of the usual account. That is, proponents of the zeitgeist, social deterministic, maturational, or culturological explanations tended to (1) ignore the uniqueness of individual contributions in an inordinate enthusiasm for abstract, generic categories of events; (2) overlook when one researcher was dependent on supposed anticipators and accordingly not fully independent; (3) blur the essential contrast between simultaneous multiples and rediscoveries or anticipations; and (4) propound an unsubstantiated doctrine of inevitability that obscures the distinction between necessary and sufficient causality.

Furthermore, should we choose to accept the data on face value, we shall still find that stochastic models can explain the observations on multiples while leaving the deterministic theoretical baggage outside. Indeed, models predicated on a random-generation process handle the facts with superior precision and comprehensiveness. In particular, such models can account adequately for (1) the probability distribution of multiple grades (even accommodating any tendency to underreport cases), (2) the occurrence of simultaneous duplicates (by introducing a communication mechanism implied by the theory), (3) the variation across researchers in the odds of participating in a multiple (by extending the logic of the constant-probability-of-success model of chapter 4), and (4) the a priori temporal orderings of contributions dictated by necessary conditions. The stochastic processes reproducing these phenomena are clearly more compatible with a theory, such as the present one, in which creativity requires trial after trial, each allotted a negligible chance of success.

Finally, to consolidate yet further the argument on the side of the chance-configuration theory, a series of six Monte Carlo models were described that simulated various processes by which multiples can emerge. By progressively elaborating the models, we developed such ideas as the random generation of trials, communication constraints, and the exhaustion of the pool of potential contributions. Gedanken experiments based on these models further vitiated the plausibility of the standard account of multiples.

I hasten to admit that neither the mathematical models nor the Monte Carlo simulations conclusively prove that the present theory is correct. Other processes may lead to the same observations. Nonetheless, the analyses may make the current explanation the most plausible of the published alternatives (cf. Lamb & Easton 1984). Advocates of the old interpretation have yet to test models that address the same facts with a comparable degree of accuracy or completeness. Moreover, the new interpretation presented here is part of a larger explanatory framework that can successfully deal with other facets of exceptional scientific creativity, as we saw in the preceding chapters. The conclusion thus appears sound, however tentative, that multiples are the result of a fundamental stochastic mechanism, one that entails chance permutations that are selectively retained, articulated, and disseminated. And we can surmise with far more assurance that the appearance of multiples cannot be taken as evidence contradicting the chance-configuration theory and that the characteristics of multiple emergence refute the traditional explanation. Given these inferences, the creative process in the sciences does not fundamentally differ from that in the arts. Depending on how we define our terms, we can compile lists of artistic multiples and maintain the historical inevitability of aesthetic products with the same degree of confidence.

7 Creative genius in science

Recapitulation

This book began by outlining the basic components of the chance-configuration theory of scientific genius. After the first chapter introduced the core concepts – mental elements, permutations, chance and communication configurations, self-organization, and social acceptance – the five following chapters developed the theoretical framework. Chapter 2 indicated how the chance-configuration theory accords with introspective reports and anecdotes regarding discovery and invention, such as the curious phenomenon of serendipity. Chapter 3 documented the theory in terms of the star scientist's personal characteristics, including both cognitive and motivational attributes. At that time the chance-configuration theory was tied to an earlier model of intuitive versus analytical information processing in order to generate an instructive typology of personalities. Chapter 4 examined the three principal facets of scientific productivity: the distribution of output across careers, the longitudinal fluctuations in output within careers, and the connection between the quantity and quality of output both across and within careers. The theory accounts for the conspicuously élitist cross-sectional distribution in productivity, predicts quite accurately the several features of agewise changes in productivity (as well as the positive covariation of precocity, longevity, and productivity rate), and supports a more comprehensive theoretical foundation for the constant-probability-of-success model of the quantity–quality relation. In addition, the theoretical scheme can handle the Ortega hypothesis, the Yuasa phenomenon, and Planck's principle. A central concept to emerge from this fourth chapter was that of creative potential, an idea adopted in chapter 5, which treated the developmental antecedents of scientific innovation. In particular, family background, formal education, role models, marginality, and the zeitgeist all were shown to affect creative development in ways consistent with the theory's chief tenets. Finally, in chapter 6 we discussed multiples, a key phenomenon in science and technology. After describing the factual and conceptual aspects of independent discovery and invention and presenting some Monte Carlo simulations, we found that the chance-configuration theory offers a better interpretation of this phenomenon than does the traditional, social-deterministic account. I maintain that the theory constitutes a promising psychology of science, at least in understanding scientific genius.

Admittedly, the theory's status with respect to each of these sets of topics varies appreciably. Although the theory helps explain all the substantive issues – introspections and anecdotes, personality, productivity, development, and multiples – its predictive capacity is obvious only in chapters 4 and 6. The fourth chapter derived equations directly from the theory that predict how creative productivity changes over a career, and the equations treated with some elegance both individual differences and interdisciplinary contrasts. In the sixth chapter the theory subsumed the stochastic models that predict precisely the distinctive empirical features of the multiples phenomenon. It would be advantageous, no doubt, to deduce comparable predictive equations for the facts reviewed in chapters 2, 3, and 5, but such an ability currently escapes us – and is probably most unlikely for the impressionistic data. Nonetheless, no other theory developed to date accounts for such a wide range of facts and at the same time makes precise predictions with respect to many of these facts. But perhaps this assertion is not so bold a claim, as only the sociology of science has attacked the question of scientific creativity on a broad front. Even this enterprise has not dealt with all the topics examined in the preceding chapters, and only for productivity have elaborate predictive mathematical models been formulated. Hence at this juncture the chance-configuration theory faces minimal competition from other theoretical quarters.

All of this is not a blind affirmation that this theory, as currently constructed, is necessarily true, or even that it is fully plausible. The efforts in the preceding chapters notwithstanding, the theory still requires considerably more development, especially in those empirical realms in which accurate prediction yet eludes us. These amendments cannot proceed, however, until many more empirical data are collected on the diverse aspects of scientific genius. Especially urgent are more inquiries into the personality and developmental variables related to distinguished scientific creativity. In chapters 3 and 5 I suggested many research questions that I hope will receive serious attention by future investigators. Now we are left with a theory clearly incomplete but still apparently adequate in light of the empirical data currently available.

Even so, I can consolidate yet further the theoretical discussion. In the next section I shall present an analogy that illustrates some central points of the theory. Then I shall describe some potential applications of the theory, after which I shall compare this theory with the three alternative metascientific perspectives. I shall conclude by discussing how the chance-configuration theory contributes to the psychology of science.

A game analogy

Imagine a game that I shall call *pseudo-Scrabble*. We have a large, flat board divided by evenly spaced horizontal and vertical lines into contiguous squares. Each square contains a number ranging from, say, 1 to 10. Then we have the playing pieces, namely, little thin squares having the same dimensions as the squares on the board. Each piece contains a letter of the alphabet plus a number (also ranging from 1 to 10). At the beginning of play these pieces are placed in a large bag that conceals their identity. Finally, each player has a little rack on which seven of these pieces can be arranged in any linear order. The game begins with the first player drawing from the bag seven pieces, which are then placed on the rack and examined by manipulating them in various orders (physically or mentally). If the player can form a word in the English language from some or all of these pieces, the word will be placed on the board, in a horizontal or vertical direction, and new pieces will be drawn from the bag to replace the ones just used. The next player continues this procedure, only from this time on, each player has the option (but is not required) to use the letters already on the board to form another word, as in real Scrabble games and crossword puzzles. Whenever a player cannot form a word from the English lexicon, one to seven pieces may be returned to the bag, and a new sample obtained from the same source. Because we assume that the playing board is immense, the game can continue indefinitely, each player taking his or her turn in an unending cycle (or until the party is over).

The object of the game is to accumulate as many points as possible, the number of points gained in a given turn being equal to the sum of the products of the two numbers on the squares and pieces. If a player takes advantage of the letters already on the board as part of a new word laid down, then those letters will also contribute points to the total received on the play. Thus there is some incentive to link the words in crossword fashion. However, unlike true Scrabble, players do not have to connect their pieces to those put down in previous turns. If the players wish, they can find some neglected corner of the board to arrange letters into legitimate words, presumably to take advantage of some empty square with a large number. This feature makes it possible, by the game rules, to earn a phenomenal number of points by placing pieces so that two arrays, hitherto unconnected, become fused into a single configuration. Players who form such syntheses are granted all the points in both arrangements. Even though a player can always explore unknown territory, a nice reward awaits those who connect two or more clusters of pieces set down in isolation on previous moves. We can add one other method of increasing a player's total score that is equally unique to pseudo-Scrabble. In any given turn a player has the option of rearranging a set of contiguous pieces already on the board, with the sole proviso that the new arrangement yields more points than did the old arrangement. The player earns as many points as were gained in the arrangement, including any points acquired from the addition of pieces from his or her own rack. Excess pieces are returned to the bag so that the player still has only seven at the end.

Before we contemplate how a typical game might proceed, let us first establish the analogous terms between the chance-configuration theory and the pseudo-Scrabble game. The board represents the raw data, the empirical facts known to experience, whether via experiment or observation. Related phenomena are contiguous, so that biological phenomena occupy one area of the board, geological phenomena another area, and so forth. The different numbers, or weights, assigned to each square reflect the differential significance of each datum. It is evident in science that some phenomena are recognized as more important than are others. In astronomy, for instance, the daily, monthly, and yearly cycles (of the sun, moon, and seasons) are facts that must be explained by *any* astronomical theory, whereas the nutation of the moon or the precession of Mercury are not nearly so important, the retrograde motion of the planets across the zodiac falling somewhere between these two extremes. In this case, variable significance likely mirrors phenomenological prominence, for almost every human being from time immemorial has noticed the calendrical cycles, whereas other facts require more care to be noticed, whether systematic observation as in the instance of planetary motion or precise measurement as in the instance of nutation and precession. However, sometimes the weights assigned to various facts emerge (as a "contextualist" epistemologist would argue) from more arbitrary social or disciplinary values. For as long as American psychology was dominated by radical behaviorism, facts about behavior were more highly regarded than were facts about mental states, such as motives and feelings – this when the phenomenological status of these facts is approximately equivalent.

The weights on the pieces more explicitly represent societal values, for these may be taken to correspond to preferred types of scientific treatment. The most points may be given for those explanations that are mathematical and hence the most predictively precise and deductively solid, somewhat fewer points for explanations that are merely logical, and the fewest points for those accounts that are largely linguistic (e.g., descriptions and nomenclature). Presumably the scientists in a given discipline have reached a consensus on the relative values of different styles of explanation, a consensus that probably contrasts greatly with the values held in other creative endeavors, such as poetry or religion.

In any case, a piece placed over a square means that a datum has been scientifically explained, and the product of the two numbers, one on the piece and another on the square, indicates the extent to which a significant fact has been handled in an esteemed way. (Here we posit that the product of significance times rigor is not a constant, as is sometimes cynically claimed.) The points that a player consequently receives parallel the honors and recognition a scientist earns during his or her career. The requirement that all letters concatenate into a legitimate word in English roughly represents the need for the mental elements in a configuration to satisfy some a priori or a posteriori structure. That is, constraints are imposed on how the components of a theory or model can be ordered to define a coherent system, even if merely a consistent nomenclature. Last, each player is limited to seven pieces on the rack to mimic the finite capacity of human information processing, which confines the number of distinct elements that can be subjected to free permutation in any given moment. Seven was obviously adopted in light of Miller's (1956) "magical number seven, plus or minus two."

Now a little Gedanken experiment can be easily performed to visualize how a game of pseudo-Scrabble would usually be played. We begin with the general observation that during the game, the playing board will be overlaid with a configuration of pieces. The arrangement of these pieces, moreover, will be systematic rather than random. Pieces with high weights will tend to be placed disproportionately on those squares with high weights, as each player attempts to maximize the number of points earned. The pieces will also be coordinated by a common set of rules, for they all form legitimate items of English vocabulary. This apparent order notwithstanding, the fundamental generating mechanism is random. Each player takes pieces from the bag to obtain a haphazard sample of seven pieces, which then are permutated until reaching a stable configuration that can be placed on the board. In other words, the player's role is to select and retain these chance permutations that will maximize the number of points earned, under the restrictions imposed by the game's rules. Because the selection process apparently requires an intellectual evaluation, one might miss the point that pseudo-Scrabble is very much a game of chance. Yet it would be relatively easy to construct a computer program to play the game; a random-number generator would pull out samples of letters to be checked for "spelling" against a dictionary, removing all but the permissible permutations, which then can be tried out on the screen subject to the rules and goals of pseudo-Scrabble.

The fundamental chance nature of the game would become especially apparent if many games were run using the computer program, inspecting the configurations that resulted each time. The configuration of pieces would never be the same from one game to the next, even though there would be a noticeable family resemblance in shape, reflecting the distribution of weights across the board squares. "Philosophers of science," observed Kuhn (1970, p. 76), "have repeatedly demonstrated that more than one theoretical construction can always be placed upon a given collection of data." By thus recognizing that the configurations are to some extent arbitrary, we preserve the basic identity of the creative process in the arts and the sciences. We can allow the belief that in Price's (1963, p. 69) words, "there is . . . only one world to discover," just as we have assumed the existence of only a single playing board, yet that is not identical with claiming that there is only one way to discover that world. Nevertheless, the arrangement of pieces is not entirely arbitrary (in the arts or sciences); however varied the configurations from game to game, certain squares will be more likely to be covered with a piece, whereas others will be more likely to remain empty. A systematic method would thus dwell in the seeming madness. The overall shape of the configurations will mirror, albeit with considerable distortion, the underlying structure of the data.

Like pseudo-Scrabble, scientific history also has a prominent chance component. Any one history, such as the history of science in Western civilization, is only one of a nearly infinite number of potential realizations, rendering history arbitrary and capricious rather than inevitable in its unfolding, a point I repeatedly stressed in our discussion of multiple discovery in chapter 6. As I observed then, this indeterminacy survives the intrusion of multiples. It is not uncommon for one Scrabble player, while awaiting his or her turn, to become frustrated at seeing a preceding player put down the exact same pieces over precisely the same squares on the board (e.g., making a verb past tense or a noun plural) and thus be "anticipated." The act of communication by one player preempts that of the other players and therein makes simultaneous multiples more, not less, probable. Moreover, if we had a very large number of players and kept track of the number of times that these multiples occurred, we would expect the distribution of grades to be just as Poisson-like as actually observed in the history of science. So, despite the appearance of multiples, the game's fundamental chance basis remains. This conclusion remains, even though it is obvious that certain moves in the game will often depend on necessary conditions – on specific pieces already having been placed on the board in previous moves.

Pseudo-Scrabble has another feature that deals more directly with scientific creativity on the individual level. Clearly there are several approaches to acquiring points on a given turn, and these inspire a taxonomy of scientific contributions that parallels that introduced in chapter 5. First, a player may place pieces on the board without attempting to link them to others already there. Such a move is analogous to being a *pioneer* or *precursor* in science, one who ventures into unexplored domains of inquiry without regard for the preoccupations of predecessors. This type of scientist is more prone to make "premature" discoveries or inventions that do not as yet fit in with the systematic arrangement of objective knowledge or practical expertise and so looks ahead of his or her time.

Second, a player might try to build on a configuration already present by adding letters to those on the board. Such a player is acting like a scientific *advancer,* a practitioner of normal science in Kuhn's (1970) terms. Actually, advancers can be distinguished by the degree of their contribution to the prevailing paradigm. Some are like players who merely add more pieces to a single configuration on the board (e.g., making a compound word); these are the *extenders* of the paradigm to contiguous substantive locales. Other advancers may behave like players who manage to bridge two (or more) hitherto separate configurations of letters, thereby earning all the points in both configurations (and the bigger the clusters so integrated are, the larger the score will be, on the average); these are the *synthesizers* who often found new disciplines through the merger of established endeavors (e.g., molecular biology).

Third, some players will be bold enough to attempt to rearrange the pieces in order to gain more points than the pieces originally earned. These players, who make more intimate and elegant the match between fact and theory, are analogues of true scientific *revolutionaries.* A revolutionary rejects the received configuration of elements for one that is more comprehensive and yet often more parsimonious as well. Lavoisier's new chemistry recast most of the same findings discussed by adherents of the phlogiston theory into a far more elegant exposition that nonetheless accommodated all the key facts. The greater is the gain in explanatory power over the previous configuration, the more critical will be the revolutionary's scientific contribution.

The pseudo-Scrabble analogy leads us to expect another benefit to arise from such a revolutionary arrangement of configurations. Anyone who has played a game of real Scrabble has observed that gaps normally appear in the configuration of pieces, gaps that persist throughout the remainder of the game. A word simply does not exist that will fit into these residual spaces and still form valid words with the pieces enclosing the gap. In crossword puzzles these regions are indicated in black to be ignored, but in Scrabble (and in pseudo-Scrabble) these overlooked squares may bring many points to that player who can find a way to cover the hole. According to the rules of pseudo-Scrabble, a rearrangement of the pieces may just do the trick. In scientific revolutions, too, a novel domain of knowledge is often opened up that would have been foreclosed under the traditional paradigm. For example, Einstein's special relativity theory did more than provide a more parsimonious account of the Michelson–Morley interferometer experiment than could be extracted from classical physics (e.g., the Lorentz–Fitzgerald contraction), for the theory spawned areas of inquiry that could not be comprehended within the classical framework (e.g., the mass–energy relation, space–time, etc.).

Even though the analogy thus provides a useful typology of scientific contributions, pseudo-Scrabble cannot explain with any elegance the individual differences in creative potential. As it now stands, all players are treated equally, making it impossible to distinguish genius from talent, talent from mediocrity. To be sure, we can always argue that some players are far more adept at generating permutations than others are; and some players have richer vocabularies for recognizing more permutations as legitimate words (or stable combinations) – a case of chance favoring the prepared mind. Even so, I do not think that we can capture the full variation in personal capacities without first modifying the game. Pseudo-Scrabble, like the original game, was designed so that all players could enjoy an equal chance of success, this to make the game fair. Yet life is unfair: In the real world, initial inequalities are to be expected, and so we may wish to fix the rules accordingly. To illustrate, instead of all players drawing from the same bag of letters, a separate bag may be allotted to each player. Some of the bags will contain all the letters of the alphabet, whereas others will contain fewer, even only one, in the extreme case. Indeed, if we have recruited enough players to try out this new game, we can make the number of players who have a specified number of letters follow the normal distribution (or, rather, the binomial approximation). We then will have a situation like that treated in chapter 4, in which the distribution of creative potential (i.e., the number of words that are feasible given the set of letters) is far more skewed, and hence élitist, than is the distribution of intellectual capacity (i.e., the number of letters). In line with what we described in chapter 5, individual differences in the number of letters allotted would presumably reflect certain features of each player's biography. In any case, given such modifications in the game regulations, pseudo-Scrabble can approximate the finer details of the phenomenon of scientific creativity.

I do not want to push the Scrabble analogy too far, as that would be as dangerous as taking too seriously the analogy between biological and cultural evolution. The pseudo-Scrabble game certainly cannot capture all the complexity of the chance-configuration theory, and its congruence with scientific creativity is more remote still. Even so, I find the analogy a useful illustration of some of the theory's features.

Applications

Besides offering a predictive and explanatory foundation for comprehending scientific luminaries, the chance-configuration theory supports many broader implications regarding how we might measure and encourage creativity in science.

Measurement

In some respects, the theory could make us pessimistic about the prospects for devising psychometric indicators of scientific "creativity." Although some global creativity tests have displayed correlations with ratings of research contributions (e.g., Jones 1964; Mullins 1963), these validity coefficients are often small and inconsistent and accordingly may have minimal predictive utility (see, e.g., Mansfield & Busse 1981). The main drawback of these measures is that they gauge cognitive skills that are not nearly specific enough to tap directly into the creative process in science. According to this theory, the capacity for generating chance permutations in a given scientific domain depends on an individual's mind holding an impressive supply of richly interassociated mental elements *within* that domain. Yet seldom, if ever, do instruments assess such particulars (cf. Gough 1976). Although Amabile (1983) defended the distinction between creativity-specific and domain-specific skills, all of her research concentrated on artistic rather than scientific creativity. In most of the arts, such as poetry and painting, a respectable proportion of the elements that are aesthetically manipulated are available to almost every intelligent person. A poet deals with common experience and emotions, using a mostly everyday vocabulary, and a painter takes advantage of sensations and perceptions that are part of the visual repertoire of almost everyone. In most sciences, by comparison, the key mental elements that must feed into the creative process are extremely unusual inasmuch as they must be acquired via specialized training with rare techniques and instrumentation, like mathematical functions, telescopes, barometers, and microscopes. It is for this reason, indeed, that a scientist's childhood and adolescence can be more traditional, or conventional, than an artist's can, for the artist must conceive even commonplace objects and events in novel terms.

We would therefore expect standard creativity tests, such as those that measure divergent responses to different mundane stimuli, to have more predictive value for artistic than for scientific creativity, and this appears to be the case (see e.g., Helson & Crutchfield 1970; Hudson 1966; Nicholls 1972). Probably only musical creativity among the arts requires the expertise that puts it closer to the scientific end of the implicit specificity scale (Schubert et al. 1977). On the other hand, tests that are better tailored to match the requirements of particular scientific domains often have more honorable validity coefficients (see, e.g., Flanagan 1963; Gough 1976; Owens 1969).

Certain other personal attributes do provide a necessary though not sufficient foundation for scientific creativity. High intelligence, as detected by IQ scores, does not guarantee that a person has a talent for doing innovative science, yet a person whose intellectual ability is average or lower has virtually no chance whatsoever of making the grade (Simonton 1985a). Likewise, enthusiasm for, and commitment to, a single scientific field is a sine qua non – but excitement and energy may also be present to no avail. Some researchers have suggested that creativity may be better predicted by dispositional traits than by cognitive attributes (e.g., Nicholls 1972), and creativity measures have been devised with that notion in mind (e.g., Cattell 1963; Davis 1975; Gough 1979). Such an approach was also adopted for predicting scientific productivity (e.g., Rushton, Murray, & Paunonen 1987). Nevertheless, we cannot deny that these traits do not ensure that an individual will be creative even when it has been shown that the traits are essential to creativity.

There is a more subtle reason that personality inventories may not serve as useful measures of creativity: Many of the personality traits that the theory holds as connected with the creative process are not stable over the life of any given individual. We have repeatedly observed that a creative person expends creative potential in the very act of self-organization, gradually converting from an intuitive to an analytical genius. Accordingly, many personality characteristics that prevail at the beginning of a scientist's career will not always be identical with those that are most conspicuous at the career's close. For instance, the youthful creator will likely be more intuitive, curious, impulsive, risk taking, receptive to new ideas, and introverted, whereas the creative elder will probably be more analytical, deliberate, conservative, and extroverted. There is some evidence, though based on studies of educators rather than scientists, that both divergent thinking abilities and a preference for complexity decline with age, even though intelligence displays no parallel descent (Alpaugh & Birren 1977; see also

Bromley 1956; McCrae, Arenberg, & Costa 1987). Such longitudinal personality contrasts should become conspicuous whenever individuals are first matched on initial levels of creative potential. In any case, existence of life-span development shifts in personality help explain why correlations between personality attributes and creative performance are often modest; much of the cross-sectional covariation is confounded by within-subject changes in character corresponding to the curve shown in Figure 4.3. Hence the theory leads us to expect that the validity coefficients for predicting creativity via personality should increase once career age differences are controlled for. I know of no data on this point, but this prediction can be easily exposed to empirical scrutiny (cf. Mullins 1963).

If the personality characteristics presented in chapter 3 cannot help us, then perhaps the developmental antecedents discussed in chapter 5 will prove more useful. Not surprisingly, a number of investigators have tried to invent biographical inventories that pinpoint those with creative potential, by using clues from family background, education, and other developmental variables (e.g., Buel, Albright, & Glennon 1966; Smith et al. 1961; Taylor 1963; Taylor & Ellison 1967; Whiting 1972). At times the correlations of these indicators with criteria of creative performance are fairly good, suggesting that this procedure holds promise, and yet the results are not always reliable. Needless to say, if we adopt this approach, then the methodological orientation will clearly convert from the measurement of creativity to the identification of creative persons, which may be an easier task. Even so, here, as earlier, we are stymied by the omnipresent problem of necessary versus sufficient causality. Certain developmental factors may help us identify who may not have much chance of achieving success in science, but something more is needed to take the identification farther. It is one thing to exclude contestants, another to choose the winners.

These difficulties with traditional indicators of creativity have led many investigators to look for still other alternatives. Perhaps the best procedure for assessing a person's creativity is to examine actual creative performance. One psychologist concluded after an exhaustive review of the available indicators that "an inventory of self-reported creative activities and accomplishments is the most defensible technique for selecting creative individuals" (Hocevar 1981, p. 450). By its very nature, a behavioral indicator will automatically be domain specific. That is, under normal circumstances, scientists will seldom list artworks that they have exhibited, nor will artists enumerate the articles that they have published in scientific journals–except for the few Leonardo da Vincis that straddle both universes. In fact, by so operationalizing creativity, we come close to applying the conclusions expressed in chapter 4, namely, that creative individuals of all species are characterized by phenomenal productivity. This exceptional output begins early, continues at an unusual rate, and persists, unless artificially constrained, until a creator's last years.

Naturally, in some respects we have begged the question, for if we define creativity in terms of total lifetime output, we will have a measure with no predictive utility. For example, this definition will not allow us to predict who will show the most promise, and it makes no sense to anticipate creativity posthumously. However, we can maneuver around this objection by using the tendency for creative potential to reveal itself in precocious and prolific contributions. The age at which a scientist first begins to publish and the rate at which that scientist produces in the following years may be the best hint we have in identifying prospective talent. Hence, there is some truth, perhaps even understatement, in the conclusion drawn decades ago that it is "probably impractical to predict with useful success, which individuals will in fact be creative until almost the time they actually begin demonstrating their productivity" (Golovin 1963, p. 20).

In the last analysis, indeed, precocious and prolific contribution merely facilitates the identification of those with creative potential. We still have to grapple with predictors that are not sufficient indicators. Access to lifetime productivity will also not help us circumvent this objection. The constant-probability-of-success model maintains that quality is positively but loosely correlated with quantity, with noticeable scatter around the regression line. We can never know for sure, therefore, whether the prolific scientist we have identified as creative is actually a mass producer or whether the relatively unproductive scientist we have rejected as nearly silent is in fact one of those rare perfectionists. To be sure, we can cheat by gauging quality more directly, by using citation indices, professional honors, or historical acclaim, yet to go this far is to give up the search for bona fide *predictors* of scientific creativity. The more validity and reliability that we demand of our measures, the less well we can anticipate outcomes far in advance. Hence, the measurement problems are complex and perhaps insurmountable if we are truly seeking a nontrivial solution.

Encouragement

Whatever the outcome of attempts at measuring or identifying scientific talent, we have at our disposal, courtesy of the theory, the wherewithal to encourage the development and expression of creativity in science (cf. Bavelas 1987; McGuire 1988; Stein 1974). Specifically, the theory outlines the general conditions that favor discovery and invention. As Campbell (1960, p. 397) summarized them, "a creative solution is more likely the longer a problem is worked upon, the more variable the thought trials, the more people working on the problem independently, the more heterogeneous these people, the less the time pressure, etc." Any cognitive, developmental, personality, or sociocultural variable that overlaps with one or more of these favorable conditions will affect the prospects for scientific advance. For example, general economic prosperity, if coupled with specific financial investment in the scientific enterprise, should increase the amount of time and the number of scientists devoted to a problem and concomitantly decrease the time pressures (cf. Rainoff 1929; Schmookler 1966). Similarly, open research institutions that recruit scientists from diverse backgrounds may expand the heterogeneity of the investigators attacking a problem, thereby increasing the odds of success accordingly (see, e.g., Andrews 1979; Pelz & Andrews 1976). Moreover, the introduction of various brainstorming devices can help scientists learn how to make their thought trials more variable and proportionately productive (cf. Osborn 1953; Parnes & Meadow 1963). And an educational system that nurtures more contrasts of opinion and variety of expertise may be highly desirable. Certainly, rote memorization as an educational technique appears ill advised to the degree that it hinders the acquisition of mental elements that are richly interconnected by largely intuitive associations.

Because the previous chapters, especially the fifth, discuss the origins of creativity, we need not expound this point any further. Suffice it to say that the theory suggests many means for augmenting scientific creativity, if not the frequency of genius. Yet it cannot be stressed too much that these conditions are probabilistic rather than deterministic in nature, the effects operating only on the average. As a case in point, even though the probability of producing a significant finding is a function of the total number of chance permutations generated, departures from expectation will be scattered about both sides of the curve. Within a single scientist's career, there will be fruitful years in which every publication is a hit, and dry years with uninterrupted strings of defeats. This happens because quantity and quality will fluctuate not in tandem but in casual correspondence. The probabilistic nexus between output and social acceptance is perhaps more striking when we turn to the variation across careers. At one extreme, as we observed when we discussed the Ortega hypothesis, a relatively ungifted scientist may have only one idea to present to the world yet be lucky enough for that one contribution to mark a spot in the history books. Gregor Mendel, who published few papers for a scientist of his renown, may figure in this category: Had he picked a plant other than *Pisum* or had he run his tabulations on different genetic traits, he might not have arrived at the clean ratios that led him to adduce his laws of inheritance.

At the other extreme, even the most creative scientists will generate many failed ideas for every grand success. Charles Darwin admitted in his autobiography that "I cannot remember a single first-formed hypothesis which had not after a time to be given up or greatly modified" (F. Darwin 1892, pp. 55–56). And Hermann von Helmholtz, when honored by a great banquet on his 70th birthday, warned his admirers how much his self-view contrasted with their image of him:

the chief difference lies here: what I have seen slowly growing from small beginnings through months and years of tedious and often enough of tentative work, from invisible germs, has suddenly sprung out before your eyes like the armed Pallas from the head of Jupiter. Your judgment was modified by surprise, mine not: it may indeed, if anything, have been depressed by the fatigue incident on work and by annoyance at all the many irrational steps that I had made by the way. (quoted in Koenigsberger 1906, pp. 400–401)

The haphazard nature of scientific creativity is one of the main points to be gleaned from the chapter on introspective reports and anecdotes. This fact should demystify the scientific genius and thereby encourage young scientists intimidated by the myths concerning the scientific heroes of the past (see also Weisberg 1986). As Campbell (1974b, p. 155) expressed it in another paper, "too many potential creators are inhibited by a belief that gifted others solve problems directly." It is not surprising, then, that many notable scientists have offered advice to the novice that strives to undermine intimidating misconceptions about how to do great science. Hadamard (1945, p. 55), for example, recommended that "one rule proves evidently useful: that is, after working on a subject and seeing no further advance seems possible, to drop it and try something else, but to do so provisionally, intending to resume it after an interval of some months. This is useful advice for every student who is beginning research work." Too many times an inexperienced researcher reduces the variability of thought trials by advancing up a conceptual cul de sac – often on the basis of some analytical preconception, conventional heuristic, or false hunch – and doggedly remain trapped there. Warned Herbert Spencer (1904, p. 465),

While thought continues to be forced down certain wrong turnings which had originally been taken, the search is vain; but with the cessation of strain the true association of ideas has an opportunity of asserting itself. . . . [Q]uiet contemplation of the problem from time to time, allows those proclivities of thought which have probably been caused unawares by experiences, to make themselves felt, and to guide the mind to the right conclusion.

On the flip side of the same coin, the behavioral psychologist B. F. Skinner (1959, p. 363), in an autobiographical essay that illustrates his own conspicuous willingness to use serendipity, proclaimed "a first principle not formally recognized by scientific methodologists: when you run onto something interesting, drop everything else and study it." Illustrious contributors to the scientific enterprise succeed in part because they are willing to take advantage of opportunities as they arise, rather than insist on pursuing a predetermined plan. Indeed, there are data supporting the proposition that those scientists who change topics tend to be more productive than are those who stick to the same restricted research program (Garvey & Tomita 1972). The Muses cannot be coerced, but they do offer spontaneous gifts if they are left alone.

It is not important for us to pin down the precise reason that the myth of the infallible and deliberate genius enjoys such wide currency. But I suspect that this false impression results from two sources. First, just as Kuhn (1970) blamed the authors of textbooks for blurring the discontinuities imposed on scientific progress by revolutionaries, so may our conceptions of genius be distorted by narratives that detail where a great scientist was right while concomitantly ignoring major missteps in the belief that these are mere historical curiosities. The tendency of text writers to transpose earlier thoughts into modern nomenclature, notation, and deduction aggravates this misperception all the more, making past figures in science far more foresightful than is justified by the primary documents. Second, the notion of an instantaneously perspicacious intellect may ensue from personal contacts that many of us have had with intimidating analytical geniuses who, when given well-defined problems that have solutions directly derivable from received knowledge, can toss off an answer in a flash, almost without meditation. If so, then we should remind ourselves that even idiot savants can display such prodigious applications of routinized thought. Something qualitatively different is necessary for true innovation. And here what distinguishes the genius is the cognitive and motivational capacity to spew forth a profusion of chance permutations pertaining to a particular problem. This generative ability is not attached to any equally awesome gift for bypassing all the false starts and fallacious conjectures. Geniuses are right more often only because they are wrong more often, too.

To summarize, creativity in science may be fostered by means both indirect and direct or, rather, impersonal and personal. At the indirect, impersonal level, we know what conditions maximize the chances for arriving at discoveries and inventions. And at the direct, personal level, we can describe how scientific creativity actually operates, rather than watch talented youths intimidated by unsubstantiated myths of analytical prowess (see also Beveridge 1957, 1980).

Comparisons

Let us next compare the present theory with the perspectives provided in the several metasciences, with an eye toward showing how the chance-configuration theory provides a constructive contribution. In particular, we shall look at the philosophy, history, and sociology of science.

Philosophy of science

Except for the implicit assumption that a psychology of science is feasible in principle (see Barker 1988; Houts 1988), every effort was made to avoid broaching epistemological issues when expounding the theory. This unwillingness to commit the theory philosophically held despite my personal predilections for an evolutionary epistemology, such as that advocated by Donald Campbell (1974a). Whatever the desirability of having the two disciplines converge on the subject of science, a psychology of science can be divorced from a philosophy of science (cf. Stevens 1939). To use a distinction made by Feyerabend (1975) and perhaps too often repeated, we are more intrigued with the "context of discovery" than with the "context of justification" (see also Popper 1959; cf. Hanson 1958). It is for this reason that the common division between discovery and invention is ignored in favor of the larger designation, creativity. Here we approve Hadamard's (1945, p. xi) assertion that the separation of discoveries and inventions "does not truly concern us; and, as a matter of fact, psychological conditions are quite the same for both cases." And he added, "Indeed, it is obvious that invention or discovery, be it in mathematics or anywhere else, takes place by combining ideas" (p. 29). Not only have discoveries and inventions been discussed in the same breath as psychological equivalents, but the differences between scientific and artistic forms of creativity have been somewhat obscured. Because the theory purports to apply as well to the arts as to the sciences, scientific knowledge is judged in the context of self-organization, of aesthetic appeal, rather than in terms of truth criteria (Simonton 1987b).

This contrast in intent between two metasciences also constitutes my response to those who may criticize the theory's emphasis on "irrationality" rather than "rationality" in the creation of science (cf. Caws 1969; Lamb & Easton 1984, chap. 2; Simon 1977). Rationality, or the symbolization of ideas in experiment and logic, is certainly a central requirement for successful communication configurations. Scientists must justify their thoughts to colleagues in the accepted manner. P. A. M. Dirac (1963, p. 47), after discussing why Schrödinger failed to publish a relativistic wave equation, stated that "it is more important to have beauty in one's equations than to have them fit experiment." Even if we accept Dirac's argument "that if one is working from the point of view of getting beauty in one's equations, and if one has really a sound insight, one is on a sure line of progress" (p. 47), no scientist, including Dirac, would ever be so bold as to justify a theory on so irrational a basis as "beauty" or, to use Poincaré's phrase, "emotional sensibility" – however much sense this may make from the standpoint of self-organization.

On the other hand, monumental breakthroughs in science require such drastic departures from received wisdom that a "random-search" procedure becomes mandatory, thereby allowing more latitude for the injection of irrationality into scientific creativity (Golovin 1963). That the initial quest for a novel configuration must be unrestrained by logic is reflected in this curious story: Niels Bohr, after hearing Wolfgang Pauli present to a professional audience a new theory of elementary particles, summarized the subsequent discussion by saying that "we are all agreed that your theory is crazy. The question which divides us is whether it is crazy enough to have a chance of being correct. My own feeling is that it is not crazy enough" (quoted in Cropper 1970, p. 57). Even so, the irrationality implied by the theory is considerably qualified. First, for the reasons discussed in chapters 2 and 3, much of the quest for viable configurations happens at the infraconscious or subliminal level of awareness. Consequently, a scientist's core consciousness may yet be preoccupied with more rational cognition, in contrast with that of artistic creators.

Second, the chance-permutation procedure is rational insofar as it is rooted in associative networks that have been established through experience. Because creative individuals are raised in enriching environments, their mental elements are connected with weak but active associations, a condition that enables numerous, mostly equiprobable connections among diverse concepts. Yet even the wildest juxtapositions of ideas are grounded in personal experience, however autistic. Speaking of his own creative leaps, Einstein observed that "to these elementary laws there leads no logical path, but only intuition," adding that the latter is "supported by being sympathetically in touch with experience" (quoted in Holton 1971–1972, p. 97).

Finally, because mental aggregates are rejected and only configurations are retained for further processing, rationality is imposed in yet another fashion; the individual is engaged in self-organization and thus seeks intellectual coherence. That cohesion of thought, to be sure, may be at times more subjective than objective, or more psycho-logical than fully logical, but it remains bounded by some guise of rationality nontheless (cf. Faust

1984; Polanyi 1968). Order, even in the shape of beauty, is more reasonable than is chaos and so is nearer to the truth – at least by instinctual assumption.

In any case, there is a definite place alongside the philosophy of science for a psychology of science (see also Singer 1971). The two metasciences deal with different problems. One concerns how scientific knowledge can be justified against some abstract epistemological scheme, the other how prospective knowledge originates within the creative mind of the individual scientist.

History of science

I may have relied too much on Thomas Kuhn's *Structure of Scientific Revolutions* (1970), ignoring the other descriptions of the course of science advocated by Lakatos (1978) and Laudan (1977), among others (see Gholson & Barker 1985). Kuhn's seminal ideas have been much used and abused in the social sciences, in part as a defensive reaction to whether a particular discipline is "pre-paradigmatic" (Harvey 1982; Peterson 1981). Nonetheless, that I have occasionally used Kuhn's terms does not signify that I totally subscribe to his theory. On the contrary, I have merely mentioned a portion of his nomenclature – the notions of "paradigm" and "anomaly," and "normal" and "revolutionary" science – for the simple reason that these concepts are well known to scholars in both the humanities and the sciences. Whatever Kuhn's success at describing the progression of scientific events, he undoubtedly succeeded in disseminating a set of useful labels for important ideas, labels that provide a lingua franca for discussion. Consequently, the validity of the chance-configuration theory as an account of the genesis of scientific creativity does not depend on the acceptance of Kuhn's own theoretical propositions.

Of course, this theory, like Kuhn's work, proposes a number of general principles that purport to overlay the specifics of historical narratives. Many historians distrust generalizations supposedly abstracted from events originally tagged with particular names, dates, and places (e.g., Barzun 1974). These skeptics act according to the aphorism attributed to Alexandre Dumas *fils* that "all generalizations are dangerous, even this one." Countering to this disposition, the chance-configuration theory clearly tries to explain the "laws of history" in science, and in a scientific language. With such an aspiration, some hostile historians could brand it a mere "philosophy of history," for many a pejorative label. Even so, my enterprise departs from philosophical history, for the generalizations are mostly founded on quantitative techniques (Simonton 1984d, chap. 1). The nomothetic findings that permeate the theoretical developments consist largely of statistical relations among observed variables. Whenever possible, the theory is reduced to mathematical equations that can be verified empirically. Except in chapter 2, qualitative speculations that could not be translated into more formal terms were avoided. Hence, our approach is scientific rather than humanistic, unlike the philosophy of history.

Because much of the theory depends on the statistical analysis of historical and biographical data–particularly in the chapters on productivity, developmental antecedents, and multiples–historians of science may encounter another source of irritation in these pages. As a group, historians are wary of quantitative approaches to the facts of history. That they find such techniques objectionable is revealed in the generally adverse response of the discipline to "cliometrics" (cf. Erikson 1975). Ironically, this antagonism holds equally well for probably the majority of those historians who supposedly appreciate science by studying science. To be sure, Derek Price was himself, though nominally a historian of science, a practitioner of the quantitative and nomothetic examination of science and scientists. The Price law of productivity and his principle of exponential growth illustrate his commitment to such methods (Price 1963). Nevertheless, because Price first did graduate work in the physical sciences, he may represent the exception that proves the rule. I remember vividly the antagonisms that Price provided when he addressed the International Symposium on Quantitative Methods in the History of Science, held at the University of California at Berkeley a decade ago. Despite the nominal sympathies of those attending the conference, it was quite evident that a large percentage of the audience was adamantly opposed to a full-fledged quantitative analysis.

I emphasize, therefore, that this book does not try to contribute to the history of science, as it is usually conceived. Rather, my desire is merely for a comprehensive theory of how psychological processes are involved in the advent of novel scientific ideas. The theory does not attempt to explain specific scientific events, as is the primary goal of historians of science. As long as historians focus on the idiographic rather than the nomothetic, there can be no grounds for conflict. Only when historians generalize about the basis for scientific genius would they be encroaching on the theory's explanatory turf.

Sociology of science

Although sociologists of science, especially those belonging to the Mertonian school (e.g., Cole & Cole 1973; Gaston 1978; Zuckerman 1977), are more obviously dedicated to quantitative and nomothetic analyses, their nomenclature and theoretical constructs differ from those favored in the present sociopsychological enterprise. Indeed, the same data are often treated in contrary ways. Thus, in the chapter on productivity we did not evoke the doctrine of accumulative advantage in order to explain the chief facets of variation in output across and within scientific careers; these phenomena are held to ensue from the information-processing requirements intrinsic to the creation of knowledge, as articulated by the theory, without any intrusion of the reward structures of science. This is not to say that the reward system may not exaggerate initial inequalities in creative potential but only that such social effects operate on an already heterogeneous pool of applicants for honors and prestige.

Also absent from discussion is any mention of the "Mertonian norms," such as universalism and disinterestedness, that are presumed to keep scientists honest and to hold science on track toward the accumulation of objective and permanent knowledge (cf. Mulkay 1980). Rather than impose social norms from outside the individual, we assumed that the individuals are themselves responsible for the self-discipline that checks extravagance, fraudulence, and error in science. Specifically, the inherent quest for self-organization convinces scientists that extraneous regulation is largely superfluous. As a consequence, there can be serious scientists without an institution or a community of scientists and without a consensus on norms, something incredible if established and enforced norms were essential to maintain law and order (cf. Mulkay 1980). In other words, this theory can handle the earlier era of "little science," when each scientist stood largely alone against the world, as well as the current period of "big science," when scientists form large social enterprises. All the same, the principle of self-organization is not omnipotent or infallible. Even if the need for self-organization serves as the dominant motive in scientists of genius, that need still has to compete with rival motives, including motives that may compromise scientific integrity, such as the desire for fame and fortune (see, e.g., Mahoney 1976; Maslow 1966). Even worse, self-organization can misguide scientists, forcing them to stray from a full commitment to what we, in our wise hindsight, see to be the truth. Planck's principle, discussed in chapter 4, as well as the confirmation bias, mentioned in chapter 1, illustrate this point (see also Faust 1984; Holton 1982).

To summarize, rather than incorporate key concepts from the sociology of science, I have tried to introduce an alternative scheme that handles many of the same substantive issues in entirely distinctive terms. Insofar as the sociological factors operate at all, they presumably are imposed on the creative process from the outside, rather than serving as primary generative principles of scientific creativity. According to this intrinsically psychological theory, sociology may have more to say about the acceptance of scientific ideas than about their origination (see, e.g., Brannigan 1981).

The psychology of science

The foregoing comparisons suggest that a definite spot is reserved among the established metasciences for a psychology of science (see also Houts 1988). Even so, that such a niche exists does not automatically mean that the current theory can claim possession of it. In some significant ways, the position in this book contradicts recent attempts to subsume scientific creativity under mainstream cognitive psychology (see Faust 1984; Hayes 1981; Weisberg 1986). In particular, the chance-configuration theory does not encourage those who believe that it is now feasible for digital computers to simulate the creative process in science (see e.g., Bradshaw, Langley, & Simon 1983; Langley, Simon, Bradshaw, & Zytkow 1987). At present, to program a computer to "make discoveries" means nothing more than to translate into some Boolean algebra a set of heuristics about the best way to solve a particular class of predetermined problems. This analytical approach ignores the likelihood that sometimes half of the difficulty in exhibiting creativity is identifying the problem. Great scientists often spot puzzles where others think nothing is amiss. Even worse, much of the other half of the difficulty in doing creative science probably is isolating the proper heuristics for the specific problems. A strict "random-search" procedure, though theoretically programmable in computer logic, also will not carry us around this last impasse. For a computer to generate the kind of chance permutations suggested by the theory, it must first acquire the rich associative networks that underpin the creative process in human heads. At some future date, computers may attain the memory capacity to absorb and retrieve the requisite (by one estimate) "50,000 chunks" of pertinent information (Simon 1986), perhaps by using the same complex developmental experiences that we described in chapter 5, but until then computers can simulate only analytical, not intuitive, genius.

Once the point is reached that we do indeed have computers with elaborate matrices of associations (and have programmed them with innate dispositions to self-organize that inchoate knowledge), we will likely learn through simulation how the current efforts to promulgate an easy "logic of discovery" served merely to trivialize the acts of scientific genius. Herbert Simon (1973, p. 479), as a case in point, would have us believe that the discovery of the periodic law of the elements engaged nothing more sophisticated than what is "required to handle patterned letter sequences." This assertion fails to grasp how hard it was for most of the scientific world to discern the "obvious" periodicities. When John Newlands, just a handful of years before Mendeléev, announced how the elements displayed recurrent properties when arranged according to atomic weight – thus presenting his "law of octaves" – a notable scientist greeted him with the derisive query as to whether better results might be obtained by placing the elements in alphabetical order! Needless to say, what is obvious in retrospect becomes far less so when an idea has yet to be printed in boldface and italics in standard textbooks. Anyhow, insofar as the chance-configuration theory implies that much of the current psychology of science has misplaced its emphasis on rational cognitive heuristics, I do not expect psychologists in this tradition to respond favorably to this treatise (but see Langley et al. 1987, pp. 15–16).

Furthermore, even psychologists sympathetic to the chance-configuration theory may have some grounds for complaint. For instance, some potential adherents may disagree with my refusal to discuss the cognitive, maybe even neurological, mechanisms responsible for the process of self-organization, including the isolation of configurations. I have chosen to be largely silent here, even though I have elsewhere observed the affinities between the present theory and the neurocognitive model proposed by Findlay and Lumsden (1988), an overlap that may offer a psychoneurological foundation for much of the discussion in earlier chapters (Simonton 1988). Other researchers may dislike my failure to treat certain fashionable topics, such as the role of gender in scientific achievement (cf. Cole 1987; Goldstein 1979; McDowell 1982). And the fact that my viewpoint aims primarily at explaining scientific genius may not satisfy those researchers more intrigued by everyday guises of creativity in science, in which routine rather than original work may be the norm. Nonetheless, these complaints would merely tell us that the theory remains open-ended with opportunities for further development in numerous directions.

More serious, I think, are the objections to the theory's conception of creative genius in science. Certainly those psychologists who subscribe to a more heroic image of genius would have much to complain about in the chance-configuration theory. Exceptional scientists are deemed more passive, less in control of their fates, than suggested by more romantic views of such luminaries. Rather than actively and deliberately make progress, in some impressive insight into the foundations of reality, the genius here can only shift through chance permutations, select some of these to present to fellow scientists, and wait for some of them to be accepted while others recede into oblivion. The genius, no matter what the magnitude, is not privileged with any shortcuts to success, whether in the generation of worthwhile configurations or in the social acceptance of those configurations.

Instead, just as chance permutations are subjected to cognitive selection on the intrapsychic plane, communication configurations are subjected to social selection on the interpersonal and sociocultural planes. Furthermore, because the constant-probability-of-success model applies as well to within-career as to across-career variation, scientists cannot improve the likelihood of winning combinations as they acquire more professional experience. No special heuristics or cognitive tricks of the trade can be mastered that accelerate the isolation of accepted breakthroughs. If it were otherwise, we would be hard-pressed to explain why, say, Einstein's unified field theory was far less well received than were his theories of relativity (cf. Bradshaw et al. 1983). The most that geniuses can hope for is to optimize their chances by producing as many ideational variations as practically possible.

Because the scientific creator, no matter how grand, must stumble upon the truth with blind determination, a primary dogma of the old cult of genius has seemingly been upset (see also Faust 1984; Medawar 1984; Watson 1930, p. 247; Weisberg 1986). Nevertheless, in other respects the chance-configuration theory revives the role of the creative scientist in history. The social deterministic, or zeitgeist, interpretation of history has been shown to be unrealistic; at no time can a contribution be considered inevitable and the individual thus epiphenomenal. At best, all discoveries and inventions will take place only eventually, for the culture helps define merely the necessary conditions for scientific creativity. Creators then serve as cultural catalysts. Moreover, in discussing the developmental antecedents of creative scientists, we repeatedly observed the importance of a scientist not being completely immersed in the prevailing zeitgeist. Frequently the missing component in a winning chance permutation can be found only outside the discipline, sometimes even outside a single culture, thus requiring the successful scientist to be to some degree marginal to the core milieu. In addition, education and other socialization practices can just as well inculcate the excessive consolidation of basic mental elements, accordingly restricting the diversity of the ideational variations that may be generated.

If this theory makes the genius a mere generator of chance permutations, with no direct line to the "truth," the role of genius in scientific creativity will be enlarged in yet another way: To the extent that not all scientists have been injected with the exact same knowledge base, each scientist will have the latitude to produce a different set of chance permutations. Even when two scientists participate in a multiple discovery or invention, their respective contributions will seldom consist of an identical set of elements, nor will those elements be ordered in the same fashion. Consequently, it is not irrelevant which scientist first succeeds in making a given contribution; subsequent generations of scientists must build on what was actually contributed, not the Platonic generic form attributed years later by historians and textbook authors. This means, too, that the creativity of later scientists will have to cope with the idiosyncratic errors along with the insights of their predecessors. Aristotle and Newton are two among many creative scientists whose peculiar mistakes or quirks decisively influenced for centuries the course of scientific history. Thus in the process of producing chance configurations, the scientific genius is also generating one particular realization of history out of an infinite number of possible paths. The more prolific and more variable the permutation process is, the more impressive a scientist's historical impact is likely to be, but that effect can retard as well as catalyze.

By so redefining the role of creative genius in science, I hope to have justified my conclusion that the psychology of science may become a worthy counterpart to the philosophy, history, and sociology of science. Without the addition of a psychological dimension, I believe, it is impossible to appreciate fully the essence of the scientific imagination. And without this appreciation, the origins of science, the emergence of new ideas about natural phenomena, must escape our grasp. Psychology is mandatory if we wish to comprehend the scientific genius as the generator of science.

References

Abelson, P. H. 1968. Relation of group activity to creativity in science. In *Creativity and Learning*, ed. J. Kagan, pp. 191–202. Boston: Beacon Press.

Abt, H. A. 1983. At what ages do outstanding American astronomers publish their most cited papers? *Publications of the Astronomical Society of the Pacific, 95*, 13–16.

Adams, B. N. 1972. Birth order: A critical review. *Sociometry, 35*, 411–439.

Albert, R. S. 1971. Cognitive development and parental loss among the gifted, the exceptionally gifted and the creative. *Psychological Reports, 29*, 19–26.

1975. Toward a behavioral definition of genius. *American Psychologist, 30*, 140–151.

1980. Family positions and the attainment of eminence: A study of special family positions and special family experiences. *Gifted Child Quarterly, 24*, 87–95.

Allen, W., ed. 1949. *Writers on Writing*. New York: Dutton.

Allison, P. D. 1980a. Estimation and testing for a Markov model of reinforcement. *Sociological Methods and Research, 8*, 434–453.

1980b. Inequality and scientific productivity. *Social Studies of Science, 10*, 163–179.

Allison, P. D., Long, J. S., & Krauze, T. K. 1982. Cumulative advantage and inequality in science. *American Sociological Review, 47*, 615–625.

Allison, P. D., Price, D. deS., Griffith, B. C., Moravscik, M. J., & Stewart, J. A. 1976. Lotka's law: A problem in its interpretation and application. *Social Studies of Science, 6*, 269–276.

Allison, P. D., & Stewart, J. A. 1974. Productivity differences among scientists: Evidence for accumulative advantage. *American Sociological Review, 39*, 596–606.

1975. Reply to Faia. *American Sociological Review, 40*, 829–831.

Alpaugh, P. K., & Birren, J. E. 1977. Variables affecting creative contributions across the adult life span. *Human Developments, 20*, 240–248.

Altus, W. D. 1966. Birth order and its sequelae. *Science, 151*, 44–48.

Amabile, T. M. 1983. *The Social Psychology of Creativity*. New York: Springer-Verlag.

Andrews, F. M., ed. 1979. *Scientific Productivity*. Cambridge, England: Cambridge University Press.

Ashby, W. R. 1952. *Design for a Brain*. New York: Wiley.

Ashton, S. V., & Oppenheim, C. 1978. A method of predicting Nobel prizewinners in chemistry. *Social Studies of Science, 8*, 341–348.

Asimov, I. 1982. *Biographical Encyclopedia of Science and Technology*, 2nd rev. ed. New York: Doubleday.

Austin, J. H. 1978. *Chase, Chance, and Creativity*. New York: Columbia University Press.

Bain, A. 1855. *The Senses and the Intellect*, ed. D. N. Robinson. Washington, DC: University Publications of America, 1977. Reprinted from J. W. Parker, London.

Baird, L. L. 1968. The achievement of bright and average students. *Educational and Psychological Measurement, 28*, 891–899.

Barber, B. 1961. Resistance by scientists to scientific discovery. *Science, 134*, 596–602.

Barber, B., & Fox, R. C. 1958. The case of the floppy-eared rabbits: An instance of serendipity gained and serendipity lost. *American Journal of Sociology, 64*, 128–136.

201

Barker, P. 1988. The reflexivity problem in the psychology of science. In *The Psychology of Science and Metascience*, ed. B. Gholson, A. C. Houts, R. A. Neimeyer, & W. R. Shadish. Cambridge, England: Cambridge University Press.

Barnett, H. G. 1953. *Innovation*. New York: McGraw–Hill.

Barron, F. 1963. The needs for order and for disorder as motives in creative activity. In *Scientific Creativity*, ed. C. W. Taylor & F. Barron, pp. 153–160. New York: Wiley.

Barron, F., & Harrington, D. M. 1981. Creativity, intelligence, and personality. *Annual Review of Psychology, 32,* 439–476.

Barron, F., & Welsh, G. S. 1952. Artistic perception as a possible factor in personality style: Its measurement by a figure preference test. *Journal of Psychology, 33,* 199–203.

Bartlett, F. 1958. *Thinking*. New York: Basic Books.

Barzun, J. 1974. *Clio and the Doctors*. Chicago: University of Chicago Press.

Bastik, T. 1982. *Intuition*. New York: Wiley.

Bavelas, J. B. 1987. Permitting creativity in science. In *Scientific Excellence*, ed. D. N. Jackson & J. P. Rushton, pp. 307–327. Beverly Hills, CA: Sage Publications.

Bayer, A. E., & Dutton, J. E. 1977. Career age and research–Professional activities of academic scientists: Tests of alternative non-linear models and some implications for higher education faculty policies. *Journal of Higher Education, 48,* 259–282.

Bayer, A. E., & Folger, J. 1966. Some correlates of a citation measure of productivity in science. *Sociology of Education, 39,* 381–390.

Beard, G. M. 1874. *Legal Responsibility in Old Age*. New York: Russell.

Beaver, D. de B. 1986. Collaboration and teamwork in physics. *Czechoslovak Journal of Physics, B 36,* 14–18.

Bednar, R. L., & Parker, C. A. 1965. The creative development and growth of exceptional college students. *Journal of Educational Research, 59,* 133–136.

Bell, E. T. 1937. *Men of Mathematics*. New York: Simon & Schuster.

Bennett, W. 1980. Providing for posterity. *Harvard Magazine, 82* (No. 3), 13–16.

Bentley, J. C. 1966. Creativity and academic achievement. *Journal of Educational Research, 59,* 269–272.

Berlyne, D. E. 1960. *Conflict, Arousal and Curiosity*. New York: McGraw–Hill.

Bernbaum, M. L., Markus, G. B., & Zajonc, R. B. 1982. A closer look at Galbraith's "closer look." *Developmental Psychology, 18,* 174–180.

Berry, C. 1981. The Nobel scientists and the origins of scientific achievement. *British Journal of Sociology, 32,* 381–391.

Beveridge, W. I. B. 1957. *The Art of Scientific Investigation*, 3rd ed. New York: Vintage.
    1980. *Seeds of Discovery: A Sequel to the Art of Scientific Investigation*. New York: Norton.

Blackburn, R. T., Behymer, C. E., & Hall, D. E. 1978. Correlates of faculty publications. *Sociology of Education, 51,* 132–141.

Bliss, W. D. 1970. Birth order of creative writers. *Journal of Individual Psychology, 26,* 200–202.

Bloom, B. S. 1963. Report on creativity research by the examiner's office of the University of Chicago. In *Scientific Creativity*, ed. C. W. Taylor & F. Barron, pp. 251–264. New York: Wiley.

Boring, E. G. 1963. *History, Psychology, and Science*, ed. R. I. Watson & D. T. Campbell. New York: Wiley.

Bouchard, T. J., Jr., & Hare, M. 1970. Size, performance, and potential in brainstorming groups. *Journal of Applied Psychology, 54,* 51–55.

Boyce, R., Shaughnessy, P., & Pecker, G. 1985. Women and publishing in psychology. *American Psychologist, 40,* 577–578.

Brackbill, Y., & Nichols, P. L. 1982. A test of the confluence model of intellectual development. *Developmental Psychology, 18,* 192–198.

Bradshaw, G. F., Langley, P. W., & Simon, H. A. 1983. Studying scientific creativity by computer simulation. *Science, 222,* 971–975.

Bramwell, B. S. 1948. Galton's "Hereditary Genius" and the three following generations since 1869. *Eugenics Review, 39,* 146–153.

Brannigan, A. 1979. The reification of Mendel. *Social Studies of Science, 9,* 423–454.

1981. *The Social Basis of Scientific Discoveries.* Cambridge, England: Cambridge University Press.

Brannigan, A., & Wanner, R. A. 1983a. Historical distributions of multiple discoveries and theories of scientific change. *Social Studies of Science, 13,* 417–435.

1983b. Multiple discoveries in science: A test of the communication theory. *Canadian Journal of Sociology, 8,* 135–151.

Bridgwater, C. A., Walsh, J. A., & Walkenbach, J. 1982. Pre- and post-tenure productivity trends of academic psychologists. *American Psychologist, 37,* 236–238.

Brodetsky, S. 1942. Newton: Scientist and man. *Nature, 150,* 698–699.

Bromley, D. B. 1956. Some experimental tests of the effect of age on creative intellectual output. *Journal of Gerontology, 11,* 74–82.

Brown, F. 1968. Bereavement and lack of a parent in childhood. In *Foundations of Child Psychiatry,* ed. E. Miller. Oxford, England: Pergamon.

Brown, R. W., & McNeill, D. 1966. The "tip of the tongue" phenomenon. *Journal of Verbal Learning and Verbal Behavior, 5,* 325–337.

Buel, W. D., Albright, L. E., & Glennon, J. R. 1966. A note on the generality and cross-validity of personal history for identifying creative research scientists. *Journal of Applied Psychology, 50,* 217–219.

Busse, T. V., & Mansfield, R. S. 1981. The blooming of creative scientists: Early, late and otherwise. *Gifted Child Quarterly, 25,* 63–66.

1984. Selected personality traits and achievement in male scientists. *Journal of Psychology, 116,* 117–131.

Campbell, D. T. 1960. Blind variation and selective retention in creative thought as in other knowledge processes. *Psychological Review, 67,* 380–400.

1965. Variation and selective retention in socio-cultural evolution. In *Social Change in Developing Areas,* ed. H. R. Barringer, G. I. Blanksten, & R. W. Mack, pp. 19–49. Cambridge, MA: Schenkman.

1974a. Evolutionary epistemology. In *The Philosophy of Karl Popper,* ed. P. A. Schlipp, pp. 413–463. La Salle, IL: Open Court.

1974b. Unjustified variation and selective retention in scientific discovery. In *Studies in the Philosophy of Biology,* ed. F. J. Ayala & T. Dobzhansky, pp. 131–169. London: Macmillan.

1986. Selection theory and the sociology of scientific validity. In *Evolutionary Epistemology,* ed. W. Callebaut & R. Pinxten. Dordrecht, Netherlands; Reidel.

1987. Neurological embodiments of belief and the gaps in the fit of phenomena to noumena. In *Naturalistic Epistemology,* ed. A. Shimony & D. Nails. Dordrecht, Netherlands: Reidel.

Campbell, D. T., & Tauscher, H. 1966. Schopenhauer (?), Séguin, Lubinoff, and Zehender as anticipators of Emmert's Law: With comments on the uses of eponymy. *Journal of the History of the Behavioral Sciences, 2,* 58–63.

Cannon, W. B. 1940. The role of chance in discovery. *Scientific Monthly, 50,* 204–209.

Capitanio, J. P., & Leger, D. W. 1979. Evolutionary scales lack utility: A reply to Yarczower and Hazlett. *Psychological Bulletin, 86,* 876–879.

Carneiro, R. L. 1970. Scale analysis, evolutionary sequences, and the rating of cultures. In *A Handbook of Method in Cultural Anthropology,* ed. R. Naroll & R. Cohen, pp. 834–876. New York: Natural History Press.

Cattell, J. McK. 1903. A statistical study of eminent men. *Popular Science Monthly, 62,* 359–377.

1910. A further statistical study of American men of science. *Science, 32,* 633–648.

Cattell, R. B. 1963. The personality and motivation of the researcher from measurements of contemporaries and from biography. In *Scientific Creativity,* ed. C. W. Taylor & F. Barron, pp. 119–131. New York: Wiley.

Caws, P. 1969. The structure of discovery. *Science, 166,* 1375–1380.

Chambers, J. A. 1964. Relating personality and biographical factors to scientific creativity. *Psychological Monographs: General and Applied, 78* (Whole No. 584), 1–20.

Chipp, H. B., ed. 1968. *Theories of Modern Art.* Berkeley and Los Angeles: University of California Press.

Christensen, P. R., Guilford, J. P., & Wilson, R. C. 1957. Relations of creative responses to working time and instructions. *Journal of Experimental Psychology, 53,* 82–88.

Clark, K. W. 1957. *America's Psychologists.* Washington, DC: American Psychological Association.

Clark, R. D., & Rice, G. A. 1982. Family constellations and eminence; The birth orders of Nobel prize winners. *Journal of Psychology, 110,* 281–287.

Clemente, F. 1973. Early career determinants of research productivity. *American Journal of Sociology, 79,* 409–419.

Cole, J. R. 1987. Women in science. In *Scientific Excellence,* ed. D. N. Jackson & J. P. Rushton, pp. 359–375. Beverly Hills, CA: Sage Publications.

Cole, J. R., & Cole, S. 1972. The Ortega hypothesis. *Science, 178,* 368–375.

1973. *Social Stratification in Science.* Chicago: University of Chicago Press.

Cole, S. 1970. Professional standing and the reception of scientific discoveries. *American Journal of Sociology, 76,* 286–306.

1979. Age and scientific performance. *American Journal of Sociology, 84,* 958–977.

Cole, S., & Cole, J. R. 1967. Scientific output and recognition: A study in the operation of the reward system in science. *American Sociological Review, 32,* 377–390.

1971. Measuring the quality of sociological research: Problems in the use of the *Science Citation Index. American Sociologist, 6,* 23–29.

Cole, S., Cole, J. R., & Simon, G. A. 1981. Chance and consensus in peer review. *Science, 214,* 881–886.

Constant, E. W. 1978. On the discovery and co-evolution of technological multiples: Steam turbines and Pelton water wheels. *Social Studies of Science, 8,* 183–210.

Cox, C. 1926. *The Early Mental Traits of Three Hundred Geniuses.* Stanford, CA: Stanford University Press.

Crandall, R. 1978. The relationship between quantity and quality of publications. *Personality and Social Psychology Bulletin, 4,* 379–380.

Crane, D. 1965. Scientists at major and minor universities: A study of productivity and recognition. *American Sociological Review, 30,* 699–714.

1972. *Invisible Colleges.* Chicago: University of Chicago Press.

Cronbach, L. J. 1960. *Essentials of Psychological Testing,* 2nd ed. New York: Harper & Row.

Crook, T., & Eliot, J. 1980. Parental death during childhood and adulthood depression: A critical review. *Psychological Bulletin, 87,* 252–259.

Cropley, A. J. 1967. *Creativity.* London: Longmans, Green.

Cropper, W. H. 1970. *The Quantum Physicists.* New York: Oxford University Press.

Crowther, J. G. 1968. *Science in Modern Society.* New York: Schocken Books.

Daintith, J., Mitchell, S., & Tootill, E. 1981. *A Biographical Encyclopedia of Scientists,* 2 vols. New York: Facts on File.

Darwin, C. 1860. *The Origin of Species,* 2nd ed. In *Great Books of the Western World,* vol. 49, ed. R. M. Hutchins. Chicago: Encyclopaedia Britannica, 1952.

Darwin, F., ed. 1892. *The Autobiography of Charles Darwin and Selected Letters*. New York: Dover, 1958.

Datta, L.-E. 1967. Family religious background and early scientific creativity. *American Sociological Review, 32,* 626–635.

1968. Birth order and potential scientific creativity. *Sociometry, 31,* 76–88.

Davis, G. A. 1975. In frumious pursuit of the creative person. *Journal of Creative Behavior, 9,* 75–87.

Davis, Richard A. 1987. Creativity in neurological publications. *Neurosurgery, 20,* 652–663.

Davis, Robert A. 1954. Note on age and productive scholarship of a university faculty. *Journal of Applied Psychology, 38,* 318–319.

Debus, A. G. 1968. *World Who's Who in Science*. Chicago: Marquis–Who's Who.

Dennis, W. 1954a. Bibliographies of eminent scientists. *Scientific Monthly, 79,* 180–183.

1954b. Predicting scientific productivity in later decades from records of earlier decades. *Journal of Gerontology, 9,* 465–467.

1954c. Productivity among American psychologists. *American Psychologist, 9,* 191–194.

1955. Variations in productivity among creative workers. *Scientific Monthly, 80,* 277–278.

1956a. Age and achievement: A critique. *Journal of Gerontology, 11,* 331–333.

1956b. Age and productivity among scientists. *Science, 123,* 724–725.

1958. The age decrement in outstanding scientific contributions: Fact or artifact? *American Psychologist, 13,* 457–460.

1966. Creative productivity between the ages of 20 and 80 years. *Journal of Gerontology, 21,* 1–8.

Dentler, R. A., & Mackler, B. 1964. Originality: Some social and personal determinants. *Behavioral Science, 9,* 1–7.

Diamond, A. M. 1980. Age and acceptance of cliometrics. *Journal of Economic History, 40,* 838–841.

1984. An economic model of the life-cycle research productivity of scientists. *Scientometrics, 6,* 189–196.

1985. The money value of citations to single-authored and multiple-authored articles. *Scientometrics, 8,* 315–320.

1986. The life-cycle research productivity of mathematicians and scientists. *Journal of Gerontology, 41,* 520–525.

Diemer, G. 1974. Creativity versus age. *Physics Today, 27,* 9.

Dillon P. C., Graham, W. K., & Aidells, A. L. 1972. Brainstorming on a "hot" problem: Effects of training and practice on individual and group performance. *Journal of Applied Psychology, 56,* 487–490.

Dirac, P. A. M. 1963. The evolution of the physicist's picture of nature. *Scientific American, 208,* 45–53.

Dunnette, M., Campbell, J., & Jaastad, K. 1963. The effects of group participation on brainstorming effectiveness for two industrial samples. *Journal of Applied Psychology, 47,* 30–37.

Eagly, R. V. 1974. Contemporary profile of conventional economists. *History of Political Economy, 6,* 76–91.

Eccles, J. C. 1975. Under the spell of the synapse. In *The Neurosciences*, ed. F. G. Worden, J. P. Swazey, & G. Adelman, pp. 159–179. Cambridge, MA: MIT Press.

Eiduson, B. T. 1962. *Scientists: Their Psychological World*. New York: Basic Books.

Einstein, A. 1933. Preface to M. Planck, *Where Is Science Going?* trans. J. Murphy. London: Allen & Unwin.

Eiseley, L. 1958. *Darwin's Century*. Garden City, NY: Doubleday.

Eisenman, R. 1964. Birth order and artistic creativity. *Journal of Individual Psychology, 20,* 183–185.

1987. Creativity, birth order, and risk taking. *Bulletin of the Psychonomic Society, 25*, 87–88.

Eisenstadt, J. M. 1978. Parental loss and genius. *American Psychologist, 33*, 211–223.

Elliott, C. A. 1975. The American scientist in antebellum society: A quantitative view. *Social Studies in Science, 5*, 93–108.

Ellis, H. 1904. *A Study of British Genius*. London: Hurst & Blackett.

Emery, O. B., & Czikszentmihalyi, M. 1982. The socialization effects of cultural role models in ontogenetic development and upward mobility. *Child Psychiatry and Human Development, 12*, 3–19.

Endler, N. S. 1987. The scholarly impact of psychologists. In *Scientific Excellence*, ed. D. N. Jackson & J. P. Rushton, pp. 165–191. Beverly Hills, CA: Sage Publications.

Endler, N. S., Rushton, J. P., & Roediger, H. L., III. 1978. Productivity and scholarly impact (citations) of British, Canadian, and U.S. departments of psychology. *American Psychologist, 33*, 1064–1082.

Epstein, S., & O'Brien, E. J. 1985. The person–situation debate in historical and current perspective. *Psychological Bulletin, 98*, 513–537.

Erikson, C. 1975. Quantitative history. *American Historical Review, 80*, 351–365.

Erikson, E. H. 1951. *Childhood and Society*. New York: Norton.

Faia, M. 1975. Productivity among scientists: A replication and elaboration. *American Sociological Review, 40*, 825–829.

Farnsworth, P. R. 1969. *The Social Psychology of Music*, 2nd ed. Ames: Iowa State University Press.

Faust, D. 1984. *The Limits of Scientific Reasoning*. Minneapolis: University of Minnesota Press.

Feyerabend, P. K. 1975. *Against Method*. London: New Left Books.

Findlay, A. 1948. *A Hundred Years of Chemistry*. 2nd ed. London: Duckworth.

Findlay, C. S., & Lumsden, C. J. 1988. The creative mind: Toward an evolutionary theory of discovery and innovation. *Journal of Social and Biological Structures*, in press.

Fisch, R. 1977. Psychology of science. In *Science, Technology, and Society*, ed. I. Spiegel-Rösing & D. Price, pp. 277–318. London: Sage Publications.

Flanagan, J. C. 1963. The definition and measurement of ingenuity. In *Scientific Creativity*, ed. C. W. Taylor & F. Barron, pp. 89–98. New York: Wiley.

Folly, G., Hajtman, B., Nagy, J. I., & Ruff, I. 1981. Some methodological problems in ranking scientists by citation analysis. *Scientometrics, 3*, 135–147.

Freud, S. 1929. *Civilization and Its Discontents*, trans. J. Riviere. In *Great Books of the Western World*, vol. 54, ed. R. M. Hutchins. Chicago: Encyclopaedia Britannica, 1952.

Fulton, O., & Trow, M. 1974. Research activity in American higher education. *Sociology of Education, 47*, 29–73.

Galbraith, R. C. 1982a. Just one look was all it took: Reply to Bernbaum, Markus, and Zajonc. *Developmental Psychology, 18*, 181–191.

Galbraith, R. C. 1982b. Sibling spacing and intellectual development: A closer look at the confluence model. *Developmental Psychology, 18*, 151–173.

Galton, F. 1869. *Hereditary Genius*. London: Macmillan.

1874. *English Men of Science*. London: Macmillan.

Garfield, E. 1979. *Citation Indexing*. New York: Wiley.

Garvey, W. D., & Tomita, K. 1972. Continuity of productivity by scientists in the years 1966–1971. *Science Studies, 2*, 379–383.

Gaston, J. 1973. *Originality and Competition in Science*. Chicago: University of Chicago Press.

1978. *The Reward System in British and American Science*. New York: Wiley.

Gentner, D., & Gentner, D. R. 1983. Flowing waters or teeming crowds: Mental models of electricity. In *Mental Models*, ed. D. Gentner & A. L. Stevens. Hillsdale, NJ: Erlbaum.

Getzels, J. W., & Jackson, P. W. 1963. The highly intelligent and the highly creative adolescent. In *Scientific Creativity*, ed. C. W. Taylor & F. Barron, pp. 161–172. New York: Wiley.

Ghiselin, B., ed. 1952. *The Creative Process*. Berkeley and Los Angeles: University of California Press.

Gholson, B., & Barker, P. 1985. Kuhn, Lakatos, and Laudan: Applications in the history of physics and psychology. *American Psychologist, 40*, 755–769.

Gholson, B., Houts, A. C., Neimeyer, R. A., & Shadish, W. R., eds. 1988. *The Psychology of Science and Metascience*. Cambridge, England: Cambridge University Press.

Gieryn, T. F., & Hirsh, R. F. 1983. Marginality and innovation in science. *Social Studies of Science, 13*, 87–106.

Goertzel, M. G., Goertzel, V., & Goertzel, T. G. 1978. *Three Hundred Eminent Personalities*. San Francisco: Jossey–Bass.

Goertzel, V., & Goertzel, M. G. 1962. *Cradles of Eminence*. Boston: Little, Brown.

Goldstein, E. 1979. Effect of same-sex and cross-sex role models on the subsequent academic productivity of scholars. *American Psychologist, 34*, 407–410.

Golovin, N. E. 1963. The creative person in science. In *Scientific Creativity*, ed. C. W. Taylor & F. Barron, pp. 7–23. New York: Wiley.

Gordon, M. D. 1984. How authors select journals: A test of the reward maximization model of submission behavior. *Social Studies of Science, 14*, 27–43.

Gough, H. G. 1976. Studying creativity by means of word association tests. *Journal of Applied Psychology, 61*, 348–353.

1979. A creative personality scale for the Adjective Check List. *Journal of Personality and Social Psychology, 37*, 1398–1405.

Gouldner, A. W. 1970. *The Coming Crisis of Western Sociology*. New York; Basic Books.

Graber, R. B. 1985. A foolproof method for disposing of multiple discoveries: Comment on Patinkin. *American Journal of Sociology, 90*, 902–903.

Granovetter, M. 1979. The idea of "advancement" in theories of social evolution and development. *American Journal of Sociology, 85*, 489–515.

Gray, C. E. 1961. An epicyclical model for Western civilization. *American Anthropologist, 63*, 1014–1037.

Green G. S. 1981. A test of the Ortega hypothesis in criminology. *Criminology, 19*, 45–52.

Green, S., Rich, T., & Nesman,, E. 1985. A cross-cultural look at the relationship between age and innovative behavior. *International Journal of Aging and Human Development, 21*, 255–266.

Gruber, H. E. 1974. *Darwin on Man*. New York: Dutton.

Guilford, J. P. 1950. Creativity. *American Psychologist, 5*, 444–454.

1959. Traits of creativity. In *Creativity and Its Cultivation*, ed. H. H. Anderson, pp. 142–161. New York: Harper.

1963. Intellectual resources and their values as seen by scientists. In *Scientific Creativity*, ed. C. W. Taylor & F. Barron, pp. 101–118. New York: Wiley.

Gupta, N., Gilbert, L. A., & Pierce, C. A. 1983. Protégés, mentors, and academic success: A feedback report to participants. Unpublished manuscript, January.

Hadamard, J. 1945. *An Essay on the Psychology of Invention in the Mathematical Field*. Princeton, NJ: Princeton University Press.

Haddon, F. A., & Lytton, H. 1968. Teaching approach and divergent thinking abilities. *British Journal of Educational Psychology, 38*, 171–180.

Haefele, J. W. 1962. *Creativity and Innovation*. New York: Reinhold.

Hagen, E. 1962. *On the Theory of Social Change*. Homewood, IL: Dorsey.

Hagstrom, W. O. 1965. *The Scientific Community*. New York: Basic Books.

1974. Competition in Science. *American Sociological Review, 39*, 1–18.

Haitun, S. D. 1983. The "rank distortion" effect and non-Gaussian nature of scientific activities. *Scientometrics, 5*, 375–395.

Hanson, N. R. 1958. *Patterns of Discovery*. Cambridge, England: Cambridge University Press.

Hardy, G. H. 1940. *A Mathematician's Apology*. Reprint with foreword by C. P. Snow. Cambridge, England: Cambridge University Press, 1969.

Hargens, L. L. 1978. Relations between work habits, research technologies, and eminence in science. *Sociology of Work and Occupations, 5*, 97–112.

Hargens, L. L., McCann, J. C., & Reskin, B. F. 1978. Productivity and reproductivity: Fertility and professional achievement among research scientists. *Social Forces, 57*, 154–163.

Harmon, L. R. 1963. The development of a criterion of scientific competence. In *Scientific Creativity*, ed. C. W. Taylor & F. Barron, pp. 44–52. New York: Wiley.

Harvey, L. 1982. The use and abuse of Kuhnian paradigms in the sociology of knowledge. *Sociology, 16,*, 85–107.

Hasan, D., & Butcher, H. J. 1966. Creativity and intelligence: A partial replication with Scottish children of Getzel's and Jackson's study. *British Journal of Psychology, 57*, 129–135.

Hayes, J. R. 1981. *The Complete Problem Solver*. Philadelphia: Franklin Institute Press.

Helmholtz, H. von (1898). An autobiographical sketch. In *Popular Lectures on Scientific Subjects, Second Series*, trans. E. Atkinson, pp. 266–291. New York: Longmans, Green.

Helmreich, R. L., Spence, J. T., Beane, W. E., Lucker, G. W., & Matthews, K. A. 1980. Making it in academic psychology: Demographic and personality correlates of attainment. *Journal of Personality and Social Psychology, 39*, 896–908.

Helmreich, R. L., Spence, J.. T., & Thorbecke, W. L. 1981. On the stability of productivity and recognition. *Personality and Social Psychology Bulletin, 7*, 516–522.

Helson, R., & Crutchfield, R. S. 1970. Mathematicians: The creative researcher and the average Ph.D. *Journal of Consulting and Clinical Psychology, 34*, 250–257.

Hocevar, D. 1981. Measurement of creativity: Review and critique. *Journal of Personality Assessment, 45*, 450–464.

Hoffman, B. 1972. *Albert Einstein*. New York: Plume.

Holton, G. 1971–1972. On trying to understand the scientific genius. *American Scholar, 41*, 95–110.

1982. Toward a theory of scientific progress. In *Progress and Its Discontents*, ed. G. A. Almond, M. Chodorow, & R. H. Pearce, pp. 202–225. Berkeley and Los Angeles: University of California Press.

Horner, K. L., Rushton, J. P., & Vernon, P. A. 1986. Relation between aging and research productivity of academic psychologists. *Psychology and Aging, 1*, 319–324.

Houston, J. P., & Mednick, S. A. 1963. Creativity and the need for novelty. *Journal of Abnormal and Social Psychology, 66*, 137–141.

Houts, A. C. 1988. Contributions of the psychology of science to metascience: A call for explorers. In *The Psychology of Science and Metascience*, ed. B. Gholson, A. C. Houts, R. A. Neimeyer, & W. R. Shadish. Cambridge, England: Cambridge University Press.

Howe, M. J. 1982. Biographical evidence and the development of outstanding individuals. *American Psychologist, 37*, 1071–1081.

Hoyt, D. P. 1965. The relationship between college grades and adult achievement. *American College Testing Program, Research Report No. 7*, Iowa City, IA.

Hudson, L. 1958. Undergraduate academic record of Fellows of the Royal Society. *Nature, 182,* 1326.

1966. *Contrary Imaginations.* Baltimore: Penguin.

Hughes, E. C. 1958. *Men and Their Work.* Glencoe, IL: Free Press.

Hull, D. L., Tessner, P. D., & Diamond, A. M. 1978. Planck's principle: Do younger scientists accept new scientific ideas with greater alacrity than older scientists? *Science, 202,* 717–723.

Illingworth, R. S., & Illingworth, C. M. 1969. *Lessons from Childhood.* Edinburgh: Livingston.

Jackson, D. N., & Rushton, J. P., eds. 1987. *Scientific Excellence.* Beverly Hills, CA: Sage Publications.

Jackson, J. M., & Padgett, V. R. 1982. With a little help from my friends: Social loafing and the Lennon–McCartney songs. *Personality and Social Psychology Bulletin, 8,* 672–677.

James, W. 1880. Great men, great thoughts, and the environment. *Atlantic Monthly, 46,* 441–459.

1902. *The Varieties of Religious Experience.* London: Longmans, Green.

Jernegan, H. W. 1927. Productivity of doctors of philosophy in history. *American Historical Review, 33,* 1–22.

Jevons, W. S. 1900. *The Principles of Science,* 2nd ed., reprinted with corrections. London: Macmillan.

Jex, F. B. 1963. Negative validities for two different ingenuity tests. In *Scientific Creativity,* ed. C. W. Taylor & F. Barron, pp. 299–301. New York: Wiley.

Johnson, D. A., & Clark, P. M. 1973. Response frequency as a function of remote associational ability, type of verbal stimulus, and serial position of response. *Journal of General Psychology, 88,* 39–44.

Jones, F. E. 1964. Predictor variables for creativity in industrial science. *Journal of Applied Psychology, 48,* 134–136.

Jungk, R. 1958. *Brighter Than a Thousand Suns,* trans. J. Cleugh. New York: Harcourt Brace.

Kahl, R., ed. 1971. *Selected Writings of Hermann von Helmholtz.* Middletown, CT: Wesleyan University Press.

Katz, A. N. 1984. Creative styles: Relating tests of creativity to the work patterns of scientists. *Personality and Individual Differences, 5,* 281–292.

Knapp, R. H. 1962. A factor analysis of Thorndike's ratings of eminent men. *Journal of Social Psychology, 56,* 67–71.

Kochen, M., & Lansing, J. 1985. On maps for discovery: Did the periodic table guide elemental discovery? *Scientometrics, 7,* 327–339.

Koenigsberger, L. 1906. *Hermann von Helmholtz,* trans. F. A. Webly. Oxford, England: Clarendon Press.

Koestler, A. 1964. *The Act of Creation.* New York: Macmillan.

Kroeber, A. 1917. The superorganic. *American Anthropologist, 19,* 163–214.

1944. *Configurations of Culture Growth.* Berkeley and Los Angeles: University of California Press.

1948. *Anthropology: Cultural Patterns and Processes,* rev. ed. New York: Harcourt, Brace & World, 1963.

Kuhn, T. S. 1963. The essential tension: Tradition and innovation in scientific research. In *Scientific Creativity,* ed. C. W. Taylor & F. Barron, pp. 341–354. New York: Wiley.

1970. *The Structure of Scientific Revolutions,* 2nd ed. Chicago: University of Chicago Press.

1977. *The Essential Tension.* Chicago: University of Chicago Press.

Lakatos, I. 1978. *The Methodology of Scientific Research Programs.* Cambridge, England: Cambridge University Press.

Lamb, D., & Easton, S. M. 1984. *Multiple Discovery*. Trowbridge, England: Avebury.

Langley, P., Simon, H. A., Bradshaw, G. L., & Zytkow, J. M. 1987. *Scientific Discovery*. Cambridge, MA: MIT Press.

Laudan, L. 1977. *Progress and Its Problems*. Berkeley and Los Angeles: University of California Press.

Laughlin, P. R. 1967. Incidental concept formation as a function of creativity and intelligence. *Journal of Personality and Social Psychology, 5,* 115–119.

Laughlin, P. R., Doherty, M. A., & Dunn, R. F. 1968. Intentional and incidental concept formation as a function of motivation, creativity, intelligence, and sex. *Journal of Personality and Social Psychology, 8,* 401–409.

Lawani, S. M. 1986. Some bibliometric correlates of quality in scientific research. *Scientometrics, 9,* 13–5.

Lawler, E. E. 1963. Psychology of the scientist IX: Age and authorship of citations in selected psychological journals. *Psychological Reports, 13,* 537.

Lehman, H. C. 1953a. *Age and Achievement*. Princeton, NJ: Princeton University Press.

1953b. The ages of scheduled participants in the 1948 APA annual meeting. *American Psychologist, 8,* 125–126.

1956. Reply to Dennis' critique of Age and Achievement. *Journal of Gerontology, 11,* 333–337.

1958. The chemist's most creative years. *Science, 127,* 1213–1222.

1960. The age decrement in outstanding scientific creativity. *American Psychologist, 15,* 128–134.

1962. More about age and achievement. *Gerontologist, 2,* 141–148.

1963. Chronological age versus present-day contributions to medical progress. *Gerontologist, 3,* 71–75.

1966a. The most creative years of engineers and other technologists. *Journal of Genetic Psychology, 108,* 263–277.

1966b. The psychologist's most creative years. *American Psychologist, 21,* 363–369.

Lehman, H. C., & Witty, P. A. 1931. Scientific eminence and church membership. *Scientific Monthly, 33,* 544–549.

Lindsay, D. 1980. Production and citation measurements in the sociology of science: The problem of multiple authorship. *Social Studies of Science, 18,* 145–162.

Lomax, A., and Berkowitz, N. 1972. The evolutionary taxonomy of culture. *Science, 177,* 228–239.

Lotka, A. J. 1926. The frequency distribution of scientific productivity. *Journal of the Washington Academy of Sciences, 16,* 317–323.

Lyons, J. 1968. Chronological age, professional age, and eminence in psychology. *American Psychologist, 23,* 371–374.

McClelland, D. C. 1962. On the psychodynamics of creative physical scientists. In *Contemporary Approaches to Creative Thinking*, ed. H. E. Gruber, G. Terrell, & M. Wertheimer, pp. 141–174. New York: Atherton Press.

1963. The calculated risk: An aspect of scientific performance. In *Scientific Creativity*, ed. C. W. Taylor & F. Barron, pp. 184–192. New York: Wiley.

McCrae, R. R., Arenberg, D., & Costa, P. T., Jr. 1987. Declines in divergent thinking with age: Cross-sectional, longitudinal, and cross-sequential analyses. *Psychology and Aging, 2,* 130–137.

McCurdy, H. G. 1960. The childhood pattern of genius. *Horizon, 2* (No. 5), 33–38.

McDowell, J. M. 1982. Obsolescence of knowledge and career publication profiles: Some evidence among fields in costs of interrupted careers. *American Economic Review, 72,* 752–768.

McGuire, W. J. 1988. The psychology of scientific knowledge: Processes for creating knowledge and criteria for evaluating it. In *The Psychology of Science and Metascience,* ed. B. Gholson, A. C. Houts, R. A. Neimeyer, & W. R. Shadish. Cambridge, England: Cambridge University Press.

Mach, E. 1896. On the part played by accident in invention and discovery. *Monist, 6,* 161–175.

MacKinnon, D. W. 1960. The highly effective individual. *Teachers College Record, 61,* 367–378.

1962. The nature and nurture of creative talent. *American Psychologist, 17,* 484–495.

MacRae, D. 1969. Growth and decay curves in scientific citations. *American Sociological Review, 34,* 631–635.

Mahoney, M. J. 1976. *Scientist As Subject.* Cambridge, MA: Ballinger.

Manis, J. G. 1951. Some academic influence upon publication productivity. *Social Forces, 29,* 267–272.

Mansfield, R. S., & Busse, T. V. 1981. *The Psychology of Creativity and Discovery.* Chicago: Nelson–Hall.

Martindale, C. 1972. Father absence, psychopathology, and poetic eminence. *Psychological Reports, 31,* 843–847.

Martindale, C., & Greenough, J. 1973. The differential effect of increased arousal on creative and intellectual performance. *Journal of Genetic Psychology, 123,* 329–335.

Maslow, A. 1962. *Toward a Psychology of Being.* New York: Van Nostrand.

1966. *The Psychology of Science.* New York: Harper & Row.

Matthews, K. A., Helmreich, R. L., Beane, W. E., & Lucker, G. W. 1980. Pattern A, achievement striving, and scientific merit: Does pattern A help or hinder? *Journal of Personality and Social Psychology, 39,* 962–967.

Mays, W. 1973. Koestler and the nature of scientific creativity. *Journal of the British Society for Phenomenology, 4,* 248–255.

Medawar, P. B. 1984. *The Limits of Science.* New York: Harper & Row.

Mednick, S. A. 1962. The associative basis of the creative process. *Psychological Review, 69,* 220–232.

Merton, R. K. 1961a. The role of genius in scientific advance. *New Scientist, 12,* 306–308.

1961b. Singletons and multiples in scientific discovery: A chapter in the sociology of science. *Proceedings of the American Philosophical Society, 105,* 470–486.

1968. The Matthew effect in science. *Science, 159,* 56–63.

Mischel, W. 1968. *Personality and Assessment.* New York: Wiley.

Miller, G. A. 1956. The magical number seven, plus or minus two: Some limits on our capacity for processing information. *Psychological Review, 63,* 81–97.

Mitroff, I. I. 1974. Norms and counter-norms in a select group of the Apollo moon scientists: A case study of the ambivalence of scientists. *American Sociological Review, 39,* 579–595.

Moles, A. 1958. *Information Theory and Aesthetic Perception,* trans. J. E. Cohen. Urbana: University of Illinois Press, 1968.

Moravcsik, M. J., & Murugesan, P. 1975. Some results on the function and quality of citations. *Social Studies of Science, 5,* 86–92.

Moulin, L. 1955. The Nobel prizes for the sciences from 1901–1950: An essay in sociological analysis. *British Journal of Sociology, 6,* 246–263.

Mulkay, M. 1980. Sociology of science in the west. *Current Sociology, 28,* 1–184.

Mullins, C. J. 1963. Prediction of creativity in a sample of research scientists. *IEEE Transactions on Engineering Management, 10,* 51–57.

Mumford, M. D. 1984. Age and outstanding occupational achievement: Lehman revisited. *Journal of Vocational Behavior, 25,* 225–244.

Myers, C. R. 1970. Journal citations and scientific eminence in contemporary psychology. *American Psychologist, 25,* 1041–1048.

Mynatt, C. R., Doherty, M. E., & Tweney, R. D. 1977. Confirmation bias in a simulated research environment: An experimental study of scientific inference. *Quarterly Journal of Experimental Psychology, 29,* 89–95.

Naroll, R., Benjamin, E. C., Fohl, F. K., Fried, M. J., Hildreth, R. E., & Schaefer, J. M. 1971. Creativity: A cross-historical pilot survey. *Journal of Cross-Cultural Psychology, 2,* 181–188.

Nicholls, J. G. 1972. Creativity in the person who will never produce anything new and useful: The concept of creativity as a normally distributed trait. *American Psychologist, 27,* 717–727.

Nisbett, R. E., & Wilson, T. D. 1977. Telling more than we can know: Verbal reports on mental processes. *Psychological Review, 84,* 231–259.

Nolan, P. D. 1982. Energy, information, and sociocultural "advancement." *American Journal of Sociology, 87,* 942–946.

Nye, M. J. 1984. Scientific decline: Is quantitative evaluation enough? *Isis, 75,* 697–708.

Ogburn, W. K., & Thomas, D. 1922. Are inventions inevitable? A note on social evolution. *Political Science Quarterly, 37,* 83–93.

Olby, R. 1979. Mendel no Mendelian? *History of Science, 17,* 53–72.

Oromaner, M. 1977. Professional age and the reception of sociological publications: A test of the Zuckerman–Merton hypothesis. *Social Studies of Science, 7,* 381–388.

  1981. The quality of scientific scholarship and the "graying" of the academic profession: A skeptical view. *Research in Higher Education, 15,* 231–239.

  1985. The Ortega hypothesis and influential articles in American sociology. *Scientometrics, 7,* 3–10.

Ortega y Gasset, J. 1957. *The Revolt of the Masses,* trans. M. Adams. New York: Norton.

Osborn, A. F. 1953. *Applied Imagination.* New York: Scribner's.

Over, R. 1982. The durability of scientific reputation. *Journal of the History of the Behavioral Sciences, 18,* 53–61.

Owens, W. A. 1969. Cognitive, noncognitive, and environmental correlates of mechanical ingenuity. *Journal of Applied Psychology, 53,* 199–208.

Park, R. E. 1928. Human migration and the marginal man. *American Journal of Sociology, 33,* 881–893.

Parnes, S. J., & Meadow, A. 1963. Development of individual creative talent. In *Scientific Creativity,* ed. C. W. Taylor & F. Barron, pp. 311–320. New York: Wiley.

Patinkin, D. 1983. Multiple discoveries and the central message. *American Journal of Sociology, 89,* 306–323.

  1985. Reply to Graber. *American Journal of Sociology, 90,* 904.

Pelz, D. C. 1963. Relationships between measures of scientific performance and other variables. In *Scientific Creativity,* ed. C. W. Taylor & F. Barron, pp. 302–310. New York: Wiley.

Pelz, D. C., & Andrews, F. M. 1976. *Scientists in Organizations,* rev. ed. Ann Arbor: Institute for Social Research, University of Michigan.

Peritz, B. C. 1983. Are methodological papers more cited than theoretical or empirical ones? The case of sociology. *Scientometrics, 5,* 211–218.

Peterson, G. L. 1981. Historical self-understanding in the social sciences: The use of Thomas Kuhn in psychology. *Journal of the Theory of Social Behavior, 11,* 1–30.

Planck, M. 1949. *Scientific Autobiography and Other Papers,* trans. F. Gaynor. New York: Philosophical Library.

Platt, W., & Baker, R. A. 1931. The relation of the scientific "hunch" to research. *Journal of Chemical Education, 8,* 1969–2002.

Poincaré, H. 1921. *The Foundations of Science*. New York: Science Press.

Polanyi, M. 1968. Logic and psychology. *American Psychologist, 23*, 27–44.

Popper, K. R. 1959. *The Logic of Scientific Discovery*. New York: Basic Books.

Poze, T. 1982. Analogical connections: The essence of creativity. *Journal of Creative Behavior, 17*, 240–258.

Price, D. 1963. *Little Science, Big Science*. New York: Columbia University Press.

   1965. Networks of scientific papers. *Science, 149*, 510–515.

   1976. A general theory of bibliometric and other cumulative advantage processes. *Journal of the American Society for Information Science, 27*, 192–306.

   1978. Ups and downs in the pulse of science and technology. In *The Sociology of Science*, ed. J. Gaston, pp. 162–171. San Francisco: Jossey-Bass.

Prigogine, I., & Stenger, I. 1984. *Order Out of Chaos*. New York: Bantam.

Rainoff, T. J. 1929. Wave-like fluctuations of creative productivity in the development of West-European physics in the eighteenth and nineteenth centuries, *Isis, 12*, 287–319.

Raskin, E. A. 1936. Comparison of scientific and literary ability: A biographical study of eminent scientists and men of letters in the nineteenth century. *Journal of Abnormal and Social Psychology, 31*, 20–35.

Razik, T. A. 1967. Psychometric measurement of creativity. In *Explorations in Creativity*, ed. R. L. Mooney & T. A. Razik, pp. 301–309. New York: Harper & Row.

Richards, J. M., Holland, J. L., & Lutz, S. W. 1967. Prediction of student accomplishment in college. *Journal of Educational Psychology, 58*, 343–355.

Riley, M., Johnson, M., & Foner, A., ed. 1972. *Aging and Society*, vol. 3. New York: Russell Sage Foundation.

Rodman, H ., & Mancini, J. A. 1981. The publishing patterns of eminent social scientists. *Sociology and Social Research, 65*, 381–389.

Roe, A. 1952a. *The Making of a Scientist*. New York: Dodd, Mead.

   1952b. A psychologist examines 64 eminent scientists. *Scientific American, 187* (No. 5), 21–25.

   1965. Changes in scientific activity with age. *Science, 150*, 313–318.

   1972a. Maintenance of creative output through the years. In *Climate for Creativity*, ed. C. W. Taylor, pp. 167–191. New York: Pergamon.

   1972b. Patterns in productivity of scientists. *Science, 176*, 940–941.

Rogers, C. R. 1954. Toward a theory of creativity. *ETC: A Review of General Semantics, 11*, 249–260.

Rosengren, K. E. 1985. Time and literary fame. *Poetics, 14*, 157–172.

Rothenberg, A. 1986. Artistic creation as stimulated by superimposed versus combined-composite visual images. *Journal of Personality and Social Psychology, 50*, 370–381.

Rubin, Z. 1978. On measuring productivity by the length of one's vita. *Personality and Social Psychology Bulletin, 4*, 197–198.

Rushton, J. P. 1984. Evaluating research eminence in psychology: The construct validity of citation counts. *Bulletin of the British Psychological Society, 37*, 33–36.

Rushton, J. P., & Endler, N. S. 1979. Assessing impact (quality?) in psychology: The use of citation counts. *Personality and Social Psychology Bulletin, 5*, 17–18.

Rushton, J. P., Murray, H. G., & Paunonen, S. V. 1983. Personality, research creativity, and teaching effectiveness of university professors. *Scientometrics, 5*, 93–116.

   1987. Personality characteristics associated with high research productivity. In *Scientific Excellence*, ed. D. N. Jackson & J. P. Rushton, pp. 129–148. Beverly Hills, CA: Sage Publications.

Scarr, S., & McCartney, K. 1983. How people make their own environments: A theory of genotype → environment effects. *Child Development, 54*, 424–435.

Schachter, S. 1963. Birth order, eminence, and higher education. *American Sociological Review, 28,* 757–768.

Schaefer, C. E., & Anastasi, A. 1968. A biographical inventory for identifying creativity in adolescent boys. *Journal of Applied Psychology, 58,* 42–48.

Schaefer, J. M., Babu, M. C., & Rao, N. S. 1977. Sociopolitical causes of creativity in India 500 BC–1800 AD: A regional time-lagged study. Paper presented at the meeting of the International Studies Association, St. Louis.

Schlipp, P. A., ed. 1951. *Albert Einstein.* New York: Harper.

1974. *The Philosophy of Karl Popper.* La Salle, IL: Open Court.

Schmookler, J. 1966. *Invention and Economic Growth.* Cambridge, MA: Harvard University Press.

Schneider, J. 1937. The cultural situation as a condition for the achievement of fame. *American Sociological Review, 2,* 480–491.

Schooler, C. 1972. Birth order effects: Not here, not now! *Psychological Bulletin, 78,* 161–175.

Schubert, D. S. P., Wagner, M. E., & Schubert, H. J. P. 1977. Family constellation and creativity: Firstborn predominance among classical music composers. *Journal of Psychology, 95,* 147–149.

Seelig, C. 1956. *Albert Einstein: A Documentary Biography,* trans. M. Savill. London: Staples Press.

Segal, S. M., Busse, T. V., & Mansfield, R. S. 1980. The relationship of scientific creativity in the biological sciences to predoctoral accomplishments and experiences. *American Educational Research Journal, 17,* 491–502.

Senter, R., Jr., 1986. A causal mode of productivity in a research facility. *Scientometrics, 10,* 307–328.

Shadish, W. R. 1988. The perception of quality in science. In *The Psychology of Science and Metascience,* ed. B. Gholson, A. C. Houts, R. A. Neimeyer, & W. R. Shadish. Cambridge, England: Cambridge University Press.

Sheldon, J. C. 1979. Hierarchical cybernets: A model for the dynamics of high level learning and cultural change. *Cybernetica, 22,* 179–202.

1980. A cybernetic theory of physical science professions: The causes of periodic normal and revolutionary science between 1000 and 1870 AD. *Scientometrics, 2,* 147–167.

Shockley, W. 1957. On the statistics of individual variations of productivity in research laboratories. *Proceedings of the Institute of Radio Engineers, 45,* 279–290.

Silverman, S. M. 1974. Parental loss and scientists. *Science Studies, 4,* 259–264.

Simon, H. A. 1954. Productivity among American psychologists: An explanation. *American Psychologist, 9,* 804–805.

1955. On a class of skew distribution functions. *Biometrika, 42,* 425–440.

1973. Does scientific discovery have a logic? *Philosophy of Science, 40,* 471–480.

1986. What we know about the creative process. In *Frontiers in Creative and Innovative Management,* ed. R. L. Kuhn, pp. 3–20. Cambridge, MA: Ballinger.

ed. 1977. *Models of Discovery.* Boston: Reidel.

Simon, R. J. 1974. The work habits of eminent scientists. *Sociology of Work and Occupations, 1,* 327–335.

Simonton, D. K. 1974. The social psychology of creativity: An archival data analysis. Ph.D. diss., Harvard University.

1975a. Age and literary creativity: A cross-cultural and transhistorical survey. *Journal of Cross-Cultural Psychology, 6,* 259–277.

1975b. Creativity, task complexity, and intuitive versus analytical problem solving. *Psychological Reports, 37,* 351–354.

1975c. Interdisciplinary creativity over historical time: A correlational analysis of generational fluctuations. *Social Behavior and Personality, 3,* 181–188.

1975d. Invention and discovery among the sciences: a p-technique factor analysis. *Journal of Vocational Behavior, 7,* 275–281.

1975e. Sociocultural context of individual creativity: A transhistorical time-series analysis. *Journal of Personality and Social Psychology, 32,* 1119–1133.

1976a. Biographical determinants of achieved eminence: A multivariate approach to the Cox data. *Journal of Personality and Social Psychology, 33,* 218–226.

1976b. The causal relationship between war and scientific discovery: An exploratory cross-national analysis. *Journal of Cross-Cultural Psychology, 7,* 133–144.

1976c. Do Sorokin's data support his theory? A study of generational fluctuations in philosophical beliefs. *Journal for the Scientific Study of Religion, 15,* 187–198.

1976d. Ideological diversity and creativity: A re-evaluation of a hypothesis. *Social Behavior and Personality, 4,* 203–207.

1976e. Interdisciplinary and military determinants of scientific productivity: A cross-lagged correlation analysis. *Journal of Vocational Behavior, 9,* 53–62.

1976f. Philosophical eminence, beliefs, and zeitgeist: An individual-generational analysis. *Journal of Personality and Social Psychology, 34,* 630–640.

1976g. The sociopolitical context of philosophical beliefs: A transhistorical causal analysis. *Social Forces, 54,* 513–528.

1977a. Creative productivity, age, and stress: A biographical time-series analysis of 10 classical composers. *Journal of Personality and Social Psychology, 35,* 791–804.

1977b. Eminence, creativity, and geographic marginality: A recursive structural equation model. *Journal of Personality and Social Psychology, 35,* 805–816.

1978a. The eminent genius in history: The critical role of creative development. *Gifted Child Quarterly, 22,* 187–195.

1978b. Independent discovery in science and technology: A closer look at the Poisson distribution. *Social Studies of Science, 8,* 521–532.

1978c. Intergenerational stimulation, reaction, and polarization: A causal analysis of intellectual history. *Social Behavior and Personality, 6,* 247–251.

1979a. Multiple discovery and invention: Zeitgeist, genius, or chance? *Journal of Personality and Social Psychology, 37,* 1603–1616.

1979b. Was Napoleon a military genius? Score: Carlyle 1, Tolstoy 1. *Psychological Reports, 44,* 21–22.

1980a. Intuition and analysis: A predictive and explanatory model. *Genetic Psychology Monographs, 102,* 3–60.

1980b. Land battles, generals, and armies: Individual and situational determinants of victory and casualties. *Journal of Personality and Social Psychology, 38,* 110–119.

1980c. Techno-scientific activity and war: A yearly time-series analysis, 1500–1903 A.D. *Scientometrics, 2,* 251–255.

1980d. Thematic fame and melodic originality: A multivariate computer-content analysis. *Journal of Personality, 48,* 206–19.

1980e. Thematic fame, melodic originality, and musical zeitgeist: A biographical and transhistorical content analysis. *Journal of Personality and Social Psychology, 39,* 972–983.

1981a. Creativity in Western civilization: Intrinsic and extrinsic causes. *American Anthropologist, 83,* 628–630.

1981b. The library laboratory: Archival data in personality and social psychology. In *Review of Personality and Social Psychology,* vol. 2, ed. L. Wheeler, pp. 217–243. Beverly Hills, CA: Sage Publications.

1981c. Presidential greatness and performance: Can we predict leadership in the White House? *Journal of Personality, 49,* 306–323.

1983a. Formal education, eminence, and dogmatism. *Journal of Creative Behavior, 17,* 149–162.

1983b. Intergenerational transfer of individual differences in hereditary monarchs: Genes, role-modeling, cohort, or sociocultural effects? *Journal of Personality and Social Psychology, 44,* 354–364.

1983c. Psychohistory. In *The Encyclopedic Dictionary of Psychology,* ed. R. Harré & R. Lamb, pp. 499–500. Oxford, England: Blackwell.

1984a. Artistic creativity and interpersonal relationships across and within generations. *Journal of Personality and Social Psychology, 46,* 1273–1286.

1984b. Creative productivity and age: A mathematical model based on a two-step cognitive process. *Developmental Review, 4,* 77–111.

1984c. Generational time-series analysis: A paradigm for studying sociocultural influences. In *Historical Social Psychology,* ed. K. Gergen & M. Gergen, pp. 139–155. Hillsdale, NJ: Erlbaum.

1984d. *Genius, Creativity, and Leadership.* Cambridge, MA: Harvard University Press.

1984e. Is the marginality effect all that marginal? *Social Studies of Science, 14,* 621–622.

1984f. Leader age and national condition: A longitudinal analysis of 25 European monarchs. *Social Behavior and Personality, 12,* 111–114.

1984g. Leaders as eponyms: Individual and situational determinants of monarchal eminence. *Journal of Personality, 52,* 1–21.

1984h. Scientific eminence historical and contemporary: A measurement assessment. *Scientometrics, 6,* 169–182.

1985a. Intelligence and personal influence in groups: Four nonlinear models. *Psychological Review, 92,* 532–547.

1985b. Quality, quantity, and age: The careers of 10 distinguished psychologists. *International Journal of Aging and Human Development, 21,* 241–254.

1986a. Aesthetic success in classical music: A computer analysis of 1935 compositions. *Empirical Studies of the Arts, 4,* 1–17.

1986b. Biographical typicality, eminence, and achievement style. *Journal of Creative Behavior, 20,* 14–22.

1986c. Multiple discovery: Some Monte Carlo simulations and Gedanken experiments. *Scientometrics, 9,* 269–280.

1986d. Multiples, Poisson distributions, and chance: An analysis of the Brannigan–Wanner model. *Scientometrics, 9,* 129–139.

1986e. Presidential greatness: The historical consensus and its psychological significance. *Political Psychology, 7,* 259–283.

1986f. Presidential personality: Biographical use of the Gough Adjective Check List. *Journal of Personality and Social Psychology, 51,* 1–12.

1986g. Stochastic models of multiple discovery. *Czechoslovak Journal of Physics, B 36,* 52–54.

1987a. Creativity: Developmental trends. In *International Encyclopedia of Education,* ed. T. Husen & T. N. Postlethwaite. New York: Pergamon.

1987b. Creativity, leadership, and chance. In *The Nature of Creativity,* ed. R. J. Sternberg. Cambridge, England: Cambridge University Press.

1987c. Developmental antecedents of achieved eminence. *Annals of Child Development, 5,* 131–169.

1987d. Multiples, chance, genius, and zeitgeist. In *Scientific Excellence,* ed. D. N. Jackson & J. P. Rushton, pp. 98–128. Beverly Hills, CA: Sage Publications.

1987e. *Why Presidents Succeed.* New Haven, CT: Yale University Press.

1988. Evolution and creativity. *Journal of Social and Biological Structures*, in press.

Singer, B. F. 1971. Toward a psychology of science. *American Psychologist, 26*, 1010–1015.

Skinner, B. F. 1959. A case study in scientific method. In *Psychology: A Study of a Science*, vol. 2, ed. S. Koch, pp. 359–379. New York: McGraw–Hill.

Smart, J. C., & Bayer, A. E. 1986. Author collaboration and impact: A note on citation rates of single and multiple authored articles. *Scientometrics, 10*, 297–305.

Smith, W. J., Albright, L. E., Glennon, J. R., & Owens, W. A. 1961. The prediction of research competence and creativity from personal history. *Journal of Applied Psychology, 45*, 59–62.

Sniezek, W. E. 1986. A re-examination of the Ortega hypothesis: The Dutch case. *Scientometrics, 9*, 3–11.

Sorokin, P. A. 1937–1941. *Social and Cultural Dynamics*, 4 vols. New York: American Book. 1947. *Society, Culture, and Personality*. New York: Cooper Square, 1969.

11963. *A Long Journey: The Autobiography of Pitirim A. Sorokin*. New Haven, CT: College and University Press.

Sorokin, P. A., & Merton, R. K. 1935. The course of Arabian intellectual development, 700–1300 A.D. *Isis, 22*, 516–624.

Spencer, H. 1904. *An Autobiography*, vol. 1. New York: Appleton.

Spiller, G. 1929. The dynamics of greatness. *Sociological Review, 21*, 218–232.

Stein, M. I. 1969. Creativity. In *Handbook of Personality Theory and Research*, ed. E. F. Borgatta & W. W. Lambert, pp. 900–942. Chicago: Rand McNally.

1974. *Stimulating Creativity*, vol. 1. New York: Academic Press.

Stent, G. S. 1972. Prematurity and uniqueness in scientific discovery. *Scientific American, 227* (December), 84–93.

Stern, B. J. 1927. *Social Factors in Medical Progress*. New York: Columbia University Press.

Stern, N. 1978. Age and achievement in mathematics: A case-study in the sociology of science. *Social Studies of Science, 8*, 127–140.

Sternberg, R. J. 1977. Component processes in analogical reasoning. *Psychological Review, 84*, 353–378.

Stevens, S. S. 1939. Psychology and the science of science. *Psychological Bulletin, 36*, 221–263.

Stewart, J. A. 1983. Achievement and ascriptive processes in the recognition of scientific articles. *Social Forces, 62*, 166–189.

1986. Drifting continents and colliding interests: A quantitative application of the interests perspective. *Social Studies of Science, 16*, 261–279.

Stewart, L. H. 1977. Birth order and political leadership. In *The Psychological Examination of Political Leaders*, ed. M. G. Hermann, pp. 205–236. New York: Free Press.

Suler, J. R. 1980. Primary process thinking and creativity. *Psychological Bulletin, 88*, 144–165.

Taylor, C. W., & Barron, F., eds. 1963. *Scientific Creativity*. New York: Wiley.

Taylor, C. W., & Ellison, R. L. 1967. Biographical predictors of scientific performance. *Science, 155*, 1075–1080.

Taylor, C. W., Smith, W. R., & Ghiselin, B. 1963. The creative and other contributions of one sample of research scientists. In *Scientific Creativity*, ed. C. W. Taylor & F. W. Barron, pp. 53–76. New York: Wiley.

Taylor, D. W. 1963. Variables related to creativity and productivity among men in two research laboratories. In *Scientific Creativity*, ed. C. W. Taylor & F. Barron, pp. 228–250. New York: Wiley.

Terman, L. M. 1954. Scientists and nonscientists in a group of 800 gifted men. *Psychological Monographs, 68*, Whole No. 378.

1955. Are scientists different? *Scientific American, 192* (No. 1), 25–29.

Thistlethwaite, D. L. 1963. The college environment as a determinant of research potentiality. In *Scientific Creativity*, ed. C. W. Taylor & F. Barron, pp. 265–278. New York: Wiley.

Thorndike, E. L. 1950. Traits of personality and their intercorrelations as shown in biography. *Journal of Educational Psychology, 41*, 193–216.

Ting, S.-S. 1986. The social psychology of Chinese literary creativity: An archival data analysis. PhD diss., University of California, Davis.

Torrance, E. P. 1962. *Guiding Creative Talent*. Englewood Cliffs, NJ: Prentice–Hall.

Toulmin, S. 1960. *The Philosophy of Science*. New York: Harper & Row.

Toynbee, A. J. 1946. *A Study of History*, 2 vols., abridged by D. C. Somervell. New York: Oxford University Press.

Trimble, T. 1986. Death comes at the end – Effects of cessation of personal influence upon rates of citation of astronomical papers. *Czechoslovak Journal of Physics, B 36*, 175–179.

Turner, S. P., & Chubin, D. E. 1976. Another appraisal of Ortega, the Coles, and scientific policy: The Ecclesiastes hypothesis. *Social Science Information, 15*, 657–662.

1979. Chance and eminence in science: Ecclesiastes II. *Social Science Information, 18*, 437–449.

Tweney, R. D., Doherty, M. E., & Mynatt, C. R., eds. 1981. *On Scientific Thinking*. New York: Columbia University Press.

Veblen, T. 1919. The intellectual preeminence of Jews in Modern Europe. *Political Science Quarterly, 34*, 33–42

Voeks, V. W. 1962. Publications and teaching effectiveness. *Journal of Higher Education, 33*, 212–218.

Vroom, V. H., & Pahl, B. 1971. Relationship between age and risk taking among managers. *Journal of Applied Psychology, 55*, 399–405.

Walberg, H. J., Rasher, S. P., & Parkerson, J. 1980. Childhood and eminence. *Journal of Creative Behavior, 13*, 225–231.

Wallas, G. 1926. *The Art of Thought*. New York: Harcourt, Brace.

Wason, P. C. 1968. "On the failure to eliminate hypotheses . . ." – A second look. In *Thinking and Reasoning*, P. C. Wason & P. Johnson-Laird, pp. 165–174. Baltimore: Penguin.

Watson, J. B. 1930. *Behaviorism*, 2nd ed. New York: Norton, 1970.

Watson, J. D. 1968. *The Double Helix*. New York: Atheneum.

Wechsler, J., ed. 1978. *On Aesthetics in Science*. Cambridge, MA: MIT Press.

Weisberg, R. W. 1986. *Creativity: Genius and Other Myths*. New York: Freeman.

West, S. S. 1960. Sibling configurations of scientists. *American Journal of Sociology, 66*, 268–274.

1961. Class origin of scientists. *Sociometry, 24*, 251–269.

White, L. 1949. *The Science of Culture*. New York: Farrar, Straus.

White, R. K. 1931. The versatility of genius. *Journal of Social Psychology, 2*, 460–489.

Whiting, B. G. 1972. How to predict creativity from biographical data. *Research Management, 15*, 28–34.

Whorf, B. L. 1956. *Language, Thought, and Reality*, ed. J. B. Carroll. Cambridge, MA: Technology Press.

Whyte, L. L. 1950. Simultaneous discovery. *Harper's Magazine, 200* (February), 23–26.

1960. *The Unconscious Before Freud*. New York: Basic Books.

Wilkinson, L. 1986. *SYSTAT: The System for Statistics*. Evanston, IL: SYSTAT.

Wispé, L. G. 1963. Traits of eminent American psychologists. *Science, 141*, 1256–1261.

Woodward, W. R. 1974. Scientific genius and loss of a parent. *Science Studies, 4*, 265–277.

Yarczower, M., & Hazlett, L. 1977. Evolutionary scales and anagenesis. *Psychological Bulletin, 84*, 1088–1097.

Yuasa, M. 1974. The shifting center of scientific activity in the west: From the 16th to the 20th century. In *Science and Society in Modern Japan,* ed. N. Shigeru, D. L. Swain, & Y. Eri, pp. 81–103. Tokyo: Tokyo University Press.

Zajonc, R. B. 1965. Social facilitation. *Science, 149,* 269–274.

1976. Family configuration and intelligence. *Science, 192,* 227–235.

1983. Validating the confluence model. *Psychological Bulletin, 93,* 457–480.

1986. The decline and rise of Scholastic Aptitude scores: A prediction derived from the confluence model. *American Psychologist, 41,* 862–867.

Zhao, H., & Jiang, G. 1985. Shifting of world's scientific center and scientist's social ages. *Scientometrics, 8,* 59–80.

1986. Life-span and precocity of scientists. *Scientometrics, 9,* 27–36.

Zirkle, C. 1941. Natural selection before the "Origin of Species." *Proceedings of the American Philosophical Society, 84,* 71–123.

1964. Some oddities in the delayed discovery of Mendelism. *Journal of Heredity, 55,* 65–72.

Zuckerman, H. 1977. *Scientific Elite.* New York: Free Press.

Zuckerman, H., & Merton, R. K. 1972. Age, aging, and age structure in science. In *Aging and Society,* vol. 3, ed. M. W. Riley, M. Johnson, & A. Foner, pp. 292–356. New York: Russell Sage Foundation.

Zusne, L. 1976. Age and achievement in psychology: The harmonic mean as a model. *American Psychologist, 31,* 805–807.

Name index

221

Subject index

abandonment, 109
acceptance, of innovation, social, 17–19,
   92–3, 97, 103
acculturation, tendency to resist, 53–4, 109,
   126–9
achievement, and age, 2, 50, 60, 66–84
adolescence
   omnivorous reading in, 108, 111–13, 124
   role-modeling effects in, 113
advancers, practitioners of normal science,
   57, 124–5, 134, 183
   synthesizers, 183
affinity, inherent, of mental elements, 9–10,
   29
   of philosophical beliefs in Western civiliza-
     tion, 10, 131–2, 135
age
   and openness to new ideas, 101–5, 186–7
   and output, 2, 50, 60, 66–84
aging, of scientific community, 100–1
aggregates, mental, 8
alcoholism, parental, 109
American Men of Science, 85
analogy, between previously unrelated phenomena, 13, 14
analytic thought, 43–8, 55, 58
   compared with intuitive, 8, 31, 70, 101–5,
     177, 186
anecdote, 21
   as evidence, in chance-configuration
     theory, 33–8
anomalies, role in scientific revolution, 18
antecedents, developmental, 21, 107–34
arts, creativity in, versus science, 21–2, 38–
   41, 55–8, 72–3, 79, 82, 107–10, 115–16,
   121–2, 185–6
associations
   free, 26, 32
   infraconscious, 44, 46, 48–9, 58
   remote, to various ideas, 43
   strength of, 10, 44
   ultraconscious, 45, 46
attention
   selective, 37
   threshold of, 44, 48

awakening, 40
   sudden illumination upon, 30
autodidacts, 108, 111–13, 117, 119, 123–7

Barron–Welsh Art Scale, 42–3, 58, 103
beauty, and truth, 15–16, 28, 56, 192–3
biology, advances in, intergenerational effects, 130
birth order effect, 108–12
bisociation, 34, 38
brainstorming, 54–5, 189

categories, mental, wide, 43, 48
chance
   defined, 7–8, 48
   and genius, 33
   pseudo-Scrabble as game of, 181–2
   serendipity, 32, 35–8, 49
chance-configuration theory, 3–6
   applications, 21–3, 185–91
chance permutation
   Ernst Mach's description, 24
   generation and selective retention, 38–9
   by group mind, 100
   individual differences in generation of, 41,
     43–8
   motivations that facilitate the process, 50–
     5
   stability of, 8, 13, 16, 20, 28–9
   tests, before general acceptance, 20–1
citations
   analysis of, 84–5
   negative, 97
class, middle or professional, 108, 111–12
cognitive style, of creative person, 40–50
combination, *see* permutation
combinations, of philosophical beliefs, in
   Western civilization, 10, 131–2, 135
communication configurations, 16–20, 26,
   27, 69, 72–4
   consensus on meaning of elements, 18, 19
   ease of translation into, and value of the
     work, 89–90
   inappropriate, 19
   social acceptance of, 103, 122–3